VERA B...

(1893–1970) grew up in provincial .... in the north of England. In 1914 she won an exhibition to Somerville College, Oxford, but a year later abandoned her studies to enlist as a VAD nurse. She served throughout the war, working in London, Malta and the Front in France.

At the end of the war, with all those closest to her dead, Vera Brittain returned to Oxford. There she met Winifred Holtby—author of *South Riding*—and this friendship, which was to last until Winifred Holtby's untimely death in 1935, sustained her in those difficult post-war years. In 1925 Vera Brittain married the political philosopher G.E. Catlin and had two children, one of whom is Shirley Williams.

In 1933 Vera Brittain published *Testament of Youth*. This haunting autobiography, a vivid and passionate record of the years 1900–1925, conveyed to an entire generation the essence of their common experience of war. It was a bestseller in both Britain and America on its first publication and again in 1978 when it was reissued by Virago and became an acclaimed BBC Television serial. In 1940 Vera Brittain published *Testament of Friendship*, in which she commemorated the life of Winifred Holtby. This was followed in 1957 by *Testament of Experience* which continued her story, covering the years 1925–1950. These Testaments are also published by Virago, along with *Testament of a Generation*, the journalism of Vera Brittain and Winifred Holtby, edited by Paul Berry and Alan Bishop.

A convinced pacifist, a prolific speaker, lecturer, journalist and writer, Vera Brittain devoted much of her energies to the causes of peace and feminism. She travelled widely in Europe and lectured extensively in the USA and Canada. She wrote twenty-nine books in all: novels, poetry, biography and autobiography and other non-fiction. Of her fiction Virago publish *Account Rendered* (1945) and *Born 1925* (1948).

Winifred Eden-Green organised Vera Brittain's 'Letters to Peace Lovers' during the war years and continued working with Vera Brittain as her personal assistant until 1964. Alan Eden-Green worked in London on emergency information during the war and later in public relations. The Eden-Greens now live in Teddington, Middlesex.

TESTAMENT
OF A
PEACE LOVER

LETTERS FROM
VERA BRITTAIN

EDITED BY
WINIFRED AND ALAN EDEN-GREEN

Published by VIRAGO PRESS Limited 1988
20-23 Mandela Street, Camden Town,
London NW1 0HQ

British Library Cataloguing in Publication Data

Brittain, Vera, *1893–1970*
Testament of a peace lover : letters from
Vera Brittain
1. English literature. Brittain, Vera—
Correspondence, diaries, etc.
I. Title   II. Eden-Green, Winifred
III. Eden-Green, Alan
828'.91209

ISBN 0–86068–843–7

Typeset by Florencetype Limited of Kewstoke, Avon
Printed in Great Britain by
Cox & Wyman Limited of Reading, Berkshire

PREFACE

Vera Brittain wrote one hundred and seventy Letters to Peace-Lovers during the Second World War and the publishers required us to select little more than a third of them. In doing so we have tried to choose those which most threw light on the personality and character of Vera herself and which related to some of the most important (though not always recognised as such) events of the war. We resisted the temptation either to include Letters simply because we agreed with the views expressed in them or to exclude them because we disagreed. We have made cuts in several of the Letters (and in some cases have only included short extracts) because the material omitted was either repeating views previously expressed, or was only of passing interest.

We would like to record our thanks to Ursula Owen and Jane Parkin of Virago and to Shirley Williams, all of whom have greatly encouraged us in this somewhat daunting task; to Paul Berry and Geoffrey Handley-Taylor for permission to reproduce the Letters, and to Alan Bishop of McMaster University, Ontario, where the Vera Brittain archives are held.

All readers of these Letters owe a debt to the work of several volunteers who, nearly half a century ago, made their first publication possible, especially to the many hours contributed by Irene Mills and Derek Edwards.

Winifred and Alan Eden-Green

INTRODUCTION

When, in 1939, Vera Brittain asked me to organise her Letter to Peace-Lovers, Dick Sheppard House offered us free office space – in a bathroom. Like life itself in those days, it seemed a very temporary arrangement and little did I think, as I put boards across the bath to accommodate my already ageing typewriter, that forty-eight years later I would again be working on the Letters.

We had no backer. Vera financed the Letters herself though later she just managed to cover the costs with the half-crown subscriptions which came in surprisingly quickly. The half-crowns were more important to me than the names, but I recall Sir Robert Mayer, Sybil Thorndike and Arthur Creech-Jones MP as being among the earliest subscribers. Eventually there were over two thousand.

The practical problems were daunting, but to the bathroom in Bloomsbury came a loyal band of helpers – including Vera's mother, then in her late seventies – to assist with the various mundane jobs involved in the prompt despatch of the Letters. At first envelopes were addressed by hand but later we managed to buy a rickety old hand-operated Addressograph machine.

Later, when the bombing forced us to move the office to our flat in Blackheath, I had to pack the envelopes in a suitcase and wheel them to the post office balanced across the saddle of my bicycle. This led to an unfortunate incident. One day I took my husband's cycle by mistake, walked to the post and, when I emerged, seeing a male bike in the place of mine, accused a nearby policeman of allowing a 'swap' to take place under his very eyes and reluctantly handed my husband's bike to him. Several days later we discovered the mistake but had some difficulty in convincing the police, whose sergeant said he'd never heard of a bicycle changing its sex before.

The police, like most people, were very tolerant, but I was not surprised when they knocked on the door – tactfully leaving their car round the corner – to investigate. They took away specimens of the Letters (but not the subscription list) and we heard no more.

Vera was a brave woman to undertake this venture. She could have continued her career as a successful writer; instead she placed it in jeopardy, standing by her own unpopular convictions and addressing the Letters not so much to the committed pacifist but to the doubters who could not reconcile their beliefs and ideas with the expediencies demanded by war.

There was a constant flow of correspondence. Subscribers sometimes wrote questioning Vera's views, but often, floundering in an environment which was unsympathetic, hostile or sometimes abusive, they were seeking guidance and reassurance. Vera had time for them all, and she was never late with her copy, preparing it in trains, air-raid shelters or wherever circumstances demanded.

Her intractable opposition to saturation bombing and her deep concern about the sterility of the government's war aims, which for most of the time went no further than 'unconditional surrender', found many an echo among her readers in the armed services of whom there were a surprising number, including Paul Berry who became one of Vera's pacifist converts and ultimately her literary executor.

I sometimes thought she looked back with nostalgia at the heady days when *Testament of Youth* made her one of the leading writers of her time. She was egocentric, she liked popularity and she found criticism difficult to take; I do not think she enjoyed having to swim against such a strong tide of public opinion. She said she was a natural coward but she overcame her fear of the bombs, determined to carry on what she had set her hand to do. In a different context she quoted Van Dyke: 'True courage is not incompatible with nervousness and heroism does not mean the absence of fear but the conquest of it.'

She was a family woman. When I first knew her they all lived in Cheyne Walk, Chelsea. Her husband was Professor George Catlin who did not share her pacifist views and was a Catholic, unlike Vera who was an Anglican.

The two children John (11) and Shirley (9) were lively and talkative. I well remember her father saying to Shirley: 'Poppy, you talk too much, you're destined for politics.' How right he was. It is a pity that Vera died in 1970, too soon to see Shirley become Secretary of State for Education and Science (in 1974) and, later, co-founder and president of the Social Democratic Party which, in 1987 merged with the Liberals to form the Social and Liberal Democrats. Shirley Williams was never a pacifist, but I know she is proud of her mother's courage and integrity.

The decision to send the children to America in 1940 caused Vera deep distress. Many friends, including her publisher, urged her to join them there, but I do not believe she ever seriously considered it, although there was much she could have achieved there.

Vera had no illusions about Nazism; she was proud of the fact that her name appeared on the same page of the Gestapo Black List as Churchill's. She was among the first to ventilate the plight of the Jews in Germany and occupied Europe. Anti-semitism in Britain was also one of her targets.

Even from a pacifist viewpoint, some of her writings now seem naive. But we must remember that they were written not with the benefit of hindsight but amidst the physical and emotional stresses of war, when information about actions and attitudes was invariably slanted and unreliable. In the circumstances she remained remarkably objective.

The Letters were one of the ways Vera flew her own personal flag, the flag of her own faith and principles which rose above the patriotism which she genuinely felt. They undoubtedly gave strength and guidance to many of her readers who were confused by the morass of conflicts in which they suddenly found themselves, and they made some small contribution towards maintaining those values which are always at a premium in wartime. Bombs may overcome a specific tyranny, but it is ideas that overcome tyranny itself.

Winifred Eden-Green
Teddington, 1988

Let me begin by telling you why I am writing. Last spring, when the final stage of the crisis opened in earnest with Herr Hitler's occupation of Prague, my usual quota of letters from unknown correspondents started rapidly to increase.

A few of their writers belonged, of course, to organised peace movements, but the majority had joined no group with which they could share their views or discuss their perplexities. So, in hope or in desperation, they wrote as a last resort to an individual whose name they knew.

Some wanted to help, others to be helped. All were anxious to stop war, and especially this war. As its outbreak moved nearer, a few were seized with despair. They implored me to do something to save them from their oncoming fate. One suggested that a million women should simultaneously raise their voices against war. Another proposed that women of the world should immediately call a truce between the combatants. In a subsequent issue of this letter – if any of you ask for subsequent issues – I hope to comment on these pleas and suggestions.

As I was considering what replies to make and how to find time to make them, the idea suddenly came to me of a weekly letter addressed to my friends and readers who care for peace, and believe that human reason should be capable of finding a substitute for war as a means of settling even the worst disputes between nations. The idea of a weekly circular letter is not, of course, original. Several eminent publicists have successfully run similar experiments for years. But apart from the leaders of peace organisations whose job it is to circularise their members, there is, I believe, no one writing regularly on the topics in which you and I are specially interested. And, so far as I know, no woman has entered the ranks of these letter-writers at all.

I do not call this informal document a News-Letter, for my main purpose is not to give information. That, for those who want it, is already obtainable from many sources, both good and bad. Nor is my object to criticise the Government and its military machine, for though I regard every form of mili-

1

tarism as the tragic evidence of human failure, there are organisations already at work on this courageous and important type of criticism.

What I do want is to consider and discuss with you the ideas, principles and problems which have concerned genuine peace-lovers for the past twenty years. In helping to sustain the spirits of my readers (and through writing to them, to invigorate my own), I hope to play a small part in keeping the peace movement together during the dark hours before us. By constantly calling on reason to mitigate passion, and truth to put falsehood to shame, I shall try, so far as one person can, to stem the tide of hatred which in war-time rises so swiftly that many of us are engulfed before we realise it. I want repeatedly to examine those popular slogans and hate-images by means of which we work up one another's emotions. I shall try to keep unimpaired the rational view we had of those whom we now call our enemies, and their needs and hopes, before our blood became heated, or we had suffered at their hands as they have suffered at ours.

In a word, I want to help in the important task (the most important of all tasks from the standpoint of future peace-making) of keeping alive decent values at a time when these are undergoing the maximum strain.

Only if a minority – let us hope a growing minority – is able to keep sane in this fashion, can we hope to win popular support for a just and lasting peace. Because free democracies gave way to their passions twenty years ago, the Treaty of Versailles has led direct to the catastrophe of today. Another such peace – and let us make no second mistake about this – will only condemn our children and their children to the World War of 1960.

Surely we who now see the second of two great wars and are still – some of us – only in early middle age, would give all we have to save those young people whom we thought we were bringing into a better world from yet another epoch of chaos and destruction!

I hope that you whose name I know, and to whom I therefore feel that I am writing personally, will sometimes write in turn and tell me your own particular hopes, beliefs and difficulties.

You will understand that I cannot reply to each correspondent individually, but whenever you or one of the others raises some question that seems to me of special interest or universal application, I shall try sooner or later to deal with it in my letters.

Although many of you are women, I shall not as a rule address these letters to women as such though I may do so occasionally. But perhaps because I am a woman myself, and a devoted wife, and the mother of a beloved son and daughter aged eleven and nine, I shall be able to understand what my women correspondents feel about peace and war in a way that only a writer of the same sex could do.

Let me finally make it clear that these letters will not be written with a view to getting profit for myself. My only object is to keep in close personal touch with all who are deeply concerned that war shall end and peace return; who wish to be wise and merciful; and who understand what Johan Bojer meant when he wrote: 'I went and sowed corn in mine enemy's field that God might exist.' By getting in touch with you I want not only to help in keeping the peace movement alive, but even during war to strengthen it so that when the chance of sanity returns, we may seize it at once instead of allowing our hatred to overcome our commonsense.

I have correspondents in twenty-five countries, and with the censor's permission I hope to make contact with these friends through my letters. If I succeed, even this humble personal campaign for peace will have its international character, and I shall sometimes be able to tell you what your 'opposite numbers' in other nations are saying and thinking. At present, I am afraid, it may not be possible to write to friends in so-called enemy countries, but perhaps even this will become feasible when our respective leaders begin once more to feel that it is time to treat one another as normal human beings, with the same needs, hopes and affections.

I wish I could offer you this weekly letter for nothing, but printing, paper, stamps and secretarial work cost money, especially in war-time, and I estimate the cost at about 1d per letter. If you would like to go on receiving a letter will you please fill

3

up the form below and send it to me, c/o Dick Sheppard House, 6, Endsleigh Street, London, WC1. So many correspondents have kindly enclosed stamped envelopes for my reply to their private letter that I hope this will not be too much. I have suggested an initial period of six months in view of the uncertainty of the future, but I will ask subscribers if they desire to continue before that period expires. The weekly letters will begin as soon as sufficient requests are received, and the more friends they make for the ideas we share, the better pleased you and I will be!

Lift up your heart, remember that war will not last for ever, and let us begin NOW to work together for peace after strife.

On 7 March 1936 Hitler, claiming that due to the signing of the recent Franco-Soviet Pact he needed to 'secure the German frontier', sent a small military force into the Rhineland, which had been de-militarised under the Versailles Treaty (1919) and put under the control of French and British forces. To the surprise of his generals (who had only four brigades at their disposal), they met with no resistance and reoccupied the whole of the lost territory.

On the same day Hitler, perhaps recognising that he had reached a make-or-break point, dissolved the Reichstag and called a general election and a referendum on the Rhineland reoccupation. On 29 March his policy was approved by 98.8 per cent of the 45.5 million voters, though how free the election was is open to question.

*Herr Hitler and National Socialism are the fruits of the defeat of
a great nation in war*

— Sir Nevile Henderson

My first visit to Cologne was in October, 1924, when British
troops occupied the city. Wherever I went I found the German
population sullen and depressed from shame, poverty and
malnutrition. The only visible displays of nourishing food
were in the British canteens, where cheerful Tommies ate
beef-steaks before the envious infantile eyes of the future Nazi
youth.

One Sunday evening I looked out of my hotel window on to
Cologne's main thoroughfare, the Hohestrasse. There, in the
dim half-lighted street, I watched the morose population
walking up and down in couples, hardly speaking and never
laughing. Without money, entertainment or hope, they resembled a troupe of shades condemned to patrol some lampless
Teutonic inferno.

I did not see Cologne again until 1936, when I went there to
describe for a Sunday newspaper the election that followed Herr
Hitler's march into the Rhineland.

On a bright afternoon of early spring, I arrived to find the
Domplatz, just beyond the station, crammed with an eager,
expectant crowd. They were waiting for Hitler himself; in half
an hour he was due to arrive in the city for his eve-of-the-poll
address. Doorways and windows everywhere were garlanded
with flowers, which were thrown excitedly into the air as Hitler's
car drove by to the sound of cheering and singing.

Since he had chosen to dine at my hotel, which was strongly
guarded by police, it was midnight before I was able to cross the
square and take possession of my room. To obtain my press
ticket for Hitler's speech in the Messe-halle across the Rhine,
I had to make a long circuitous journey to the Ministry of
Propaganda on the outskirts of the city.

When the hour arrived, my press seat was not twenty yards
from Herr Hitler's place on the platform. While the packed

hall waited for him for over an hour, I watched the stewards assiduously beating the red velvet curtain at the back of the stage to eliminate possible bomb-throwers. When Hitler arrived the audience rose to cheer and I rose with them – not to cheer, but to get a clear view of the Nazi leader whose face I had hitherto seen only in press photographs and Low's cartoons.

I saw a man in early middle-age, fresh complexioned, of medium height, well set up and with no trace of the growing portliness which we are now told is characteristic of him. His smile looked friendly, even conciliatory. Cartoonists had not exaggerated the tooth-brush moustache and loose lock of thinning dark hair. Apart from these, he was indistinguishable from numerous middle-aged sergeant-majors whom I had met during the war.

But no sergeant-major could have made his speech. It started, and for nearly an hour continued, on a quiet, rational note. My German is far from first-class, but I could follow his thesis without difficulty. It ran on lines to which we were then less accustomed than we are now, and dealt with the wrongs done to Germany by the Treaty of Versailles. He might have been a Member of Parliament explaining the international situation to his constituents.

Suddenly, when he had spoken for about an hour and reached the subject of the Rhineland reoccupation, there came a change. With the instantaneous effect of switching on an electric light, it seemed to me that he allowed some subconscious quality to take control. The formerly measured tones rasped, roared, finally shrieked, as he waved his arms and stamped his feet. Sincerity degenerated into hysteria, exposition into denunciation. I felt myself in the terrifying presence of a religious fanatic with the ruthless one-track mind of a Grand Inquisitor.

'If,' I said to myself, 'you could have added Horatio Bottomley to Mrs Pankhurst and multiplied the combination by ten, the result would be Hitler.'

Modern psychiatrists who run clinics for 'problem' adults and children are familiar with this type of dual personality and the obstinate intransigence of which it is capable. Of the many methods of dealing with it which have been evolved, reciprocal violence is usually regarded as the least successful.

When the speech was over, cheering crowds singing the Horst Wessel song swept me with them out of the building. Borne along by the surge of Stormtroopers and Brownshirts, I hurried across the great Hohenzollern Bridge which spans the Rhine like the arched skeleton of a prehistoric mammoth. As I reached the centre, I saw that the cathedral and other beautiful buildings on the opposite bank were floodlit, gleaming like fairy palaces against an indigo velvet sky. The warm spring air was filled with shouting, singing, cheering, and the excited sound of thousands of marching feet.

It was a changed Cologne on to which I looked from my hotel window that night. Floodlights and flowers had replaced the dark depression of 1924; the pale ghosts flitting up and down the Hohestrasse, unsmiling and unspeaking, had changed to noisy, jubilant crowds. Beneath the exuberant surface, perhaps, there existed no spiritual reality such as that which commands the allegiance of our democratic Anglo-Saxon people. Liberty was gone, and personal security; there was no more freedom of speech, publication or assembly.

But glamour, stimulus, the sense of achievement against heavy odds, were there; no one, I imagine, would deny that these things contribute to the morale of a state.

Two days later, in Frankfurt, I asked an English official who had spent many years in Germany how far the 99 per cent support for Hitler supposedly revealed by the election represented the truth. It was, he said, partly engineered, as I imagined; but the sincere supporters probably numbered 80 per cent of the population. Then, the reason was the dread of Bolshevism; today it is the fear of another dictated peace.

You may wonder, perhaps, that at this time, I have chosen to share these memories with you. It is because I want to explain why I do not believe that the Nazi regime can be ended by force, but only by the voluntary acceptance of a nobler ideal on the part of the German people. It is for us to see that democracy genuinely represents that nobler ideal: that the advantages which

8

it offers its supporters are so great that no sane man or woman would choose an alternative.

As the Archdeacon of Stoke remarked in a fine speech the other day at Birmingham: 'Nazism will only be conquered when those who call themselves Christians begin to live in the spirit of Christ!'

— Extract: 30 November 1939 —

A few days ago, I returned to London from a provincial town which provided me with one of the strangest and saddest experiences of my life. I had been summoned to the Assizes as a witness for the defence at the trial of a personal friend – a distinguished doctor whose responsibility for the death of his beloved wife had brought him into that court on a capital charge.

The story was one of bitter tragedy, relieved only by the fine record of the accused man and the determined courage with which he faced his ordeal. At some period of the day that the Germans invaded Poland, he and his wife had presumably resolved to die together. Exactly what happened after that, nobody knows; but the next morning both were found in their gas-filled study, she dead and he just living.

Why, you may well ask, should these two valuable people, both only in early middle-age, be driven to make so terrible a decision? The evidence produced at the trial – a fair and patient hearing which was an excellent example of British justice – supplied the answer. It showed that the doctor, as a boy of nineteen, had been a shell-shock case, insufficiently recognised and never properly treated, in the final year of the Great War.

During an important action in the summer of 1918 he lost his memory, and simultaneously acquired a subconscious horror of the mutilations which he had seen at the front. Later he suffered from similar lapses in which his normal control disappeared, but despite this legacy of the war he rose to a leading position in the world of industrial medicine, and by his organised research work brought comfort and healing to thousands of lives.

In the witness box he referred to the tragic irony of making people fit only to destroy them. Some of his hearers were conscious of the further irony that the same society which drives thousands anonymously into battle will also spend three days in patiently examining a man's personality and discussing his future.

Today, though the law justly treated my friend with mercy, his work has been as ruthlessly destroyed as the cities of Poland. Because a new outbreak of barbarism revived the horrors of the first, one of the most highly civilised of men is a social casualty whose shattered career must be rebuilt at the cost of intolerable pain.

Before the war Vera accepted an invitation to go on a lecture tour in America. It was an engagement she was determined to fulfil. Travel was difficult. American ships and planes were forbidden to land in belligerent countries but there was a regular flying-boat service by Yankee Clipper from Lisbon to New York, so Vera had to make her way to Lisbon.

Special permission was needed for anyone to leave Britain and numerous regulations made entry into all other countries difficult.

Always do what you are afraid to do
— Old French Proverb

How I wish you could have shared with me one of those long war-imposed journeys which, for all their fatigues and mischances, have so strange a quality of glamour!

For many years I have believed that the stimulus of such journeys, so alarming in advance, so memorable in retrospect, arose from the naive zestfulness of one's twenties. But now, being far from my twenties, I know that their peculiar enchantment lies in the ageless delight of discovering unfamiliar countries and peoples at unusual seasons, in the overcoming of inordinate obstacles in order to accomplish some worth-while mission.

The preliminary obstacles consisted in the number of permits, visas and other documents now required before an unoffending citizen can leave England by the Yankee Clipper. My exit permit involved a wait of three weeks. The Portuguese, Spanish and French visas (the latter requiring four separate visits to the French Consulate) accounted for another two. Then there were forms — forms relating to cross-Atlantic passages, money, food, baggage and trains. I lost count when I had filled in nineteen. The total must have reached the neighbourhood of thirty.

The next obstacle was the capricious behaviour of the Yankee Clipper itself. After storms had delayed it and caused a large accumulation of passengers at Lisbon, the probable date of my passage became so indefinitely distant that I was obliged to transfer to an Italian boat which fortunately called at Lisbon on the very day that I had arranged to leave by the Clipper.

Finally, on January 5th, my Paris aeroplane was cancelled owing to 'low visibility' leaving me with the distinct impression that this latest method of man-made transit, so much at the mercy of climate and chance, is infinitely inferior to the older, staider but more reliable expedients of rail and boat. Cursing the inauspicious conjunction of war and weather, I transferred to the night cross-Channel steamer which offered the last chance of reaching Lisbon in plenty of time. Later I learnt that Portuguese floods round the Tagus had held up the Sud-Expresse for two days, so that had I caught my aeroplane it would merely have compelled me to spend an unforeseen night on the Spanish frontier.

Travelling at evening to the English port, I read an article, which I commend to you, in the Reader's Digest for January, 1940. It is called 'Prayer for Peace,' by Anne Morrow Lindbergh, and suggested to me that the airman's wife has a personality at least as distinguished and a mind perhaps rarer than that of her famous husband.

My journey to Paris was uneventful, though it took twenty-one hours. In the care of our picturesque escort on a calm, misty sea far smoother than that of most August crossings, we encountered neither mines nor submarines. It was weather, not war, which again created anxiety by obliging us to anchor for an hour outside the French harbour till the morning fog had lifted.

In Paris, where I spent three hours and dined in a little restaurant near the Gare d'Austerlitz, I found the black-out much less severe than ours; roads and pavements, though dim, were clearly visible. In France, too, ARP 'black-out' material is not black but royal blue, which wears both by day and night a more cheerful aspect than our sombre black curtains. Altogether, Paris seemed to me totally different from the tense, tragic city that I remember during the last war. Perhaps the change lay partly in myself, but it seemed to me to possess a confidence, an equilibrium, even a gaiety, of which there was little trace between 1914 and 1918.

In the south-bound *wagon-lit* from the Gare d'Austerlitz, I slept so soundly that when the conductor brought me coffee and rolls at Bordeaux, I thought we had only just started. As we passed through Dax, Biarritz and St Jean de Luz, the mild soft air and warm lovely sunshine seemed incredible after the harsh, bitter cold of war-time London.

My first real and somewhat disconcerting adventure occurred in Spain, a country which still seems, under the ubiquitous supervision of General Franco's portrait, to be more genuinely at war than England or France. All of war's cruelty, resentments,

13

and desperation are here; they speak alike in the ruthlessness of officialdom and the lorries hurtling down muddy roads regardless of human life.

At Irun on the frontier, devastated by fire and slaughter at the outset of the Civil War, the Spanish police arrested and detained me for two hours for bringing pesetas into Spain. Not only, apparently, is this forbidden, but my travel agency, with the best intentions, had presented me with currency changed at an international rate which is illegal within Spanish territory. This double crime automatically rendered me a highly suspected person. Since the Spanish policeman knew no French and I no Spanish, a long time elapsed before I could convince him – with the help of some English and American travelling companions – that I was the innocent victim of an error and not the deliberate perpetrator of a fraud.

I did not really mind being arrested, nor even the summary confiscation of £15 worth of pesetas for which compensation is remotely improbable, since I had enough money to carry me to Lisbon. But I did mind being compelled to lunch at 3.30, and thus have only one hour of sunset light in which to look at Irun.

But it was enough. The little town's mixture of gaiety and grimness, of new houses and uncleared debris, brought back memories of villages on the Western Front a year or two after the Great War. Buildings with their insides bombed away still stand starkly amid heaps of stones and rubble, their twisted iron balconies pointing like grotesque skeleton fingers into the air. I saw one large deserted villa, fronting the main street, which must once have been an elegant home; its impressive exterior was blackened with fire, its windows gaping, its roof blown away. In front of it only a few patches of tussocky grass showed where once a garden had been. As the evening mists rose from the Bidassao river, there rose with them a smell once familiar to me – the smell of French villages where the unburied dead rotted anonymously beneath heaps of fallen stone.

Such is, and was, war. The relief of moving away from it into Portugal this morning was beyond description. I began to write this letter at twilight, sitting exultantly in my lighted carriage

14

beside an uncurtained window as the train sped past the flooded Tagus, running through a vast shallow lake for mile upon mile. Why, I had asked myself earlier in the day, has no one ever described to me this lovely astonishing country of rocks and pines and rushing streams, with its wonderful vistas of rocky valleys climbing upwards to rugged ranges of cloud-capped violet hills?

And tonight, sitting in mild spring air at my open hotel window, and looking up the broad slope of the Avenida da Liberdade with its brilliant lights, I think to myself: 'This is peace. May it soon bring the light and life of Lisbon to London once more!'

The 'repeal of the embargo' to which Vera refers was the lifting of the ban imposed by the Neutrality Act on the sale of arms to belligerent countries. Following an appeal by Roosevelt on 21 September 1939, the US Congress agreed that arms could be sold if paid for in advance and carried by the buyer's own ships. This was a clear advantage to the Allies who could provide the necessary naval protection.

Leslie Hore Belisha, Secretary of State for War, had recently visited France. He urged Field Marshal John Gort (Chief of Imperial General Staff) to have more defences built in the gap between the end of the Maginot Line and the coast, through which the Germans would be most likely to invade – as indeed they did three months later. The army brass hats apparently resented his interference and complained to Chamberlain, who demanded Hore Belisha's resignation. It created a sensation, though the reasons were, of course, not known at that time.

Excessive partially for one foreign nation and excessive dislike
for another cause those whom they actuate to see danger only on
one side, and serve to veil and even second the arts of influence
on the other — George Washington's Farewell Address
(quoted by the *Chicago Sunday Tribune*, 21 January 1940)

I write to you from Chicago, which scintillates in the cold and
cruel wind from Canada that has pushed the mercury, even in
usually mild Kentucky, down to twelve below zero.

In this country of uncensored news, I have learnt more about
our war in a few days than you or I have gathered from
the official semi-fog of the past five months. It wouldn't, I am
afraid, be much good my trying to tell you anything unusual that
I have heard, for the result would probably only be the complete suppression of this letter. America tacitly expresses her
opinion of war-propaganda in a small inset caption which
appears on the main page of nearly every newspaper – 'Remember that all news from Europe is subject to censorship and
propaganda.'

The quotation which recently appeared in the *Chicago Sunday
Tribune* and is reproduced at the head of this letter, is another
indirect comment on British censorship in particular, for our
determination to examine American mails on the high seas (thus
interfering with the operation of the Clipper) has produced a
kind of minor rage in America which is not confined to the
newspapers. In this anti-British city it probably reaches its
height.

English people who imagine that the entire United States is
watching the European conflict with deep sympathy for the
Allied cause which a little encouragement would turn into active
participation, are either indulging in wishful thinking, or know
only the Eastern seaboard of America. In Chicago-dominated
Illinois, the debt question and one or two other problems,
hopefully disregarded by ourselves, over which England and
America have not seen eye to eye, remain obstinately unfor-
gotten.

17

Wherever I go, I collect opinions about what is known here as 'the European war situation'. Since I arrived late for my lecture tour, and was only able to remain for less than a day in New York, the views that I have heard are those of the Middle West, rather than those of the East which are so much more often relayed to England.

One very intelligent and well-informed American exponent from Wisconsin describes as follows the typical reactions of his own community. 'The lessons of the last war – the futility of it,' he writes, 'have sunk deep out here. And there is no sense of European history; all our history here really dates from 1917, and what people remember are the secret treaties, the vindictiveness of Versailles, the defaulted war debts and the post-war blindness of France and England. There is also a deep-seated suspicion of British and French motives, based partly on these recent memories, and partly due to the suspiciousness which people feel when they are up against something they don't understand – the European system. In the East people feel more at home in discussing Europe – not so here.'

This particular American divides his countrymen who opposed the repeal of the embargo into four groups – and these groups, he says, represent the majority in the area under the influence of Chicago. A large group – perhaps half – were totally indifferent to the fate of England. Europe, ran the argument, will be Europe whatever happens – and whatever does happen, we must take care of ourselves. A second, and smaller group, while professing to hate Hitler, showed actual hostility to England for reasons difficult to analyse but perhaps due to an inferiority-complex based on a reluctant ultra-respect for their own British ancestors.

A third, and still smaller, section actively sympathised with Germany, though not with Nazism, on the ground that the Germans had a 'raw deal' after the Great War. A fourth group took that view that somebody sooner or later must unify Europe administratively, and that Germany was the only country strong enough to do it.

The pro-repealers, I gathered, were less easy to classify. They

18

included outraged Catholics who identified Hitler with communism and both with anti-Christ; ardent Liberals of the 'Bill of Rights' variety; and a Rooseveltian group which blindly follows the President in everything. Only one or two lone highbrows favoured repeal from a sense of historic unity with England.

A few days ago, on the train from Washington to Louisville, Kentucky, I asked a conversational business man whom I met in the lounge car what interest that southern section of the Middle West felt in the war. He replied that it was the main topic of every intelligent discussion – and that radio programmes from Europe were still eagerly followed, if not with quite the all-absorbing enthusiasm of the opening weeks.

Certainly my first lecture audiences – both of them Women's Clubs – catechised me assiduously on Europe's problems, though my lecture had been only indirectly on the subject. Why had Hore-Belisha resigned? How long would Mr Chamberlain last as premier? What did I personally think about American participation in the war? On the other hand, apart from the great *Chicago Tribune*, the Mid-Western newspapers that I have seen appear as a rule to relegate the European war news to a back page.

The Peace Pledge Union was founded in 1934 by Canon Dick Sheppard (see p. 46). (see p. 46) Members signed a pledge which read 'I renounce war and never again, directly or indirectly, will I support or sanction another.' By 1936 there were 100,000 members. Sponsors included Eric Gill, Aldous Huxley, Siegfried Sassoon, Donald Soper and Vera herself.

The organisation still exists today with Sir Michael Tippett OM as its president.

It may not be easy to preserve the critical attitude when you love; that attitude is gone, without hope of recovery, as soon as you hate

— George Saintsbury

In a recent issue of these Letters, I promised to explain why I believe that an early peace by negotiation would be better for our own country than the bitter war required to 'smash Hitlerism.'

Let me assure you straight away — in spite of one or two journals which for years accused me of being a communist, but launched out on a series of quite contrary allegations when I joined the Peace Pledge Union — that I hold no brief for the Nazis and their methods. Even if there had been no war, no Jewish persecutions, no concentration camp at Dachau, I need not explain to any other lifelong feminist my reasons for detesting the Nazi regime.

Between 1933 and the outbreak of war, one of the lectures most in demand on my list was entitled 'The anti-feminist reaction in Europe'. It ended with a challenge to women everywhere to combat those fascist doctrines which emphasised a woman's functions at the expense of her citizenship, and turned her into a subject auxiliary whose status was hardly better than that of the villeins on the medieval manors of Norman England.

Like most people of this country, I would far rather negotiate with a more rational, less aggressive and less brutally humourless adversary. I know that an honourable peace with Nazidom would be hard to achieve. I fully realise its difficulties, and the intransigence of those with whom negotiations would have to be conducted. I only wish I could believe that the advocates of a 'fight to a finish' recognise the disadvantages of their position as clearly as I perceive the complexities of mine.

But, unlike the 'wishful thinkers' who see the downfall of Nazidom looming ahead every time a ship is scuttled or a raider defeated, I ask myself constantly what the alternative to early negotiation is likely to be.

A short time ago, at an unofficial political dinner, I sat next to a man whose conversation reminded me of the slogan used by the wounded Tommies in my Army hospitals between 1915 and 1919 – 'The first seven years will be the worst!' Meditatively and without emotion, my acquaintance remarked that judging by the power and resources of both sides, he saw no reason why the present war should not last for fifteen years.

I do not wish to suggest that I endorse the gloomy estimate of this contemplative pessimist, any more than I accept the optimistic predictions of certain 'crush Hitler' enthusiasts. But, before it is too late to prevent it, we should, I think, consider and face as realistically as possible the probable consequence of a long and cruel war.

At present, even amongst ardent militarists, an attitude of reasonable humanity towards the other side prevails. But what – judging by the evidence of the Great War – is likely to happen to our national mood after years of conflict?

On a Birmingham platform which I shared with him not long ago, the Archdeacon of Stoke remarked that, however terrible the toll of death and suffering which war exacts, perhaps its worst feature is the universal moral degeneration that occurs during its progress. Early in November, Dr L.P. Jacks, the veteran pacifist who clearly remembers the good intentions of statesmen at the outset of the last war and their dismal failure to fulfil them, wrote a letter to *The Times* to make a similar point.

'There is the same tendency,' he wrote of this war and the last, '. . . to overlook the operations of the time factor, under which the conditions of a good peace deteriorate with every day the war is prolonged . . . In our idealist ardours we had failed to foresee that if the war went on long enough – as it did – the end of it would find the victors in a condition so exhausted, impoverished and embittered that the one thought uppermost in their minds would be that of recouping their losses and getting compensation for their sufferings at the expense of the beaten foe, a state of mind fatal to the prospect of a wise, just and honourable peace.'

From these and other conclusions Dr Jacks drew the moral

(which, he added, he had drawn during the last war and offered to the combatants in vain): 'Agree with thine adversary *quickly*' – an exhortation that one greater than he had already made to the world with similar results.

Has it ever occurred to you, I wonder, that it is much more difficult for a democratic country to conclude a just peace after a severe war, than for a dictatorship or an oligarchy which leaves its international affairs in the hands of official diplomats? I remember how surprised I was when a German woman professor at Cologne University told me after the Great War that Germany had regarded our war propaganda as more bitter than that of the other Allies.

'You were not a conscription country like France or Italy,' she pointed out. 'Your men had to be *persuaded* to go to war. When the time came to make peace, you could not suddenly change your attitude after four years of such propaganda.'

In criticising the Treaty of Versailles, Mr Lloyd George has repeatedly emphasised that he was unable to go beyond the mandate of the people. I, myself, remember the change of attitude which came about the end of 1916, when the long list of futile casualties from the battles of the Somme intensified the deepening misery of that bitter winter. Was it surprising that after another two years, the mandate of a people free to direct its rulers demanded reparation and revenge?

So far our propaganda is less crude, our posters fewer, than those of the last war. But if we fight for three or four years and are again 'victorious', I venture to predict that the same kind of people who shouted at the Khaki election of 1918 that the Kaiser must be hanged and Germany must pay, will do it again at the General Election of 1943.

This time, no doubt, they will agree with the French in demanding a treaty to break up Germany into a number of small and powerless states – a policy which will guarantee that the next twenty-five years will be spent in reuniting them, with yet another bloody war to complete the process.

I recommended those optimists who believe that an efficient nation of ninety millions can be forcibly suppressed, to read the story of Prussia's resurrection under Stein, Scharnhorst and Humboldt between 1806 and 1812, after her utter defeat by Napoleon at Jena.

Knowing how often history repeats itself, I suggest that we devote our minds without delay to considering the possibility of a new type of peace treaty, lest our passions and resentments land us yet again in the very mistakes that we now desire to avoid.

The ill-planned British landings in Norway in April failed to prevent the German invasion and resulted in a humiliating evacuation. Neville Chamberlain had come under severe criticism, especially from the Labour opposition, during a Commons debate on 7 May. He saw the need to form a National government and realising that Labour ministers would not be willing to serve under him, he tendered his resignation to the King, nominating Winston Churchill as his successor.

Churchill became Prime Minister on 10 May 1940, the very day the Germans invaded the Low Countries and started their drive to the sea.

While these mighty events were taking place, a minor struggle was going on in Bow Street police court where several of Vera's fellow luminaries in the Peace Pledge Union were on trial for sedition, having published a poster which carried the simple statement 'War will cease when men refuse to fight.' It says much for British justice that, within a few days of the return of our defeated army from Dunkirk, the Chief Magistrate concluded that the offence only merited the six defendants being bound over in their own recognizances in forty shillings and sharing £36 in costs, with 14 days to pay!

Vera no doubt had the poster in mind when, in a Letter two months later she told a story of a conscientious objector in the 1914–18 war:

He was serving a prison sentence when an attack of measles compelled the authorities to put him into the same hospital ward as a number of serving soldiers. Next morning the medical officer doing his rounds discovered the category of his new patient, and proceeded vehemently to state his opinion of conscientious objectors. 'What', he thundered, 'would have happened in 1914 if everybody had behaved like you?' As he turned his back and marched up the ward, the soldier occupying the next bed was heard to remark, in language now made familiar by *Pygmalion*: 'Bl——y fool! No b——y war, of course!'

I would love to close my life in freedom from strife, but if we are to save civilisation, we must still take part in the great crusade based on the eternal truth that man-made evils can by man be remedied

– George Lansbury

On the morning that Germany marched into Holland and Belgium, I went down to Bow to bid a last farewell to George Lansbury.

The door of his pleasant cottage stood open to admit all those who came in from the wide Bow Road. Behind the purple-lidded coffin standing in his drawing-room amid the spring flowers brought by his friends, the open window showed a green radiance of garden where birds were singing. The sculptured features of his dead face, so calmly beautiful, seemed the last assurance of peace left in this world.

For the time being, the forces of cruelty and hatred – those evil powers against which George Lansbury and Dick Sheppard struggled throughout their lives – dominate all of us in Western Europe. As I write, the physical havoc now rampant across the Channel has barely touched our shores, though it may well have penetrated them by the time you read these words. But the spiritual havoc of war – its bitterness and blind vituperation, its swift, demoralising eclipse of the noblest human values – is here already. To deny this would be to join the ranks of those wishful thinkers who prophesied that Herr Hitler, abandoned by the German people who supported his transformation of their country from a world pariah to a world menace, would fall from power in two or three months.

Today, like those small countries which have already gone down in a war fought to defend them, we confront the two greatest tragedies which history offers to a people. We face the ruin of those private worlds which hold all the warmth and sweetness of our existence; we contemplate the loss of our sons, the shattering of our homes, the ruthless termination of maturer lives which walked with death a quarter of a century ago. But, worse still, we risk the temptations which destroyed Judas and vanquished Peter; we live in a darkened world where the spiritual forces of love and truth are themselves the earliest casualties.

Perhaps, like many of us in the first World War, you are among those for whom the former tragedy tends to obliterate the latter. Mr Winston Churchill has offered his new Government the sole reward of 'blood and toil and tears and sweat'. They are spectacular words, likely to echo through the corridors of time. But the blood and toil, the tears and sweat, are actually being contributed by 'Class 1940', which Will Dyson, in his famous prophetic cartoon drawn for the *Daily Herald* in 1919, perceived as a child crying behind a pillar while Clemenceau and his fellow assassins of peace emerged from their job of treaty-making. In war, as Mr Arthur Greenwood recently remarked to the Labour Party Conference at Bournemouth, there is no such thing as equality of sacrifice, since nothing that man offers can weigh beside human life. It is not the elderly politicians, but the young soldiers, whose blood is shed for the crass blunders made by the Old Men during the fourteen years in which peace might still have been restored. Youth, and youth only, pays the real price of war.

It is too late now to save Class 1940. Difficult as we may find it in these days when heaven is falling and earth's foundations have fled in a sense more complete than A.E. Housman dreamed of, we who are peace-lovers must begin at once to consider Class 1960. All the more because our hearts are breaking and our lives are threatened, we must guard that capacity for thinking in terms of constructive principles which distinguishes the architects of society from its destroyers.

In the midst of such a war as this has now become, pacifism is for the time being a lost cause. It has no hope of triumphing, and little of increasing its power. At present, such possibilities of a negotiated peace as existed before total war came upon us, have vanished with other rational objectives. But, as the hero of the film 'Mr Smith Goes to Washington' remarks, perhaps the lost causes are the only ones worth fighting for. Notice those phrases that I have just used – 'for the time being' and 'at present'. They are phrases to which, for the sake of our own courage, we must cling with all our strength, remembering that Christianity did not end with the crucifixion, nor the cause of slave emancipation with the death of John Brown.

Today many well-meaning people are arguing that because, for the moment, force has triumphed, the doctrines urged since 1919 by peace-lovers were mistaken. Force, they say, has been proved the only valid argument in an evil and perilous world. Actually, the exact contrary is true. The present catastrophe has arisen, not from the application of pacifism, but from the total failure of statesmen in all countries to practice its principles when their acceptance was a political possibility. Far from the pacifist doctrine being proved wrong, the present calamity demonstrates its correctness; yet peace-lovers are universally expected to forswear their creed at the very moment when the dire consequences of repudiating that creed are violently apparent. The anarchic chaos of contemporary Europe proves one thing and one only: that they who sow the wind will reap the whirlwind. Fully and completely, it justifies those who struggled to prevent the sowing of the wind because they knew that, once the whirlwind was ready for reaping, their power to save their fellows would be temporarily ended.

We cannot now stop this war, for wars will cease only when men have passed through suffering and spiritual revolution to a new conception of human brotherhood. So long as they are prepared to hate, fight and kill each other for political purposes, governments are likely to compel them to do so. Pacifism is the very reverse of that 'peace at any price' political defeatism which those who most rabidly misrepresent it endeavour to maintain; it is a way of life, beginning with a personal affirmation of love which it is now clear that centuries of inspired teaching can alone make universal.

War will cease when the great majority of mankind are persuaded – as at long last they were persuaded of that world-wide institution slavery – that its practice arises from the abnegation of human reason and the violation of all that is best in the human spirit. The minority who refuse war when the majority accept it serve merely as the advance guard of protestants; they are the John Browns of the peace movement, creating a precedent to which the majority will one day look back. To convert the majority means a world-wide educational campaign of a kind which has never yet touched more than the few. And, as Lord Ponsonby has said, the time for such an educational campaign is not during a war, but before it begins, or, better still, in the period of fierce anti-war reaction after it has ended. That such a time will ultimately come we know, and for that you and I must live and hope.

___ 20 June 1940 ___

When we come near death or near something which may be worse, all exhortations, theory, promise, advice, dogma, fail. The one staff which, perhaps, may not break under us, is the victory achieved in the like situation by one who has preceded us, and the most desperate private experience cannot go beyond the Garden of Gethsemane

– Mark Rutherford, *Catherine Furze*

Twenty-two years ago, on Saturday, June 15th, 1918, my only brother, a gifted young musician, was killed in action fighting for Italy. He was the companion of my childhood, the loyal confidant of my youth, and his loss has been one that no time can assuage. But it is not in any spirit of self-pity nor even of grief for a valuable life uselessly sacrificed with a million others, that I revive this personal tragedy. I mention it because it epitomises the cruelty and futility of modern war.

Today the beautiful country for which my brother died is aligned with the forces that seek to destroy us. You will have heard and read, as I have, the bitter vituperations of a Minister and of editorial writers against not only Signor Mussolini, but the gay and kindly people whose lack of political-mindedness has made them the prey of the furious factions which now dominate our world. You will be glad that even amid this rage of recrimination, there were Members of Parliament who emphasised the efforts made for peace by the Pope and other eminent Italians.

For my part, I can feel nothing but regret that the callous manoeuvrings of an armoured doctrine should have turned the Italian people into our official antagonists whose lives we shall take and whose lovely cities – the irreplaceable treasures of beauty-loving mankind – we shall perhaps destroy. Just as 'the enemy', when German, recalls to me the pitiful prisoners whom I nursed at Etaples in 1917, so our new 'enemies' bring back to my mind the friendly stewards on the Italian ship which recently took me to America, and the courteous hotel-keeper from Bassano who helped me to find my brother's grave when I first visited the Asiago Plateau in 1921.

Thinking that I might be afraid of the steep mountain roads and the forbidding loneliness of the pine-clad plateau, the hotel-keeper took his little son with us to prove that there was no real danger. Today, I suppose, this charming child, as a member of the fascist youth, has become my 'enemy'. But perhaps he still recalls the day on which, with the instinctive sympathy of childhood, he picked a bunch of scabious and white clover for a young English woman as she left the mountain cemetery among the pine-woods at Granezza.

With Mussolini's decision and the collapse of France, this sad world approaches a period in which 'total war' becomes not merely a military but a geographical reality. Already hostilities have extended to Africa. The voice of President Roosevelt, broadcast from Virginia in competition with the triumphant echoes of the Horst Wessel song from Germany, has indicated that Europe's catastrophe must involve the peaceful democracy of the United States. At such an hour, all lovers of peace are inevitably asking: 'What shall I do now?' For the rest of this letter, I shall try to give you the answer that one pacifist has made to herself.

In the terrible wars of today there are, I think, two distinct stages which may well be followed by a third before they finally

31

resolve themselves into a fourth. The first is the preliminary period, which in this war continued for several months after hostilities had broken out. During this stage it is the unquestionable obligation of peace-lovers to do everything in their power to prevent the active development of the war, and to urge peace by negotiation while this is still feasible.

With the advent of 'total war', the peace-lover's duty changes. I do not mean that he should cease to be ready for one of those miracles which have sometimes changed the course of history. But unless he wishes to be a mere 'wishful thinker', he cannot base his calculations on the accidental intervention of a miracle. When war is at its height and the prospect of peace remote, he has I think a double obligation: first, to do what he can to save the rational values of civilisation from being submerged in the flood of hatred and panic fear; secondly, to relieve, by every opportunity that he is able to seize, the suffering of war's innocent victims. Of these the most obvious are children, refugees, and civilian casualties, but I do not exclude wounded soldiers or prisoners of war.

This is not, I know, the position of the absolute pacifist. War, he says, is evil, and logically its opponent should stand aside even from its victims. I respect this view, but I cannot share it, for I believe that when war becomes 'total', the logic of pacifism, as distinct from its spirit, ceases to exist. If genuinely obeyed, it would become a purely suicidal principle, involving the refusal of food because sailors have carried it, and a deliberate self-exposure to bombs because air-raid shelters are military precautions.

I believe that life, so long as we possess it, carries the obligation to fulfil its responsibility to ourselves and others. We are not therefore entitled to lay it down for the sake of logic, and to bury ourselves in an ivory tower; we are part of a community, and cannot escape the demands that citizenship lays upon us. In such a war as this, the community reaches – as we are now reaching – a point at which all the agencies designed to relieve suffering must co-operate or prove ineffective. The time will soon be past for debating whether we sully the purity of our pacifism by collaborating with the government, for at a certain stage of horror, every government is compelled to mitigate the consequences of its own war policy by the organisation of mercy.

You will not, I am sure, misunderstand the kind of work that I suggest we should undertake. I do not regard a comfortable, well-paid job in a war-waging Ministry as one which a sincere pacifist could contemplate. The work that we should now prepare is of a humbler but nobler order. Like that of the soldier, it should, I think, repudiate all prospect of gain for ourselves, while accepting the risk of personal sacrifice. Our attitude towards our fellow-sufferers should be that of the Master who healed the sick, fed the poor, and washed His disciples' feet, because 'He was moved with compassion toward them'.

The time is coming upon us in this island when the ability to stop a haemorrhage, put on a bandage, or even have a cup of tea ready to offer a panic-stricken householder, may make all the difference between life and death, between sickness and health. Let us therefore co-operate with anyone who is willing to co-operate with us, provided that our object is to save life and mitigate suffering.

Before our country reaches the final stage of anti-war reaction, it may go through a third so terrible that war, by its own consequences, will stop itself. In *The Shape of Things to Come*, Mr H. G. Wells presents mankind struggling helplessly against a cholera epidemic produced by the ravages of war. Those of us who recall the influenza epidemic which attacked our lowered resistance in 1918 and the typhus which stalked like a scourge of God over Russia and Poland, will realise that the present welter of destruction – the full story of which is withheld by all governments from their stricken populations – may well end by breeding some form of pestilence unequalled since the Black Death. Before such an onslaught of outraged Nature, political creeds and doctrines would become as chaff before the hurricane, and human 'enemies' would stand together, puny atoms stricken down by their own arrogance of destruction, to combat the superhuman power which avenged their betrayal of civilisation.

33

Even for such an outcome, the peace-lover must be prepared. The field for his tilling is the post-war world. By whatever route it comes, he must be ready to recognise its advent and to make the best of its opportunities.

Victor Gollancz, although entirely disagreeing with Vera's pacifism, was predominantly a humanitarian and, as will be seen in later Letters, they often supported each other. He sharply criticised the government and published a series of 'Victory Books' of which the best known was *Guilty Men*. The authors ('Cato') were Michael Foot, Peter Howard and Frank Owen and the book was an indictment of Chamberlain, Lord Halifax, Sir Samuel Hoare, Ramsay MacDonald and several other leading politicians for their conduct of the war and the events leading to it.

Winifred Holtby's name will often recur in these Letters. Vera met her in 1919 and a rare and deep relationship quickly developed. But it was not, as has often been rumoured, a lesbian one. Just before Vera died in 1970 she wrote 'I loved Winifred, but I was not in love with her.'

Vera depended on Winifred emotionally, spiritually, and often practically. Winifred gave her great encouragement when she was struggling with *Testament of Youth* and often minded John and Shirley when Vera went on lecture tours. Winifred was only thirty-seven when she died. Vera was at her bedside and afterwards wrote: 'We all exploited her. She had so much to give. She gave with both hands.'

Hyde Park Corner provided Londoners with a surprising measure of free speech throughout the war.

There were 584 barrage balloons around London and diagonal trenches had been dug to prevent enemy planes from landing.

William Joyce (Lord Haw Haw, whose regular broadcasts in English from Germany became a joke) was tried for treason after the war and hanged at Wandsworth on 5 January 1946.

Duff Cooper was Minister of Information.

— 15 August 1940 —

If an earthquake were to engulf England to-morrow, the English would manage to meet and dine somewhere among the rubbish, just to celebrate the event

– Douglas Jerrold

Two Sundays ago, on the twenty-sixth anniversary of August 4th, 1914, I went to Hyde Park to hear the week-end orators proclaiming their opinions.

You will doubtless remember that afternoon as one of the hottest and sultriest of this ironically brilliant summer. But for the war, it would have been Bank Holiday Sunday. Never since last September have I seen the Park so crowded or the orators so numerous. The usual contingent were all there – International Socialism, the Salvation Army, the Ministry of Information, the Catholic Evidence Guild, and the New and Latter House of Israel. Two adjacent platforms, the Peace Pledge Union and the Anti-Fifth Column League, between them attracted the largest crowd of perspiring listeners.

When a noisy indefatigable heckler seemed liable to cause a breach of the peace, the young PPU speaker wisely abandoned his meeting. His hearers drifted across to the Anti-Fifth Columnist, whose peculiar brand of vituperative eloquence suggested an obsession with three *bêtes noires* – Mr Duff Cooper, Lord Haw-Haw, and the British Union of Fascists.

'Ever seen such tripe as the Silent Column?' he thundered. 'Walk about with faces like dish-rags, don't say a word! ... Lord Haw-Haw – yes, that's Bill Joyce – a cowardly rat if ever there was one ... Don't you know I'm trying to crush the rottenest filthiest ideology – kill this dirty murderer of children and his rotten gang ...!'

The crowd listened indulgently. Their several expressions of mild amusement suggested that children slain in Hull or Hamburg were as unreal to them as Duff Cooper and William Joyce. Above their heads the barrage balloons hung low beneath thundrous clouds. Some distance from the rostrums, another section of holiday-makers surged incongruously round the

37

fenced-in military area which causes the centre of Hyde Park in this war to resemble the Western Front in the last.

I noticed several fathers and mothers, their shoes comfortably kicked off, resting their backs against the anti-parachutist sand-heaps while they ate their sandwiches out of paper bags. Despite exhortations to evacuate, they had brought their families to town for the day. At the bottom of one long diametrical trench, several children were making pies with the perilous assistance of discarded tins. One charming baby, dressed only in a pair of pink and blue check gingham knickers, played blithely on the top of a dug-out reinforced with piles of sandbags. Only a few yards from the barbed wire entanglements, a laughing throng drank its cups of tea beneath the orange umbrellas of the open-air restaurant.

Perhaps you, too, were in Hyde Park last Sunday week. If so, I am sure you would agree that this characteristic scene could hardly have occurred in any country but Britain. Remembering my American friends in times of crisis, I recalled their habit of 'downing tools' and listening by day and night to the radio broadcasts coming through on their perfect transmitters from half the capitals of Europe. The state of tension produced by this keen, nervous, intelligent interest was something, I felt, which an English Bank Holiday crowd would regard with amazement. Last September, just before he went to the Continent and gathered the material for his vivid little study 'Inside Germany', Mr Oswald Garrison Villard, the ex-editor of the American *Nation*, told me that the absence of alarm and excitement impressed him more than anything in London.

Though I shuddered at the bare possibility of an air raid in that crowded park with its scores of pretty children, I could not help wishing that Herr Hitler and Dr Goebbels could be trans-ported here to see the vast London population which they have so often described as panic-stricken. So accustomed has that imperturbable populace now become to military preparations of the most sinister type, that they have ceased to think of their meaning or even to notice them – except as props for their backs or convenient sandpits for their toddlers.

Nevertheless, admirable as our national placidity may be in one sense, it has disadvantages arising from its close relation to apathy, inertia, lack of foresight, failure of imagination and other negative qualities, which Mr Villard apparently did not recognise. I realised this later the same day, when I heard Lord Gort broadcasting during the Sunday evening service.

Though we have failed, he stated, as a nation of worshippers, 'we are responsible neither for the ambitions of the leaders of great nations who are today our enemies nor for the failure of their peoples to check their lust for domination.' But is it indeed true to say that we have no responsibility for these calamities? Lord Gort, it seems to me, went back too short a distance into those causes which produce the results that we record as history. It is true that, once they were in the saddle, we were not responsible for the rate at which the ambitions of the fascist leaders grew. But how far was the post-war humiliation of the conquered by the conqueror responsible not only for the driving venomous bitterness of those ambitions, but for the fact that the men who entertain them got into the saddle at all?

For fourteen years after Versailles, there were elements in Germany which feared the rise of Hitlerism and foresaw its consequences more clearly than we did. They knew that fascism was being created by the policy of the Allies and especially of France. The people of this country did nothing to support those German elements or to stop that French policy. In their cheerful apathy they left the circumstances which made Hitler inevitable to be created by a group of 'Guilty Men'. (My own list of names is by no means identical with that given in 'Cato's' book recently published by Victor Gollancz, though several are the same for different reasons.)

Nobody knows better than myself how little interest this liberty-loving democracy – then totally unhampered by the restrictions on speech and publication now beginning gravely to disturb its more intelligent members – took in the actions and policy of France. I remember, throughout 1923, speaking up and down England against France's occupation of the Ruhr. I spoke to tiny audiences, benevolent but a little sceptical of the consequences of French policy as foreseen by a girl in her twenties. But young as I was, I was right in what I foresaw. Any intelligent person who troubled to study the situation could have been as right as I was. But very few people did trouble. The rest were too cheerful, imperturbable, casual, good-humoured, unconcerned. To use a less complimentary word, they were too apathetic.

Over and over again, since this war began, I have asked myself why the earnest, well-meaning peace movement of the nineteen-twenties failed so completely. Why I failed. Why Winifred Holtby failed. Why those who shared our platform failed. In Hyde Park, on the twenty-sixth anniversary of the outbreak of the first World War, I found one answer.

We failed because we were too easily satisfied. We assumed that the keen enthusiasm of an energetic minority signified a desire for peace on the part of the whole people. Perhaps it did; but it signified only a negative, apathetic desire which was never sufficiently alive to count the cost of peace and be ready to pay it – the desire of those who today challenge pacifists with the too familiar words: 'Of course, we *all* want peace . . . but . . .' I remember the excitement of the League of Nations Union – a real influence for peace in those early years, before 'collective security' had come to mean just England, France and Russia versus Germany, Italy and Japan – when its membership touched a quarter of a million. It should not have been excited. It should have been beating its breast because a quarter of a million is only one two-hundredth part of a population of fifty millions. For in the end, when the testing time came, it was not the quarter-million but the forty-nine and three-quarter millions who decided (or rather, failed to reverse) the policy of this country.

We are an admirable, imperturbable, good-tempered, kindly people. Yes, we are. You and I know it and are proud of it. But when the time for a peace settlement comes once more, for God's sake and that of civilisation, do not let us again accept cheerfulness, patience, composure and good-tempered resignation as desirable substitutes for energy, knowledge, foresight, vitality and intelligence.

40

The war had entered a desperate stage. The Battle of Britain was at its height and many people believed a German invasion was imminent.

Some pacifists felt a need to reappraise their position. They knew that in Germany pacifists were among the first to be sent to concentration camps and conscientious objectors had few illusions about what would happen to them under a Nazi occupation. Should they now put their principles aside and join up? Most stood firm; some went to jail while many got involved in various kinds of relief work – some official, some unofficial – in the bombed areas.

The tolerance of the British public, so far remarkably generous, was getting frayed at the edges. Pacifists were called Quislings (after the Norwegian traitor), white feathers were distributed. Two attempts were made to set the Blackheath Peace Shop on fire and an army major (very untypically, for members of the services were usually much more tolerant than the general public) even threatened to shoot the organiser of these Letters and her husband.

Vera must have felt the pacifist's dilemma very keenly. She could easily have joined the Ministry of Information or the BBC. Instead she insisted on proclaiming her unpopular views.

O war, I hate you most of all for this, that you do lay your hands on the noblest elements in human character, with which we might make a heaven on earth, and you use them to make a hell on earth instead. ... You take our loyalty, our unselfishness, with which we might make the earth beautiful, and using these our finest qualities you make death fall from the sky and burst up from the sea

– Harry Emerson Fosdick,
Apology to the Unknown Soldier

During the past three weeks, you and I have watched from near or far the fiercest and most momentous aerial battles which history has ever known.

In smoke and flame the most highly trained young airmen of two nations have fallen from the sky, and with them a young American, gay, fortunate, brilliant, an only son whose best years should have lain before him. However heroic and daring these boys may be, any one of us with imagination can picture what they must go through before each of their swift, intense flights.

By sea and land, co-operating with the Air Force, our sailors are watching the sinister waters which protect us, dodging bombs and torpedoes, convoying vital cargoes; our anti-aircraft gunners and searchlight batteries are standing by continually under fire. This island is filled with regiments holding perilous positions, and boys on duty at aerodromes which are main targets of enemy bombers.

Even this is not the end. Never, I suppose, has the sum total of civilian courage in this country proved so great as it is today in response to the intense and perpetual strain placed upon it. This courage is not even confined to the civilian defence forces, those ordinary men and women in steel hats who patrol the streets during raids, fight fires, rescue casualties from the debris of buildings, and lay down their lives at first aid posts, like the young pacifist warden who was recently killed at Portsmouth. Day after day, men and women working in offices, in factories, or in their own homes fight their human fears with a brave show of cheerful indifference. Even the children sing in their shelters, subjecting themselves prematurely to adult self-control – with what long-range effects on their nervous systems we do not yet know.

In addition to raids, the inhabitants of London and the south-eastern counties face the possibility of shells and rockets being dropped on their houses and streets. At any moment death may descend upon any one of us from the brilliant noonday skies or the serene moonlit clouds. We have learnt, and are learning, to confront fate with a heroism which is none the less magnificent because it is universal.

And for what? You and I are growing so accustomed to the demand made upon our endurance, our humour, and our self-control, that we have almost ceased to ask ourselves just why they are required. Let me repeat my question. For what end is this nation showing its superlative courage? For what purpose is it making, at incalculable cost, the emotional sacrifices involved in parting with children, abandoning homes, leaving husbands or wives in danger, closing down businesses, terminating professions or social experiments which have embodied the hopes and dreams of a lifetime?

We are doing, permitting and enduring these things in order that we may destroy another nation whose airmen, soldiers, sailors and civilians are showing the same gallantry as ourselves. Our finest qualities are demanded of us in order that grief, terror and despair may be inflicted not only upon a hostile government, but upon the people who accepted it. The outcome of our nobility can only be their greater suffering, their more prolonged ordeal.

It may be that now we have no alternative but to press on to victory over the men and women who have endorsed and practised the militaristic creed which now forces us to perfect the arts of destruction. It may be that we have no choice but to convert those conquered countries which were once our friends into starving hostages whose clamorous needs will cause them to rise against their conqueror. Many pacifists who have grown old in the service of peace now feel themselves compelled to take this

43

view. I refuse to attack or condemn men and women of such proved honesty and rare nobility as Bertrand Russell and Maude Royden.

There are, I know, quite a number of eminent persons who have so successfully boxed the compass in this war, that they have not only avoided persecution but have cleverly furthered their own interests in the process of recantation. Nobody could put either Maude Royden or Bertrand Russell into this time-server's category. I believe I understand the days and nights of self-questioning which led them, with painful reluctance, to change their minds. But I cannot myself accept the view that there is not – much less that there was not – any other possibility than the heroic recklessness of our present resistance.

Am I, who so dearly love my country and so sincerely admire its brave, imperturbable people, really playing the part of a defeatist when I inquire what would have happened if all the energy, courage and resourcefulness which is now dedicated to the work of destruction, had been given to seeking a solution for Europe's problems while time still remained? This war, we say, was brought upon the world by one nation's ruthless ambition. Supposing that to be the whole truth and nothing but the truth, could not the national genius which we possess, and are now displaying, have suggested a policy which would have prevented the rise of those ambitious rulers, or a plan which would have compelled even them to negotiate a tolerable peace in their own interests as well as ours? The aggressor is never solely to blame, since aggression must always prove abortive unless it is assisted from without by provocation, incompetence or indifference.

Why must it be only in war that we awaken from our inertia, put a government with driving energy into power, rouse the world to a chorus of praise for our achievements? Suppose that the crusading courage of our young pilots, the vigilant energy of our soldiers and sailors, the brave uncomplaining endurance of our civilians, were harnessed to the imaginative construction of friendly international relationships based on mutual sacrifice and co-operative good will? Imagine what would happen if they were dedicated to revitalising the Church, rebuilding the slums,

44

re-invigorating literature, music and art, reorganising from top to bottom the economic system based on privilege and power, tackling the vexed problem of distribution, making equal education and opportunities available for all?

Should we not even in one decade be appreciably nearer to building the City of God in the green lanes and pleasant villages where now the incendiary bombs make hell upon earth and the German planes crash in an inferno of blazing oil and splintering steel?

'Do I not have an account to settle between my soul and him?' wrote Dr Harry Emerson Fosdick, the famous minister of Riverside Church in New York, as he apostrophised in penitence the Unknown Soldier. 'They sent men like me into the camps to awaken his idealism, to touch those secret, holy springs within him so that with devotion, fidelity, loyalty and self-sacrifice he might go out to war. . . . If wars were fought simply with evil things, like hate, it would be bad enough, but when one sees the deeds of war done with the loveliest faculties of the human spirit, he looks into the very pit of hell.'

Have we not, too, an account to settle with the Unknown Pilot, whose ashes we take from his burnt-out aeroplane and cover with earth and grass? Is not the apathy or the misdirected energies of numerous Guilty Men responsible for the fires which consume those ardent young lives, and the years of promise and achievement which should have been theirs? And are not you and I responsible for choosing those Guilty Men, or for failing to remove them when they allowed our neighbours to become our enemies?

By the sacrificial heroism of our youthful airmen, by the vigilant courage of our soldiers and sailors, by the bravery of our civilian defenders, and by the quiet endurance of men and women who guard their homes and save their children while scorning to save themselves, let us vow that never, never again shall we ask a young generation to die for their land instead of using their superb qualities for the building of permanent peace.

Hitler's bombing of London was intensified by a heavy raid on the afternoon of 7 September 1940. It continued every night and often in the day until 17 November. After that there were spasmodic and sometimes very heavy raids for most of the war.

Dick Sheppard's name inevitably recurs in several of these Letters, as he was the source of much inspiration to Vera.

He was the Very Reverend Hugh Richard Lawrie Sheppard, Canon and Precentor of St Paul's Cathedral; also one of the King's Chaplains. He became well known and popular as a broadcaster when vicar of St Martin-in-the-Fields from 1914 to 1927. As has already been recorded, he founded the Peace Pledge Union in 1934 and died in 1937.

The gods are not angry for ever. . . .

– Homer, *The Iliad*

If you live, as I do, in London, you will not easily forget the brilliant Tuesday, September 3rd, on which we celebrated the first anniversary of this second World War of our generation.

You will remember the raid warning – our thirty-second since August 15th – which lasted from 10.30 till 11.30 a.m. and ended precisely a year from the first pseudo-warning that sounded over London immediately after Chamberlain had broadcast the declaration of war. The siren of September 3rd, 1940, was no fake alarm; all morning, from the misty blue-grey ceiling, came the throb of invisible aeroplanes – the British light, the German dull and heavy. Whatever part of London you live in, they always seem, by day or by night, to be passing just overhead.

Then, when the disturbed morning had ended and a second afternoon warning was over with one of the hottest days of this grimly beautiful summer, you looked up in the late evening to a perfect pale blue sky, with feathery drifts of cloud sweeping like celestial brooms across the peaceful heavens from which death and disaster so incongruously descend. Perhaps, to your pre-occupied imagination as to mine, the rooks flying home resembled miniature black bombers, strangely menacing in their flight. But away to the west, a luminous cirrus-cloud formation took on the appearance of a distant sea-shore with snow-white sands, where tired humanity, wearied of the terrible futility of destruction, might rest at last. Perhaps, I thought, that placid evening sky after hours of battle is a symbol of the life of this generation. Perhaps, when the too eventful days of our years have drawn nearer to their close, we who have known so much war and catastrophe will find peace at eventide.

All over this lovely island which peril has rendered dearer than ever to most of us, we look as I write, upon the same warm harvest beauty which greeted the outbreak of war a year ago. But there are desolate areas now – London districts with houses, streets or factories demolished, seaside towns and ports with acres of ruin behind a proud façade of normality, damaged regions in Scotland, Wales, the Midlands and the West. There is little, perhaps, as yet which rivals the devastated areas of the last Great War – but at last we in England know warfare as it has not appeared here since the Civil War four hundred years ago, nor from outside these shores for nearly nine centuries.

When I walk a hundred yards from my house and inspect the craters made by three bombs which crashed last week into the pleasant square where my children played as babies, I realise that war now appears much the same to me as it looked to the mothers of France and Belgium twenty-five years ago. We need not now – as some of us did then – put on a uniform and take a train and boat in order to find it. In spite of the normal appearance of our homes and gardens, of the household routine which we refuse to allow raid warnings to disturb, the war is with us always whether we like it or not. We defeat its influence best by going steadily on with our job – whether this be guarding an aerodrome, working in an office or factory, tending patients in hospital, cooking the dinner, or writing a book – with the maximum concentration of which we are capable. The better we wrest order out of potential chaos, the more effectively we counter not merely the attacking Nazis, but war itself.

Sometimes, in the midst of this determined self-discipline, we pause to think – a function which those of us who have the luck to survive will probably perform rather better when the present period of curtailed nights and interrupted days recedes into the past. When we do think, we realise what a year of history lies behind us; a twelvemonth of almost uninterrupted calamity. We remember the invasions of Poland, Norway, Denmark, Holland and Belgium; the thundrous collapse of France; the astonishing rescue of the British Expeditionary Force from Dunkirk; the change of government at Westminster; the air fights over Kent, Essex and London. We recall the galloping sequence of events which has left us alone to carry on a war that need never have occurred if we had been ready to show the same unsupported courage at the council tables of Europe as we are now displaying on the battlefields of Britain.

How many of us reflect that, hitherto, history has recorded man's disasters rather than the constructive tale of his achievements? 'Happy is the country which has no history' is an aphorism taken by most of us to mean 'How fortunate is the nation which has had no calamities to interrupt the story of its progress.' I remember lecturing at Middlesbrough on the evening of Edward VIII's abdication, and remarking that, like most of my audience, I belonged to a generation which had known too much history in the accepted sense of the word. How much more we were still to experience I did not then realise – although, having visited Germany that spring and heard Hitler speak at Cologne, I perceived possibilities which I still hoped that Europe's politicians might have the belated wisdom to forestall.

Now we are right in the midst of an epoch which for tragedy and intensity has probably never been equalled. You and I are unlikely to agree with Churchill that a period of unmitigated destruction could ever be 'our finest hour'; yet, peace-lovers though we are, we tend with each day of isolated struggle to become more and more consciously citizens of this land. In every department of life we have incomparable opportunities (if not quite the kind that many of us would choose) of serving the community of which we are part. If we seize, in accordance with our conscience, whatever chances of service come our way, they will make other and better opportunities for us when the war is over. For over it will be one day – leaving behind it a trail of human wreckage and social problems, whoever is the winner and whatever the terms of peace may be.

That day is not yet in sight, but we know that some of us will see it, and must prepare to write another type of history when it comes. The service of re-dedication last Sunday at St Martin-in-the-Fields, with the memories of Dick Sheppard's life and Winifred Holtby's death, recalled to me a morning spent in the English Church at Boulogne twenty-three years ago, commemorating the third anniversary of the first Great War. The Chaplain-General to the Forces then read the collect which concludes with the words: 'Spare us, good Lord, spare Thy people whom Thou hast redeemed with Thy most precious blood, and be not angry with us for ever.' And I remember how, as I knelt with the khaki-clad congregation in the soft light that filtered through the high stained glass windows, a phrase slipped into my head from my recent classical studies at Oxford: 'The gods are not angry for ever. . . .'

But now I know – as I knew even then – that when the gods cease to be angry, it is not their doing, but ours. We cannot save our rocking civilisation by reliance upon some supernatural effort, some divine intervention; we alone can redress the blunders and barbarisms for which we have been responsible, and find some new basis for the future which we must build. And we need not wait for the end of the war to admit our mistakes, and discover – as we never discovered in 1918 – the foundations of that better society which will develop out of our failures.

Never, perhaps, has an English generation suffered so much as yours and mine if you were born, like myself, in the closing years of the nineteenth century – a century which, in the unparalleled speed of its material achievements, had lost the spiritual vigilance which alone can rescue the race of man from its own tendency to self-destruction. But if, when this second Great War of our lifetime is over, we can weave from the stuff of our experience a pattern of civilisation quite other than the stereotyped design which formed the background of our youth, then we may even find it to have been expedient that one generation should suffer for posterity.

South Riding was Winifred Holtby's now well-known novel about the lives of people in her native Yorkshire, the way they were affected by local government and the complex motives of those responsible for it. Her mother was Yorkshire's first woman councillor.

Vera, as Winifred's literary executor, was responsible for its publication in 1936, a year after Winifred's death. The book (reprinted Virago, 1987) was later made into a film and television series.

He who would valiant be
'Gainst all disaster,
Let him in constancy
Follow the Master.
There's no discouragement
Shall make him once relent
His first avowed intent
To be a pilgrim.
— John Bunyan, *Pilgrim Song*

Again I have to apologise to you for the lateness of your letter. This time it is partly due to the extent to which I myself have been involved in the Blitzkrieg.

Writing from the blessed seclusion of a weekend in Berkshire after five weeks of bombing, I realise how little those who have the good fortune to live in the country know of the ordeal which London and other industrial areas are now enduring. As one who has had a good deal of 'blitz' to contend with – though not, I fear, nearly so much as some of you – a brief résumé of my experiences may lead you who are mercifully distant from London to forgive this retarded letter.

For those of us whose homes are in south or south-west London, bombing and gunfire began to disturb our nights as long ago as August 15th. But it was not until September 7th – when the church-bells rang as though for an invasion, and London was brilliantly lighted by the great dockyard fire caused by the afternoon raid – that the Nazis began to show what they could do. That very night a bomb fell on the roof of a house which backed on to one where I was staying in Kensington. The windows were open, and the blast hurled me downstairs. Two days later, a suburban train on which I was travelling ran into an afternoon raid, and was bombed and machine-gunned while I lay on the floor among the cigarette ends expecting every moment to be my last. In another three days, my Chelsea house had to be evacuated because a time bomb fell a few yards away. This is still unexploded, and as others have since joined it, I have not yet been allowed in to rescue the manuscript of *South Riding* and other valuable papers which I rashly allowed to remain there.

Today, homeless and a refugee, deprived even of my family because my children are at school in America and my husband went over some weeks ago to fulfil a university contract made while Hitler was still behind the Maginot Line, I am nevertheless aware how universal amongst Londoners are occurrences such as I have described. I feel ashamed to have found so shattering the combined experiences of solitude and peril, and to realise how much less of courage and philosophy I possess than the men and women of the East End who have borne the worst fury of the aerial attack. I understand now how difficult of attainment is the ideal of courage expressed in the lines at the head of this letter – lines which I quoted so often on pre-war peace plat-forms. Quite apart from my own insignificant trials, I confess that my heart sometimes fails as I watch the gradual transforma-tion of the London that I love from a city of beauty and dignity to one reduced with a diabolical thoroughness to the squalor of destruction and dislocation. It needs Christ himself to remember constantly the seventeen-year-old pilots compelled by their masters to this horror of indiscriminate ruin, and to say of them – as of our own young men who are raining nightly death upon the French coast and the Ruhr: 'Father, forgive them, for they know not what they do.'

I cannot be sure whether it is the East End or the West End which gives me most thoroughly the sense of having gone to sleep and woken up in the midst of H. G. Wells' film *The Shape of Things to Come*. The East End, of course, is the heart of human tragedy, but bombing has made less difference to its physical appearance – most of which was anyhow due for rebuilding, if only safe alternative accommodation had been provided for its tragic families.

The other day I walked through Regent Street and Oxford Street, when the fire hoses were still playing on John Lewis's gutted store. From the shattered window-ledge of one upper storey, an orange silk vest hung poised to remind passers-by of the luxurious prosperity which has already vanished. In Regent

Street, not one dignified shop seemed to have escaped with windows unsmashed or frontage unblackened. At the top of the street, Peter Robinson's magnificent store with a huge ugly gash in its side dominated the forlorn scene. The air was filled with the smell of burning wood; the wide empty street lay ankle-deep in glass. In one elegant furniture shop, where the plate-glass window had been completely destroyed, two beautiful yellow porcelain vases stood untouched on their pedestals. Up and down the pavements moved a silent throng of spectators, bewildered and aghast. They passed indifferently under dangerous walls; showers of glass fell round them as they moved. A stalwart steel-helmeted policeman remonstrated with weary resignation: 'Naw, then, show a little common sense, cawn't yer!'

The previous day, I had been down to the East End to take part, as a visitor and observer, in an Emergency Relief Committee called at Kingsley Hall by that finest of Quaker leaders, John Hoyland. With him had come a vigorous group of young Friends from Birmingham to help tackle the problems created by the bombing of the crowded boroughs. Just as I arrived the siren went for about the hundredth time, and our committee meeting was held in a white-washed dug-out beneath Kingsley Hall, with a concrete ceiling, and cushions on the floor.

Only a few days before, an aerial torpedo had fallen just outside the Settlement, turning the surrounding region into a devastated area. It was hardly surprising that we shared our business meeting with numerous mothers and children who sought refuge in the friendly shelter. For some reason, I was reminded of Swinburne's poem, 'Watchman, what of the night?' If anything could have given assurance that dawn would eventually come, it was the tranquil determination of John Hoyland and his group of young men to do what they could towards clearing up the chaos brought to London's poorest areas by generations of irresponsible politicians, who never really believed that they who sow the wind must reap the whirlwind.

The Committee was obliged to conclude that the problem of the East End – its wrecked houses, its homeless families, its inadequate shelters and the increasingly grim conditions inside them – is one of such magnitude that only the government itself, or bodies such as the LCC and the local borough councils, possess sufficient resources to tackle it on an adequate scale. It is beyond the scope of voluntary organisations, though these can usefully put pressure on the authorities to take defence measures – such as the provision of deep shelters – which ought to have been put in hand months ago. There is, however, one way in which peace-lovers who live in the country can help, and that is by finding empty mansions which can accommodate large numbers of evacuees, by forming friendly groups which will be responsible for billeting them in private households. There is practically no limit to the number of families which need and are now ready to accept accommodation. If you or your friends have a concrete offer to make, I know that Doris Lester, the Warden of Kingsley Hall, Bow Road, E, will be only too glad to receive and make use of it.

Well, this is war as Madrid, Pekin and Helsinki have known it. For all the warnings that I used to issue at public meetings, I don't think I ever quite believed that it would come to London, and I don't suppose that you did either. There is not much, now, that you and I can do, except to seek the courage that comes from carrying on our work as best we can, however often the conditions of our lives may threaten to break our hearts and extinguish our spirits. Whether you are an ARP Warden who now, after months of boredom, have maximum danger to face; whether you are a civil servant, a journalist, a housewife, or, like myself, a creative worker confronted with the baffling task of writing a book containing some measure of hope and encouragement in a world which holds too little of either, you can say to yourself: 'I'll pull it off! I won't be done, not even by war itself.'

And if, like myself, you are a natural coward, tormented by grim sights and terrified by destructive sounds, you can also add: 'I know I'm afraid. Let me admit that, and get it over without any fuss. But let me also determine that not every fear is going to prevent me from doing what I set out to do, knowing that the very shrinking of my flesh and spirit from danger gives me fellowship with an ever-growing band of men and women who, because they have now known in their own souls not only the horror, but the humiliation of modern warfare, will one day work against its recurrence as no generation has ever worked before.'

_____ 2 January 1941 _____

Be kind, for most folks are fighting a hard battle
— National Wayside Pulpit No. 126,
displayed outside a village chapel in North Cornwall

I begin this first letter of 1941 with the wish that the New Year may bring us all more sanity, peace and happiness than the one which has gone. I should like also to thank you for the many cards, letters and messages of encouragement that I have received this Christmas from you and your fellow readers. I acknowledge these kindnesses with the more appreciation because my own plans for sending Christmas greetings to my friends were interrupted by an event which meant bitter grief for some sad families, and barely missed bringing tragedy to me and mine.

You will probably have noticed, in one or two of these letters, a passing reference to the absence of my husband in America, where his work has lain for the greater part of this war. On December 6th he sailed from New York for a brief Christmas visit, not merely to me, but at least as much to his bombed and battered country. The boat he chose was the *Western Prince*.

From the time that this liner was reported by the Sunday newspapers of December 15th to have been torpedoed and sunk in mid-Atlantic before dawn the previous day, until the following Wednesday afternoon when the little rescue ship arrived at a western port, I did not know whether or not my husband was among the survivors. Actually, his rescue and that of many other passengers was little short of a miracle, quite apart from the fact

56

that he did not at first hear the alarm and was the last passenger to get into the lifeboats.

The salvation of 150 persons was due, by the mercy of God, to four factors, of which the absence of any one would have meant a far greater if not a total disaster. First, there was, quite genuinely, no panic, and a very high level of behaviour on the part of everybody concerned. In his description published on December 19th, Mr James Bone, the London editor of the *Manchester Guardian*, who was also on the liner, reports that, far from the passengers fighting for the lifeboats, it was difficult in the early morning darkness for the crew to find the persons intended to occupy them.

In the second place, the high proportion of survivors owe their lives to the magnificent British seamanship which launched and kept afloat six lifeboats in a heavy rising sea. In the third, they are indebted to the gallantry of a small freighter's crew, who unanimously volunteered to go into the danger area and rescue – just before a cold stormy night which the occupants of the lifeboats could hardly have survived – a large number of ship-wrecked individuals whose transport would have left their rescuers without hope for themselves had the little cargo boat been torpedoed in its turn.

Finally, the survivors escaped owing to the mercifulness of the German submarine commander, who allowed the lifeboats to get clear of the *Western Prince* before his final attack. To quote Mr Bone again:

A ship appeared about twenty yards away on the starboard side of our lifeboat, the tower and part of the deck of the German submarine. She submerged as she passed by, and there was a flash which was thought to mean that photographs of us had been taken. I watched closely the faces of the sailors and firemen, massed in our bows watching the enemy. I saw no fear in their eyes, but a terrible tension like a white shadow passed over their faces. 'I thought he was going to give us the machine guns,' said one sailor as he relaxed.

In his broadcast to America relating this experience, my husband wanted to pay a tribute to the German commander for his observation of the rules of international law. He was prevented from doing so – not, as you may perhaps imagine, because the British propaganda authorities wished to suppress an acknowledgment of German decency, but because the broadcast might be heard in Germany and the commander penalised for sparing his victims. Silence was, therefore, a comprehensible if unexpected method of showing mercy to the merciful. My husband reports that, though some passengers spoke bitterly of an attack which nearly cost them their lives and deprived them of all their possessions, the sailors themselves showed no resentment. In their view the German was just doing his job, and it was all part of the fortune of war. Like some of us who have been bombed in London, Coventry, Birmingham, Bristol, Sheffield, Southampton and Manchester, these men to whom peril is the order of the day have no desire for reprisals.

I have written you about the sinking of the *Western Prince*, not because it so nearly became, for my family and me, a major personal tragedy, but on account of a very small incident which happened simultaneously. You may remember that [in a previous letter] I quoted from the wise and beautiful booklet: 'The First Year of War: A Review and a Re-dedication', which I had found a few weeks previously in St Paul's Cathedral. During the weekend in which the *Western Prince* was torpedoed, one copy of this letter was returned to me with these words scribbled across it: 'Will you please stop sending these letters. No one in this house wants them. We're all too busy doing our bit to bother with such nonsense.'

It is not, of course, surprising that such outbursts should occasionally reach me; what does astonish me is that amid the heated passions of a tense and costly war, they are still so few. The only significance of this malevolent message lies in the fact that it was sent me at a time when I was not only facing – like so many mothers – the first Christmas without my children, but was waiting, in a suspense which I need not describe, to know whether or not my husband had been lost at sea.

I record this incident in no spirit of self-commiseration. My husband was in fact saved, and my children's delightful cables

58

from America show that they, at any rate, are well, happy and free from homesickness. But, as Mr Bone wrote of December 14th, 'The line between wives and widows was a very close one that Saturday.' Had the captain of the British freighter displayed less courage and the German submarine commander less mercy, this particular small act of cruelty would have coincided with the moment of widowhood. And however vehemently occasional readers of this letter may object to my views (though, oddly enough, the issue selected not only endeavoured to embody the spirit of the Christian teaching, but did so with reference to the authoritative pronouncements of St Paul's Cathedral itself), I do not believe that they would wish to belabour me or anyone else at a time of acute personal disaster.

The episode, insignificant enough in itself, shows how easily today any one of us, by some thoughtless manifestation of unkindness, may intensify the human suffering which is now so widespread. It gives point to the wisdom and timeliness of the Wayside Pulpit message quoted at the head of this letter and displayed outside a chapel in the Cornish village where I am spending Christmas with my mother – who came here to live with a sister when her house in Kensington was partly demolished.

If you are one of the many non-pacifist readers of this letter, you will, I know, forgive me for reminding you that careless cruelty displayed today by the united majority towards those who hold minority opinions is likely to cause exceptional pain owing to the fact that the minorities are sharing the common burden to a more than equal degree. During the last war – when so many of us, young and ardent, put on uniforms and went out to seek adventure in France, the Mediterranean or the Near East – any pacifist who was not a young man of military age and therefore faced with imprisonment, could with perhaps some justification be criticised for voluntary dissociation from national suffering. Today, precisely the opposite is true. Without even the satisfaction of believing that he suffers in a righteous cause, the pacifist who may have spent years in striving to prevent this war is as liable as its most convinced advocate to the loss of his home, the break up of his family, and the death or injury by aerial bombardment of those whom he loves best. A bitter attack upon him for his opinions may coincide with the bombing of his house or the death of his child.

Let me emphasise, however, that the Wayside Pulpit injunction is addressed to the minority no less than the majority. Many times, in pacifist publications, I have seen statesmen, churchmen, authors and editors personally attacked with a bitterness which seems to be especially regrettable when displayed by members of our particular fellowship. Although we know that considerations of personal prestige do enter the calculations of those who occupy the high places of this world with perhaps more frequency than amongst obscurer men and women, it is none the less true that many eminent persons with whose outlook we do not agree are doing their job with an honest and disinterested regard for principles which seem as obvious to them as ours appear to us. And they, too, have private griefs and anxieties – perhaps for sons who are pilots, for wives or daughters working in danger areas, for beloved children evacuated overseas.

The sum total of human suffering today is so much greater than ever before in the history of the world, that not one of us can afford to forget for one moment our Master's exhortation: 'Be ye therefore merciful, as your Father also is merciful.'

The focus of the war at this time was on North Africa where Rommel had arrived to take over the conduct of the hitherto Italian campaign. By mid-May the Germans were in Greece, Yugoslavia and Crete.

The book Vera refers to in the third paragraph of the letter that follows was *England's Hour*. It was about the London blitz, was published in 1941 by Macmillan and republished in 1981 by Futura.

Christianity has not been weighed in the balance and found wanting; it has been found difficult and has not been tried
                                                                — G. K. Chesterton

I begin this letter sitting in the spring sunshine as it pours through the wide south window of my flat. Last week, as I travelled through southern England from Southampton – another of the blitzed but unbowed cities which I have recently visited – I noticed the pussy-willows bursting like miniature spools of grey silk from the bare black branches. Today, a hundred yards from my flat, gold and white crocuses spangle the grass in Hyde Park with the prodigal loveliness of previous years. As a friend remarked to me the other day: 'Even Hitler cannot stop the spring.'

A hundred yards in the opposite direction, a demolition squad is clearing the debris from a recently bombed building of which the ground floor was once an elegant show-room for luxury cars. The removal of the shattered masonry has revealed the grotesque transformation of those costly machines to rusty scrap heaps of twisted metal. Mentally comparing the gay affirmative crocuses in the Park with these grim symbols of a civilisation engaged in destroying its own prosperity, I find myself strenuously agreeing with the author of 'From Greenland's icy mountains' that there are indeed occasions when every prospect pleases and only man is vile.

You will probably feel, as I do, that one of the saddest consequences of prolonged warfare is the deliberate cultivation by normally civilised persons of the potentially viler qualities which are inherent in us all. The other day I was sent the cutting, from a magazine to which I used to contribute, of a review given by a distinguished novelist to my latest book. Some years ago, I remember finding in the same magazine, by the identical novelist, one of the most moving short stories I have ever read; it described, in starkly simple language which emphasised its poignancy, the trial of a mother who had murdered her son rather than see him submitted to the horrors of another war. But times change, bringing situations which cause distinguished authors, like other individuals, to revise their values. This one, at any rate, roundly attacked my point of view for being 'the antithesis of nearly everything that the Prime Minister stands for'.

Now no writer, and paricularly a writer with certain minority opinions which become disproportionately conspicuous in war-time, expects a wholly favourable press for any publication. It is even possible that some people might find not utterly objection-able qualities which are the antithesis of everything that the Prime Minister stands for. The criticism would not be worth mentioning, had not the chapter in my book which is specially selected as 'neither virile nor constructive' been the one which deals with the theme of forgiveness. The reviewer pilloried by quotation one sentence from this chapter: 'If we do not learn to forgive, this nation has already lost the peace; and if it loses yet another peace, the war of 1965 will annihilate our children and our London too.' From this she proceeds to her own conclusion: 'Let us learn to forgive by all means, but not through the con-templation of a war of 1965. It is a victory of 1941–42 that we should be concentrating on at the moment, and we can but do that by attending to the job in hand. It will be much easier to forgive the Nazis when we have delivered their victims, driven them from the field and the air and the seas, and taken stock of the new world-position that must then ensue.'

Doubtless you have noticed, as I have, a rapid recent growth of the idea that charity, forgiveness and even foresight (as in the persistent evasion of an official statement of peace aims) are effete, sentimental and 'unconstructive'. The fact that charity and forgiveness are the fundamentals of the Christian teaching which ostensibly dictates our national standards is as carefully disregarded as it was in 1914–19. Persons who identify 'virility' with vindictiveness and use 'realism' as a camouflage term for indiscriminate reprisals, do not, of course, loudly and publicly attack the teaching of Christ and the writings of St Paul. Even the most reactionary clerics might object to that. There are many humbler and safer targets for the slings and arrows of war propagandists, while it is left to little known writers like George Orwell to pour discreet scorn (as he does in his latest publication) upon the Sermon on the Mount and those who quote it.

One of the most conspicuous symptoms of this growing moral decline is the obliteration of the distinction, so sedulously observed during the early months of the war, between the Nazi leaders and the German people. Week after week, leading editors celebrate the Sabbath by urging us to annihilate German and Italian cities, to set their farms and forests ablaze, to erase the memorials of their civilisation before they can do further damage to ours. Nowhere have I seen a protest that the last persons to suffer from such a policy will be the Nazi leaders; that those who must actually feel it will be the humble dockers and woodcutters of Germany. (It has become as automatic to overlook this fact as to forget that the inevitable Nazi reprisals will be paid for by Yarmouth fishermen or helpless Whitechapel householders, and never by the well-guarded politicians and editors who identify courage and initiative with the limits of reciprocal frightfulness.) Love, humanity, pity, are qualities which now lack 'practical' value. When, as my reviewer says, we have defeated the Nazis and delivered their victims (with whom meanwhile we are presumably making ourselves popular by bombing them repeatedly), there will be plenty of time to think about forgiving them.

But will there? If you have ever really tried to forgive an injury to your pride or an insult to your family, you will know as well as I do that magnanimity is not a virtue which you can put into cold storage for the duration and take out again unimpaired at the end of the war. Save in the case of a few exceptionally noble spirits such as Dick Sheppard and Winifred Holtby, forgiveness and generosity are not instinctive qualities. They have to be fought for again and again – as those of us who sometimes suffer abuse know only too well. The impulse to 'hit back' now so universally challenged by war savings posters is always the first to arise. Most of us have an immense amount of pride-swallowing to achieve before we can conquer our natural pugnacity and return the soft answer to those who have injured us.

I do not for a moment suggest that the persons who have persuaded themselves that we must cultivate vindictiveness and ferocity are not wholly sincere. In their sincerity lies their danger. Thanks to them, when this war is over and we ought indeed to be thinking in terms of forgiveness if the war of 1965 is to be prevented, we shall find that we have lost the power to do so. Like the ugly weeds in our cottage gardens, hatred, pride and resentment are qualities which grow all too readily without cultivation. If we cultivate them deliberately and as carefully cease to cultivate their opposites, we shall find that this hellish bindweed has throttled to death the more sensitive plants of wisdom and compassion.

We need not look further back than our own time to establish the historic truth of this fact. As Mr Lloyd George's Memoirs and other war documents make clear, the 'peace' of 1919 was not lost through the malevolence of statesmen so much as by the accumulated vindictiveness of the common man – expressed in England at the 'Khaki Election' of 1918. Much of this vindictiveness was undoubtedly due to comprehensible causes, such as the loss of sons, the ruin of ambitions, and the decimation of families. But however understandable and even excusable, this partly press-created animosity had political consequences which a few of us dimly foresaw and struggled desperately to prevent, using our brief holidays and the few pounds we could then scrape together to study the situation in Geneva and Central Europe while some of those who now hold us up to contempt were taking things easily on the Riviera.

'Not a generation nor a dozen generations', wrote Winifred Holtby from Cologne in 1924, 'will heal the breaches made by centuries of folly here.' That same autumn, in that same city, I recorded a similar conclusion in my diary: 'There is a strange lack of dignity in conquest . . . Modern war is nothing but a temporary – though how disastrous! – forgetfulness by neighbours that they are gentlemen. Its only result must be the long reaping in sorrow of that which was sown in pride.'

In those days the harvest truly might have been plentiful, but the labourers were insufficient. Enjoying their years of relaxation after the rigours of the last war, too few travellers journeyed to uncomfortable places to see things for themselves, too few powerful voices gave a lead to eager struggling youth. The results are as we see them today.

With all the sincerity of which I am capable, I say to you that this historic tragedy will simply repeat itself unless – not after we have beaten the Nazis, but *now* – we begin deliberately to prepare our minds and discipline our emotions for the situation which will confront us after the war. As long ago as February, 1940, the principal of the Institut Français, speaking in London, gave it as the opinion of the French that Germany must be disarmed and placed under Allied tutelage for at least thirty to fifty years. Though the French have no longer the power to enforce this opinion, there are persons in England – who shall be nameless, though we can all name them – who hold this view. The lessons of history – not merely the rise of the Nazis, but the rearmament of Germany under Stein during the Napoleonic wars, and the resurrection of Poland after more than a century of annihilation – make no impression upon their closed minds.

It is they, and not the pacifists – the more constructive of whom are interested in exploring new ways of life in accordance with new values, and not in opposing the government – who are both sabotaging the war effort and jeopardising the peace. From the standpoint of the future, they are a greater menace to this country than the Nazi bombs, for they are helping to unite behind Hitler many Germans who would like to see his downfall if they could trust our capacity to make a just settlement. Since part of our official policy is to encourage revolt in Germany, why should irresponsible persons be permitted to advocate, with little opposition, the very plan which can be guaranteed to prevent it?

Not only from the religious and moral aspects but from the most coldly calculated political foresight, I suggest that we begin to cultivate the virtues of charity and forgiveness here and now. The difficult Christianity which has never been tried may well prove to be the truest political realism and our only source of salvation.

The world, with all its beauty and adventure, its richness and variety, is darkened by cruelty. Death, if it ends the loveliness, the adventure, ends also that. Death balances the picture. It completes the pattern. It makes even cruelty fall into place. It is completion

– Winifred Holtby, *Virginia Woolf*

There are many things which I could write to you this week, for it seems clear that the war has taken another turn which is likely to demand all our fortitude.

I might send you some comments on the Balkan campaign and the Nazi capture of Salonika – that famous port, held by us through the last war, whose defenders I nursed during my year of hospital service in Malta. Or I could discuss with you the failing fortunes of Italy, that country in which, by one of the catastrophic ironies of war, we have helped Mussolini and the Nazis to undo the work of Mazzini and Garibaldi, supported with such romantic enthusiasm by the England of that day, and celebrated in many noble poems by Swinburne and the Brownings. Italy is now as much a German province as she was before the War of Liberation, and the lamp of that civilisation which illumined both the Renaissance and the Risorgimento is quenched in the night of military disaster.

But the event which has shadowed my mind for the past two weeks is neither the downfall of Italy nor the Allied setback in the Mediterranean, but the death of Virginia Woolf, which was first made public just after I had written the last issue of this letter. To me her loss is more grievous and significant than the process of a military campaign or even the temporary eclipse of a great country's glory, since it typifies in its stark unalleviated tragedy what war does to the finest flowering of a civilisation.

My personal contacts with Virginia Woolf were few but memorable. I recall sitting, perhaps fifteen years ago, among tall spring irises in Mrs H. M. Swanwick's devotedly cultivated little garden at Kew, and listening to her reminiscences of Sir Leslie Stephen's family. She spoke particularly of his beautiful daughter Virginia, and of an early period of mental illness through which her devoted husband had nursed her and of which she always dreaded a return.

The first time I actually saw Virginia Woolf was about 1928, when a few of us who had reviewed Radclyffe Hall's novel *The Well of Loneliness*, or who knew the author, were invited to a studio in Ebury Street to discuss how we could most effectively protest against the penalisation of free speech on a difficult moral problem. Virginia Woolf sat a little apart from the rest, silently listening to the conversation. She wore a dark red velvet dress and hat, and I was deeply impressed by her tranquil beauty.

Three or four years afterwards I saw her again, when she made one of her rare public appearances in company with her close friend, Dame Ethel Smyth the composer, on an after-dinner platform at the club rooms of the London and National Society for Women's Service. The contrast between the two celebrated women was striking indeed. Dame Ethel, the senior by a quarter of a century, kept the audience convulsed by a pungent and witty speech which she evidently enjoyed delivering; it concluded, I remember, with the suggestion that the only title she would accept from her grateful country was one which would impress the local golf club – 'Ethel, Duchess of Woking.' By comparison Virginia Woolf appeared the more gentle and diffident. In a low voice, audible only through the microphone, she gave a scholarly address which she accompanied with shy but elegant gestures of her thin pale hands.

I do not think that I ever actually spoke to her, but I have three letters from her which I cherish. Two, written after the publication of my two *Testaments*, which she liked though they were so different from her own exquisite work, filled me with grateful pride. But the one which moved me the most came after the death of Winifred Holtby, whose short critical study of Virginia Woolf was in some respects the most profound of her books. I hope that its original publisher or some other will be prevailed upon to reissue it now.

When she began this short study, Winifred did not know

Virginia Woolf at all, so with conscientious humility she limited her subject's life story to a brief introductory chapter. But for this, some personal contact with Virginia Woolf was important, and Dame Ethel Smyth, who already knew Winifred through *Time and Tide*, arranged for the two to meet.

Now Virginia Woolf, in her fifties is gone, while Ethel Smyth, in her gallant eighties, is left to mourn. The 'appreciations' written of Virginia Woolf by friends and critics on the Sunday following the announcement of her disappearance struck me as extraordinarily inept. Even the poem in *The Observer* by V. Sackville West, costly as it must have been to write, was one of the least adequate that I have ever read of her beautiful verses. It seemed to me that these friends had been hurried over their threnodies, as though the manner of Virginia Woolf's death at this time was an embarrassment best tidied out of the way.

How far it was a deliberate protest against the sorry situation to which war has brought literature and its exponents throughout Europe, we shall probably never know. But her last pitiful letter makes clear to us the effect of London bombs and the planes incessantly roaring over her Sussex home upon a sensitive mind always living in fear of its own infirmity. One newspaper recently stated that the house in a famous Bloomsbury Square where Leonard and Virginia Woolf ran the Hogarth Press had been partly demolished, but this seems to be exaggeration. I passed the house only the other day; the windows had been shattered and a notice on the door announced the removal of the Press to Letchworth. But less than fifty yards away yawned a large ugly gap where three or four old houses together had been destroyed. I have now seen many damaged districts in London and elsewhere; few seem to me to have been reduced to a more sordid grimness than the area surrounding this once most dignified of London's squares.

The minds of those who deliberately seek death are seldom open to analysis. It may be that Virginia Woolf felt that the war, for too long, had put an end to all she cared for; that she had no contribution to make to the 'tough' society which it is in the process of evolving. Her end was perhaps a kind of protest, the most terrible and effective that she could make, against the real hell which international conflict creates for the artist.

Of all those whom war penalises, musicians, painters and writers probably suffer the most. Their world is always so full, so deeply interesting, that they have no need of acute political crises to give them excitement or provide them with occupation. The society in which they can create most effectively is one spiritually and intellectually on the up-grade – a society such as the Greeks enjoyed in the time of Pericles, the Italians during the Renaissance, Shakespeare and Spenser in the Elizabethan age, the great Victorian authors during the nineteenth century. War, especially its modern variety, is the most tragic interruption conceivable of all that 'the makers' do and are. There is no escape from totalitarian warfare – not even by retiring to California like James Hilton and Aldous Huxley. It seeks out the author, painter and composer, and runs him down wherever he goes.

'At certain moments – and this is one of them,' writes Storm Jameson in her book of essays, *Civil Journey*, 'all writers who can claim to be called "living" must be political in a sense . . . A care for justice, a detestation of cruelty, are no more than one expects of an honest writer. He can sometimes – if he has taken care to be born in a more fortunate age – leave thinking directly of them. But not this day. Not this day, with us.'

The only method of adaptation for the artist under present conditions is to acquire what the Quakers call 'a concern' for the problems that war creates for mankind and for exploring the routes that lead out of these problems – an essentially political pursuit. And this – except for a few individual giants like George Bernard Shaw – means accepting the position of a minor artist because enough attention cannot be given to the full-time job of becoming a major one. Some of us have adapted ourselves in that way, sacrificing concentration upon our art to the overwhelming bludgeonings of circumstance. Virginia Woolf perhaps preferred to die. She was too fragile, and not young enough, to adapt herself to these times. In any case she would not, I think, have wished to do so. She could no more compromise with the brutalised values which are now being accepted by many civilised minds than James Joyce, the protesting invalid exile who made long lists of proof corrections for *Finnegan's Wake* with the Germans at the gates of Paris, could compromise with the circumstances that sent him out of tottering France. She preferred to say – in words written ten years ago, at the end of *The Waves*, which might stand for her epitaph: 'Against you I will fling myself, unvanquished and unyielding, O Death!'

In April 1941 Ernest Bevin, Minister of Labour and National Service, introduced compulsory registration for all women between the ages of eighteen and forty-five.

On 10 May Rudolph Hess, Hitler's deputy, flew alone to Scotland, parachuting to within twelve miles of the home of the Duke of Hamilton, with whom he wished to discuss a 'mission of humanity'. It was a sensational event, though nothing came of it and there were doubts about Hess's sanity. After the war he was sent to Spandau prison as a war criminal and remained there, guarded by British, American and Russian soldiers, until his death in 1987.

That same night most of the House of Commons was destroyed in a fire-bomb raid. For security reasons official statements rarely went beyond saying that bombs had been dropped on 'Southern England' or London, but on this occasion Churchill did not hesitate to tell the world that the Nazis had tried to destroy the seat of democracy.

Hugh Walpole and Max Plowman, both writers and the latter a well-known pacifist, died at about this time.

I believe that in a society which has decided to go to war – and the majority of our society, whether you like it or not, has so decided – conscription is fairer than the voluntary system. That is, it is fairer to those who have accepted the war as a necessary evil. And if it is to be applied to men, then – in an increasingly equalitarian society – it should be applied to women.

I came to this conclusion during the last war; and though I have changed my views about the inevitability of war, I have not altered my opinion that – granted the acceptance of war by the majority – conscription is more democratic than the voluntary system. The notion that it is the peculiar product of totalitarianism is historically inaccurate; its origin was the *levée en masse* in the most democratic of uprisings, the French Revolutionary War. I realise, of course, that conscription is part of the war machine, and that all war brings totalitarianism. But it gives no advantage to wealth and privilege; it saves from ignominy those convinced war supporters who cannot be in uniform and it spares the individual from much of the anguish inflicted by the voluntary system.

That anguish, bad enough for men, was in the last war intolerable for women. In those days every kind of voluntary service to which women were called was hampered and complicated by family claims. The parents of my youth were not to blame; they had been brought up in a Victorian world which regarded daughters as super-domestic servants whose first duty was to be available in family crises. This widely endorsed attitude involved the daughter in a constant moral tussle between her duty to her country and her duty to her family, which her brother, unable to leave the Army when he was once in it, was wholly spared. I suspect that old-fashioned parents, though less conspicuously in the majority than they were during the last war, are still in existence, so for the sake of the girls of today who have resolved that their country's interests come before any other claim, I am glad that the government has decided to place them in a position where their allegiance cannot be challenged by purely private demands.

Needless to say, this does not mean that I endorse the application of conscription to the woman pacifist. She ought, of course, to have been placed in the same position as the man pacifist and given the right to object to her summons. The fact that in practice she is unlikely to be compelled to do war work to which her conscience is opposed should not, I think, have caused Mr Bevin to deprive her of the right to object officially. Though not actually asked to kill, she may well feel herself virtually responsible for killing if she finds herself constructing instruments of death; she is thereby made an 'accessory after the fact' to exactly the same degree as the accomplice in a capital crime.

The women who hold this view have two alternatives. In the first place, they can refuse to register and take the consequences. In the second, they can register but state their objection to doing war work on the form provided for registration. Personally, since the negative attitude of objecting, protesting and resisting seems to me only half – and a very inferior half – of pacifism, if my age-group is ever asked to register, I shall state what I am prepared to do in the way of social service, first aid, or whatever form of activity is consistent with my beliefs. I should not refuse to obey the command of the state if the state asked me to undertake some form of work which was essential to the life of the community, but not part of the war machine.

This statement, I feel sure, will provoke a howl of indignation from those die-hard pacifists who feel that any form of state service in wartime is compromise, and 'touching pitch'. I can only reply that if this is true, I would rather soil my hands than remain so self-righteously pure and stainless. Die-hard pacifism seems to me as insufferably relentless, complacent and unimaginative as any other form of die-hardism. You and I may think that the state is wrong when it goes to war, but this does not mean that we are automatically right in every action that we do and every decision that we take. We cannot expect our country to adopt the humble and contrite heart which real peace-making requires unless we begin by modifying our own arrogance as a contribution.

Last week you doubtless felt, like the rest of Britain, that there is no limit to the strain placed upon human credulity by this too eventful war.

Perhaps you passed its Sunday and Monday, as I did, feeling that the debating chamber of the House of Commons, in which so much of our history has been ordained, could not possibly have vanished in a single night. Perhaps you believed, with others, the depressing rumour that Big Ben had suffered mortal damage. On this point, at least, I can reassure readers outside London, for in the usual post-blitz atmosphere of blowing dust and scattered debris, I saw with my own eyes its charred but unimpaired clock-face. A single big gash marked the stonework over the face fronting Victoria Street above the drunken-looking turret on the shattered roof of Westminster Hall.

We had barely recovered from our shock of dismay, when we learned that out of the evening skies of that Saturday, like some semi-mythical apparition from the Twilight of the Gods, had descended the martial figure of Rudolf Hess. These jolts to our credulity, whether gratifying or gruesome, have one advantage which we must not underrate. They compel us to realise that we can be forcibly severed from our dearest traditions and still survive; they provide us with concrete evidence that the most fantastic events conceivable by our wildest imaginations are not impossible; they cause us to accept, almost as commonplace, incongruities which we should never have pictured even a year ago.

This lovely May afternoon, for instance, I am writing to you from a seat in London's Green Park. In the warm sunshine I feel comfortable and almost lazy; a blackbird is chirping on the hawthorn above me; a fat sparrow, undisturbed by my presence, is pecking in the gravel beneath. Yet almost at my feet yawns a large dusty bomb-crater, one of six within a hundred yards or so – the heritage of a recent noisy night. When war brings so many grotesque surprises, who shall now dare to say that even the dream of perpetual peace, so often designated by sceptics as hopelessly improbable, is beyond fulfilment?

Of Virginia Woolf, and her deliberate choice of death rather than war, I have already written in these letters. I doubt whether the war was equally responsible for Hugh Walpole's death, for he spent most of his time in the Cumberland cottage where he had already written so many novels with a Lakeland background. Only recently he reported to a friend that he was working on his new novel and 'gloriously happy' – a phrase which suggests that he was not exactly hypersensitive to those woes of the world which most of us would agree are somewhat excessive just now. Amongst less important deficiences, he completely lacked the magnanimity which rendered Max Plowman as incapable of nourishing a grievance as Winifred Holtby – who once told me that she never felt angry with anyone for more than twelve hours, because she had always forgotten by the next morning what the offender had done. Even Max's little-known writings – so few because he never persuaded himself that anything he did was important – possessed a quality of which the famous Hugh Walpole never came within range. I am glad to learn that his wife Dorothy is hoping to publish a collection of his personal letters, into which so much of his wisdom and philosophy were poured.

Hugh Walpole's consistent inability to forgive an unfavourable critic was recorded in the unduly malicious *Times* obituary which Max read in his last hours. 'He was singularly sensitive to adverse criticism,' wrote *The Times* contributor. 'Every reviewer of his last 30 years must have had a bundle of his letters, for he always wrote thanking, remonstrating or explaining.' That this recorded weakness was a fact I can testify from personal experience. In our young days as reviewers, Winifred Holtby and I each wrote critical notices of two of Walpole's less distinguished novels. Though he was a well-established and highly successful author and we were then struggling beginners, he kept up a vendetta against us for years.

During the late nineteen-twenties, when we were both associated with the final campaign for equal suffrage, he contributed to a weekly review an article on the younger writers which derided us both as 'the Miss Beale and Miss Buss of modern letters'. Five years later, when one of my books was submitted to the Book Society by my publisher in the confident expectation of a choice as Book of the Month, Walpole, as Chairman, saw to it that the book was dismissed with a recommendation – a severe blow in the days when a Book Society choice could establish an author's career.

Two years afterwards, I met Walpole for the first and only time at a literary dinner at which we were both invited speakers. The preliminary introductions were poorly organised, and I arrived to see him standing alone with that air of arrogance which often camouflages discomfort. I asked to be introduced, and noticed with amusement that he looked startled by the insignificant feminine appearance of someone whom he had evidently pictured as large, masculine and aggressive. In my speech I chaffed him for the 'Miss Beale and Miss Buss' article, adding that I did not know which of those two highly respectable spinsters could more appropriately be credited with my two children. At the end of the evening, Walpole came up to me. Looking somewhat embarrassed, he held out his hand and said ruefully: 'I'll never call you Miss Beale or Miss Buss again.' And he never did. Despite his orthodox conservative prejudices, he recently reviewed my latest book more generously than many critics who might reasonably have been expected to display magnanimity towards opinions which they themselves shared in fair peace-time weather.

But it is not because Walpole was kind to me at the last I agree with J. B. Priestley in deploring the disparaging tone of *The Times* obituary. The moment when a man's pitiful corpse is still unburied and his friends are unadjusted to the shock of his loss, is not the time to expose his weaknesses in the public press. I refuse to believe that truth is served by such inconsiderate cruelty. Decency itself demands in the hour of death a generous interpretation of a man's life, which can easily be revised in a later, more considered estimate if the initial balance should appear too favourable.

In any case I feel sure that others who were victims of Hugh Walpole's sensitive vanity will agree with me that they had more reason for gratitude to him than for resentment. In recent years I have been unable to read his long romances, but in my youth, before I was sufficiently acquainted with grief to distinguish in books between emotions which spring from the depths of an author's experience and those skilfully manufactured by a natural story-teller's creative imagination, I found hours of enjoyment in such early Walpole novels as *Fortitude* and *The Cathedral*. I remember reading the former on night duty in France during the last winter of the first World War. Amid such dangers as we encountered during the spring of 1918 (they appear small in this catastrophic present, but they seemed real enough then), I used to keep up my spirits in our threatened camp by repeating words used by Walpole in *Fortitude*: 'Tisn't life that matters! Tis the courage you bring to it.'

So I shall always thank Hugh Walpole for giving my naîve youth the stimulus that it needed in a bitter hour. None the less, he will never rank for me in the same category as great men like Max Plowman, who not only forgave those who trespassed against him, but was seldom even conscious that he had anything to forgive.

Hitler invaded Russia on 22 June 1941, against the advice of most of his generals. He was confident that Britain would make a separate peace and that Russia's resources were inadequate for successful resistance. But Russia had bought valuable time by signing the Nazi-Soviet Pact in 1939 and hers were the first Allied troops to enter Berlin four years later, by which time she had lost 22 million of her people.

*Unless Isaiah were an editor, with the minor prophets for a staff,
how should any newspaper hope to deal adequately with a time
when new marvels and portents are added to things already on a
scale so far beyond ordinary human grasp? . . . In this War full
idealism is the only common sense for all the people who intend
to count*

– The Observer, April 1917
(commenting on the outbreak of the Russian Revolution)

In the twenty-four years which have passed since the news of the
Russian Revolution broke through the fog of obscurity shroud-
ing the Eastern Front in the first World War, the wheel of history
has turned full circle.

You may recall that the month of April, 1917, found a British
government of which Mr Churchill was a member, taking the
Americans and the Russians to its bosom with fervent impartial-
ity. The month of June, 1941, found a British government of
which Mr Churchill has become the head, enthusiastically if
belatedly encircling both the Americans and the Russians in the
same comprehensive embrace. The twenty-two-year-old record
of Winston Churchill, interventionist on behalf of the White
Russians against the wicked Bolsheviks, is now discreetly laid in
the cupboard. Whether or not they like it, whether or not we and
the Americans like it, the Union of Socialist Soviet Republics is
compelled by Hitler's policy to become the ally of the two great
'capitalist powers' which are fighting against Nazism.

I happened to spend the weekend which included the longest
day of the year with some friends in the Cotswolds. That Sunday
was not only the lightest but the loveliest of this long-delayed
but suddenly beautiful summer. From a garden in which roses,
lupins, passion flowers and half-a-dozen other varieties of
clematis had sprung into blossom overnight, I looked across lush
buttercup meadows into a wooded valley where beech, oak and
ash seemed to radiate the vivid green which usually comes in late
May or early June. As I contemplated the rich landscape – so
gentle, so English, so heart-breaking in its illusion of tranquillity

80

– and listened to the news of Hitler's invasion of Russia coming from the portable wireless under the trees in the garden, I seemed for a moment to be back in the cloudless, unendurable May which accompanied the Nazi conquest of France with shining seas and sparkling skies.

That evening, through the same wireless set in the same peaceful garden, I heard Mr Churchill address the nation on the Russian invasion. In the terms of invective now so familiar when British statesmen take to the air, I listened to a new dismissal of Hitler as 'a bloodthirsty guttersnipe'. Later I noted the description of the Nazi army as 'the dull, drilled, docile masses of the Hun soldiery plodding on like swarms of crawling locusts'. And I wondered, as I have wondered so often, why it is that those who have assumed the burden of leading this nation to that far-off goal which they describe as 'victory' should strike so many false notes in their constant appeals to the 'average man'. By the common consent of politicians and newspaper men alike, the greatest handicaps of this country in the present war are British lethargy, British indifference and British inability to put forth maximum effort before the bottom of the abyss yawns within sight. Already our newspapers, and especially the Beaverbrook Press, are pouring forth alarmed editorials which warn the British public against regarding the Hitler-Stalin duel as a heaven-sent opportunity for a long, comfortable snooze.

Now you and I know that British inertia is rooted in British complacency. The muddle-headed inefficiency of this country in war rises partly from the ordinary Englishman's confirmed belief that he is worth five foreigners – any five foreigners. In his heart he thinks of the French as 'froggies', of the Germans as 'jerries' and of the Italians as 'dagoes'. His attitude is identical with that of the editor who described a storm which rendered the Straits of Dover impassable under the famous headline: 'Continent isolated.'

In this good-tempered sense of superiority lie some of the advantages of the British character. It is the quality which enables the slum-dweller on the dole to accept poverty without abjectness, and to endure misfortune without bitterness. But it is not a quality which wins wars, though it sometimes eludes defeat. Much less, with its lack of humility and imagination, is it likely to make a successful peace.

No nation buttressed by this feeling of innate self-satisfaction is likely to put forth maximum effort either in fighting, in production, or in reconstruction. Months if not years of intense propaganda would be required to shake so deeply-rooted an assumption. Yet at the very moment when it may well prove fatal, it is to this self same quality that Mr Churchill and his henchmen appeal. By minimising the demonic power of Hitler, by underrating the fanatical, self-sacrificing devotion which his leadership inspires in the rank and file of the Nazi party, our political broadcasters encourage us to indulge our superiority complex and thus root us the deeper in our complacent lethargy.

What matters about Hitler today is surely not his origin, but his ability. If he was indeed a guttersnipe, his achievements become only the greater, his ruthless efficiency the more formidable. As for the Nazi rank and file, I doubt whether dull, docile masses would be capable of the costly devotion to duty of the Crete parachutists, or of the grim endurance of the sailors who fought to the death in the *Bismarck*. If the Prime Minister had ever been swept, as I once was, over the Hohenzollern Bridge at Cologne by the swift excitement of the singing Brownshirts whom Hitler had addressed on the eve of the poll after the reoccupation of the Rhineland, he would know that, vile as we recognise the Nazi creed to be, it produces a state of exultation far more difficult to meet than docility or dullness.

If I were a war-making politician, I should insistently remind this nation that it is engaged in a mortal struggle with the greatest military genius since Napoleon, who has not yet made the mistakes which caused Napoleon's downfall. I should repeatedly assert that this genius is supported by a people of infinite courage and greater energy than any nation except the Americans. Finally, I should emphasise by every means in my power that the movement which he and his followers have created is inspired by the religious fervour of Islam, and might

82

well be described as the greatest politico-religious crusade of modern history.

The men and women who are carrying on this war might then realise what they have to fight, and put forth an effort proportionate to the struggle. A proper appreciation of the enemy's qualities and achievements not only keeps alive the spiritual quality of generosity which is one most easily lost in wartime; it inspires in those who take part in the battle a realisation of the sacrifices required. The invective which decries and villifies our opponents is unlikely to rouse this nation to its greatest deeds. It merely suggests that those opponents are, or should be, easy to overcome; it puts to sleep the imagination of a people which not only understates its sufferings but habitually underrates its perils.

If you want to be realistic in war, and yet, despite the growing ruthlessness of propaganda, to remember that the Nazis too are human beings with human emotions and aspirations, I suggest that you glance through an anthology of modern German poetry, edited by Jethro Bithell and recently published by Methuen at 7/6. I am grateful to the article in the latest number of *New Vision*, the International Youth Review edited by G. P. Pittock-Buss, which brought this collection of poems to my notice. War policies, military deeds and patriotic slogans may be crudely and fiercely national, but the language of poetry, like that of music and painting, is an international language created by the joys, hopes and sorrows which all humanity shares.

Though the writers represented in this volume include Jewish exiles and Czech refugees, the Nazi propagandist poets are not excluded. The pathos of exiled Max Herrmann-Neisse awaiting internment, and of Ina Seidel mourning the havoc of the last World War, is finer in quality but not greater in degree than that of the Nazi, Baldur von Schirach, extolling his Fuehrer with religious devotion. Little though we may admire his sentiments, and incapable as we are of sharing them, it is less than responsible to deny that they exist. A blind refusal to recognise the qualities of our foes will neither win us the war, nor lay the foundations of a lasting peace.

P.S. A correspondent from Lancashire writes me as follows: 'I am writing to tell you of an article I read in a newspaper . . . It said that to inaugurate the "War Weapons" Week at Keswick, there was a procession and speeches with Hugh Walpole as the first speaker. During the procession he felt distressed and remarked to the man next to him that the pace was too much. The man advised Walpole to drop out, but he would not do so. It was with great difficulty that he got through his speech and afterwards had a heart attack which was the beginning of his last illness. So it seems as if war conditions were responsible for his death – he probably would never have joined a procession for any other cause, knowing his heart was weak.'

Hugh Walpole was, of course, an ardent supporter of the war, and it seems only fair to him that the extent to which he was prepared to sacrifice himself for his convictions should be recorded here.

— 31 July 1941 —

Go practise if you please
With men and women: leave a child alone
For Christ's particular love's sake
 – Robert Browning, *The Ring and the Book*

A few days ago I received a letter from an organisation known as the Freier Deutscher Kulturbund – the Free German League of Culture in Great Britain – asking for my help 'on behalf of children who are in greatest distress'. In the name of the Children's Committee, wrote my correspondent, 'we are sending you informations dealing with the position of refugee children from the Central Europe.'

The documents enclosed with the letter described some of the attempts made, in collaboration with the Children's Overseas Reception Board, to find safer and more permanent homes for these children than it is possible for a country at war to provide. I learned that there are now in England ten thousand children from Germany, Austria, Czechoslovakia, Danzig and Poland, who have found refuge here from fascist oppression. Some of them have spent the past eight years being harried in country after country. Many lived in Nazi Germany, where they witnessed the persecution, ill-treatment or arrest of their parents, and sometimes experienced persecution and humiliation themselves. Such children were first smuggled by night into Czechoslovakia: then, when the Gestapo appeared at the gates of Prague, they had again to flee. Finding their way, through deep snow, across the Czech-Polish frontier, they left their fathers and mothers behind in prisons or concentration camps. Many remain ignorant of the fate of their parents. 'During their short existence,' states the report with painful simplicity, 'these children have suffered more than most people in a long life.'

And now war has come to this country, which seemed their final refuge. Some of them are with their mothers in internment camps on the Isle of Man and elsewhere. Others had found homes with British foster-parents whose own lives are now hampered by air raids, taxation, and evacuation problems. The few still united refugee families have been broken up by the removal of aliens from protected areas. Unless compassionate householders in the United States and the Dominions can offer them homes, and shipping again becomes available to take them there, the future of these desolate children looks black indeed.

More and more, in these days, I am coming to believe that the words being spoken and the actions being organised by the eminent on both sides of this world-conflict matter little in comparison with that which is being said and done by parents, teachers, and all the other 'ordinary people' who are responsible for the care and upbringing of children. The most important and constructive work left in the world is surely to inculcate, in the young, those basic human values which war destroys; to save them from the feelings of hatred in which adults throughout the world are now so lavishly indulging; to make the terror that they suffer lead to a desire to eliminate its cause, rather than to seek revenge and to despise their contemporaries in the countries which we are now subjecting to the torments of modern warfare.

I spent last weekend a few miles inside the coast of Essex. Lying in bed in the semi-twilight of Sunday evening, I listened for an hour to the sound of our heavy bombers flying out to sea, and felt more sick at heart than I have ever been made by the clatter of the German raiders, like a set of vibrant descending tea-trays, over the heads of London's population. To realise that one's own people are suffering damage is grievous, but to know that they are about to inflict it is detestable.

How many children in Germany, I wondered, would die before the morning? – children who, whatever the faults of their parents in giving active assistance to the Nazis or in mere inertia, are not to blame for the hideous conditions of their lives. The reflection that we were now 'getting our own back' for the sufferings of our cities between September and June comforted me not at all. Even if I had desired revenge, I should have known that modern warfare seldom exacts payment from those who are responsible. Our belligerent editors and vituperative politicians often write and speak as though Hitler, Goering and Goebbels were personally damaged by every raid that we make on Germany. But it is not Hitler upon whom our bombs fall. Our air-raids, like his, wreck humble homes and decimate families living in the East Ends of industrial cities, or close to the dockyards of naval and commercial ports. It is not the Nazi leaders but the children of the German and Italian workers whom they destroy.

You would probably prefer, as I should, not to dwell upon this aspect of the war. The powers-that-be would certainly wish us to bury our heads in the sand, since compassion for the children of the enemy is weakening to 'morale'. I maintain, none the less, that 'morale' is very far from being identical with morality, and that, for some of us at least, our moral duty lies in seeing things *exactly* as they are, and in keeping our eyes resolutely upon the truth, despite the smoke-screen with which propaganda conceals it. What, then – if we can think of any children as 'enemies' – are the present sufferings of 'enemy children'? How much of it can we deduce from the ordeals of our own?

In this country we are frequently told that children have suffered less from air-raids than the authorities expected.

Presumably they are tougher, and less dependent upon a background of security, than psychologists informed us before the war. But do we really know? Recollections of my childhood and the observation of my own children seem to indicate that childhood is not so much 'tough' as reticent – sometimes because it is inarticulate, but more often owing to the pathetic pride which the very young take in concealing their particular wounds and alarms from 'grown-ups'.

I still vividly recall a long-ago winter afternoon which I spent in silent and solitary terror, concealed within the folds of a large bath-towel in the family bathroom because, a short time previously, I had heard the cook read aloud to the housemaid a newspaper extract prophesying that the world would end on the twentieth of January. I remember the agonies of apprehension suffered by my son at the age of seven, because I had given him a thermometer to put away, and foolishly warned him that it was 'precious'. It was a revelation to me that he had really expected me to scold or beat him because he had promptly broken it from excess of caution.

Most clearly of all, I recollect the aftermath of a minor operation which my daughter, aged nine, underwent in a London hospital during the week in which Hitler invaded Prague. A naturally volatile and courageous child, she had given no sign of dreading the operation, no indication that she had heard or understood the excited talk about prospective air-raids between the nurses in her ward. But a few days later, in the rooms which I had taken for her convalescence by the sea, she suddenly appeared, shaking and terrified, beside my bed in the middle of the night. Between her sobs she vouchsafed, shamefacedly, an explanation: 'Please let me come into your bed; I'm frightened to be alone. I keep on dreaming of headless bodies falling on my cot. I 'spect the operation has upset my nerves!'

Children are proud and reserved; I do not believe that they are ever indifferent, or unaffected by events, however well it may suit the purposes of political propaganda to believe them so. And today they suffer not only from bombs in danger areas, but, only too often, from the negligence of parents or the impatience of foster-parents after evacuation. (Like one charming small boy whom my indignant protests temporarily saved from a public belabouring by a hard-faced woman in the streets of Reading.)

How many children today in England, and in all Europe, have to choose between nights of terror and days without kindness? Correspondents writing to me of their childhood in the last war have often mentioned their dark recollections of tension, of telegrams, of blackened windows and decreasing rations. But what will the memories of today's children be? – many hounded from country to country, still more wakened by guns and bombs, yet others forcibly severed from beloved parents and cherished homes. What shall we, who care for peace and are responsible for children, do in order to turn these memories to account? How shall we ensure that out of them shall spring, not cynicism nor vindictiveness, nor pessimism, but the constructive determination to save yet another young generation from their own harsh experience. I believe that only by working to eliminate war, the source of their suffering, will today's children find compensation for their terrors and release from their nightmare recollections. It is for us – parents, foster-parents, preachers and teachers – to make sure that they do grow up to fight against warfare, and not, like yesterday's children, against one another.

— 25 September 1941 —

'An artist is not a man who gives the public what it wants; he is a man who makes the public want what he gives it. He may take a long time to subdue the public. The subjugation, indeed, may not be made until after his death. But sooner or later, it is achieved'

– St John Ervine, *The Observer*,
on the centenary of Henry Irving, 6 February 1938

I was lucky enough to be able to attend a gathering in London of unusual interest – the 17th International Congress of the P E N Club.

As you probably know, the P E N (its appropriate initials

standing for the words Poets, Essayists and Editors, Novelists) is an international organisation of writers. In the 'Never Again' mood which followed the last war, it was founded by an idealist, Mrs Dawson Scott, to promote friendship and understanding between the writers of different countries. As H. G. Wells emphasised at one of its luncheons last July, this body was intended to be not only international but supranational; it was quite unconcerned with the aims and values of nationalism as such.

The first president of the London Centre was John Galsworthy, who held this office until his death in 1933. His successors have been H. G. Wells, J. B. Priestley, H. W. Nevinson, and Storm Jameson, the first woman to be chosen. She was elected in 1938 and still retains the position. The recent courageous attempt to hold an international conference of writers in war-time was due largely to her inspiration.

During the two decades of its existence the P E N has held its international conferences in many great cities as far apart as Paris and Warsaw, Berlin and New York, Budapest and Buenos Aires. Those who attended it perhaps remember most vividly the 1938 Congress in Prague, summoned to uphold the fundamental values of civilisation in the tense atmosphere preceding Munich which postponed only by a year their submergence in the dark tide of war. The Stockholm Centre made brave but unavailing efforts to call together the meeting planned for 1939. Last year the Conference lapsed altogether, for reasons which those who experienced the Battle of Europe will understand only too well.

Since the suppression of one P E N Centre after another occurred in the Axis-dominated countries, and writers whose books had been burned or banned took refuge from fascism in Britain and the United States, the main problem of the New York and London P E N Clubs has been similar to that of the peace movement itself. How were they to maintain their ideals of reconciliation and international understanding, and yet show adequate sympathy and hospitality to grief-shattered and often poverty-stricken refugees whose one passionate objective was the restoration of their countries and their homes?

At the recent London Congress, attended by delegates from thirty countries of which a large proportion were represented by refugee writers, this conflict was much in evidence. The discussions swayed back and forth between expression of violent resentment against oppressors (though some of the oppressed, such as Arthur Koestler and the Chinese delegates, showed admirable restraint), and urgent reminders of the purposes for which the P E N was founded. But to me the most memorable moments of the conference were associated neither with the understandable bitterness provoked by personal suffering, nor even with the conscientious endeavours to recall to life the fading spectre of world unity. One came during the speech by Thornton Wilder, the American author of *The Bridge of San Luis Rey*; the other is connected with the treatment by Señor de Madariaga of the proper relation between art and politics in the work of a writer, which was one of the main topics of the conference.

Thornton Wilder and his fellow American author, John dos Passos, came over by Clipper to join the P E N discussions. In the midst of describing the impression made upon an American by the first sight of bomb-damaged London, Mr Wilder suddenly gripped the desk and exclaimed, with a note of real anguish in his pleasant voice, 'Forgive us our immunity!' And I remembered – with sympathy for the unhappy conscience-stricken letters which I have received during the past twelve months from so many American friends, whose sense of guilt is due less to their non-participation in the fighting than to the post-1919 abandonment of Europe by their country, which was one of the war's chief causes – some words which Winifred Holtby makes Judas Iscariot utter from hell in her short story *The Comforter*: 'Heaven is only tolerable for those who have learned how to forgive themselves. So I came here, where, if we are in torment, we may at least share the pain we have inflicted. We are not called upon to suffer the horror of immunity.'

Winifred Holtby would have understood the compulsion – contemptuously dismissed by one writing friend of mine as 'pure romanticism' – which has made many English authors who might have spent the war writing with artistic detachment in America, feel unable to join their comfortably situated British colleagues in Hollywood. For some of us who have opposed not only war but this war, the compulsion seemed greater rather than less. We are conscious that, by failing to secure the official acceptance of our policies, we carry our proportion of responsibility for the suffering which the war has caused. We therefore feel an obligation to share in that suffering, and to serve as best we can the community whose individual members bear so heavy a burden.

It is not, I believe, their cowardice, but their toughness, which rouses public resentment against British writers and film stars in America. We could forgive them their fear; it is their indifference which seems intolerable. But perhaps – as Raymond Gram Swing suggested in a recent review of the broadcasts from England to America by the American commentator, Edward Murrow – the sentiment merited by those who have abandoned their country is not anger, but pity.

Commenting on the new and deeper note which crept into Murrow's broadcasts after the blitz on London began, Gram Swing remarked that after the war the British writers who had endured the Battle of Britain would speak a different language from those who had avoided it; there would be no basis of common experience. He told me himself when recently in London that few things were more intolerable than listening-in from the United States to an air-raid on England. London, he said was a far happier city today than New York.

But the British writers in America have their reply. They might, and sometimes do, answer that politics, and the explosions which it causes, are no part of the artist's business; his function is to stand apart from the struggle in order to achieve the emotional detachment and mental concentration which works of art require. There have been, I suppose, few deeper concerns than the conflict between art and politics for the writers and thinkers of this generation, whose minds have been so largely moulded by world events and great political movements.

It is clear from this letter and some of those that have had to be omitted from this collection that Christianity was increasingly becoming a driving force in Vera's life.

The 'political expedients' which she mentions in her fifth paragraph refer specifically to the petition originated by the Bishop of Chichester and others urging the government to take the initiative in abolishing night bombing. A forlorn hope indeed!

And now we are saved absolutely, we need not say from what,
we are at home in the universe, and, in principle and in the main,
feeble and timid creatures as we are, there is nothing anywhere
within the world or without it that can make us afraid
                              – Bernard Bosanquet, *What Religion Is*

I wish you could have been with me on November 8th at the
Kingsway Hall, where the Council of Christian Pacifist Groups
held, in the name of 'Christ and Peace', one of the most beautiful
devotional meetings that I have ever attended at Armistice time.

Donald Soper took the Chair, and the two speakers were
Canon Charles Raven and a German, Pastor Franz Hildebrandt,
who is a friend of Pastor Niemoller. Pastor Hildebrandt spoke
first. There was not a stir or a murmur during the moving
speech, delivered in faultless English, in which he paid tribute to
the courage of those German religious leaders, such as Niemoller
himself and the Roman Catholic Bishop of Munster, who have
dared to criticise the Nazi regime; and testified to his own belief
that the only effective method of overcoming the evil of Nazidom is the acceptance and pursuit of the way of Christ 'through
pain, death and hell'.

Canon Raven followed, expressing his conviction that the
salvation of the world from the present tragedy is not to be
found through escape or in detachment, but by a determined and
redemptive share in the suffering which this war has brought to
its victims. 'If Christ', he said, 'is crucified afresh by the sin of
man, we ought to be with him on the Cross.'

Have you ever had the experience of doing something which is
hard to do, but which you are certain is right though you do not
quite know why, and then of hearing someone whom you deeply
respect supply you with the reason? That was my experience
when Canon Raven spoke. I understood why I had recently tried
to explain to you, haltingly enough, my feeling that 'immunity',
though it might confer detachment and freedom, is less tolerable
today than peril and sorrow. I recognised that the strange compulsion which makes us go into danger or remain there, when

commonsense sees 'no necessity', has not only a sound but a spiritual basis.

This Kingsway Hall meeting must have helped many people to realise that the 'romantic' acceptance of avoidable suffering and the 'unnecessary' act of desperate heroism – often entered into so blindly, and carried out with so many misgivings – actually brings us as near as most of us ever get to the heart of the Christian experience. It is here, and – in the spiritual sense – here only, that the alternative to war lies. Its acceptance may logically involve the trying-out of political expedients such as the one about which I wrote previously which must be urged irrespective of their chances of finding favour with majority opinion. But the essence of the Christian injunction to 'overcome evil with good' lies in the pursuit of a certain way of life, in the public affirmation of that pursuit, and in the acceptance – with charity, with forgiveness and with the resolute repudiation of bitterness – of whatever penalty this choice may involve.

Let me try to explain my meaning more concretely in terms of some recent experiences of my own. Soon after the outbreak of war, the representative of a government department assured me that, without undertaking war propaganda or departing in any way from my principles, I could do this country valuable service by helping to maintain friendly contacts with the United States. Believing as I do that Anglo-American co-operation will be a vital necessity of post-war reconstruction, I agreed to fulfil a lecture tour booked some time previously, though this involved leaving my son and daughter behind in a country at war.

As you will know if you are one of my earliest readers, I did go to America for three months during the 'sitzkrieg' period, returning just after the Nazi invasion of Scandinavia. But the anxiety of leaving my children in potential danger had proved intolerable, and in the belief – then uncontradicted – that my work of maintaining Anglo-American 'contacts' was likely to be continuous after fifteen years experience, we decided to send our family to friends in the United States. I did not accompany them because this country was then threatened with invasion and aerial blitzkrieg which my husband and friends had to face, but I had further American lectures arranged for the winter, and let my children go believing that if we all survived the débâcle, I should see them again in four or five months.

But I reckoned without the panic legislation which last year did its best to classify the honest holders of minority opinions with treacherous Fifth Columnists, and gives to worthy but limited men, under the now notorious Regulation 18b, alarming powers which supreme spiritual and intellectual genius is alone fit to exercise. When I put in for routine permission to pay another short visit to America, it was and has ever since been refused by the relevant government department. I resisted this decision by every means at my command, to realise at last that the individual is helpless against a Ministry invested with totalitarian powers by a terrified House of Commons.

Last autumn, bombed, buffeted and humiliated, I spent many hours in ruminating bitterly on the injustice of a situation in which I had, as it seemed, been cruelly deceived into parting with my beloved children before being told that, as a pacifist, I should no longer be allowed to undertake the work which the previous winter had been represented as my duty. One October day, staying with friends between Reading and Oxford, I walked along a Berkshire lane angrily meditating how easily, armed with my pen and the articulateness which is the endowment of every writer, I could one day 'get my own back' on the officials who had made such wreckage of my personal life. Suddenly, in an empty valley covered with fallen leaves, something seemed to check the direction of my thoughts. Within my mind, an inconvenient second self addressed me firmly.

'Don't you realise that this is a spiritual experience? For the past few years you have had far more honour and appreciation than you deserve. Now you know what it is to be humiliated; and this gives you a new kinship with those to whom you have hitherto felt superior – prisoners, refugees, the unemployed, and down-and-outs, and all the despised and rejected of men.' And I remembered writing four years earlier in a novel: 'I suppose, if we took a long enough view, we should feel that any sorrow bears its own compensation which enlarges the scope of human mercy. Some of us, perhaps, can never reach our honourable estate – the state of maturity, of true understanding – until we have wrested strength and dignity out of humiliation and dishonour.'

One does not always get the chance to try out, in one's own life, a conclusion written with full conviction about a character in a story, and the opportunity must certainly be regarded as a privilege. I don't say that it looks like a privilege always, or even often. My thwarted love for my lost children gives me, again and again, a deep sense of injury in which I still contemplate picturesque literary revenges on leading officials in the Ministry of Home Security. I am, unfortunately, a very imperfect pacifist and an even more imperfect Christian; and so far I have learnt only enough to recognise that this mood is wrong without always being able to avoid it. But I am so certain that it is wrong, and that the experience which Bosanquet describes as 'salvation' lies in precisely the opposite direction, that I want to refer you to three examples of the spiritual victory which I know to be possible, though as yet I am unable to achieve it myself. One comes from the symposium 'Into the Way of Peace', edited by the Archdeacon of Stoke-on-Trent, and published by James Clarke and Co. The first two chapters, 'The Suffering Servant of the Lord', by the Rev. Kenneth Rawlings, and 'The Gospel Basis of Pacifism', by the Rev. C. Paul Gliddon, are complementary studies of the greatest spiritual triumph through acceptance of suffering known to religion and history. If you are trying to get the basic conceptions of Christianity straight in your mind, these chapters will help you. To indicate their quality, I quote a passage from each.

'The Second Isaiah', writes Kenneth Rawlings, 'gave a new and more profound significance to the Messiah. He represented him, not as a conqueror, but as a sufferer; not as one who delivers the innocent from persecution, but as one who shares it, and who, although himself innocent, is despised and rejected of men, a man of sorrows and acquainted with grief. Here, then, we have in the Old Testament the dim perception that perhaps after all the real victory of righteousness is with the sufferer and not with the conqueror. A Hebrew prophet, seven centuries before

Christ, catches a glimpse of the truth revealed in the death and passion and resurrection of our Lord – the truth that to strive to save one's life is to lose it, and that to be willing to lose one's life for love's sake is to save it.'

In the next chapter, Paul Gliddon adds his similar conclusions: 'There is no other way whereby we may be saved from sin than the way taken by Jesus, and to attempt to produce the same results by methods which Christ rejected is to reject His guidance as either impracticable or inadequate. Certainly no other way of dealing with sin has met with success, for sin lives in the human will and the will is not really changed by punishment, which, when it does bring about alterations in conduct, does so by fear of consequences and not by the will freely forsaking the loving of unholy things and turning to love of another sort . . . It was not because of a rebellion in heaven that no legions of angels were sent out to destroy: not because the power was absent, but because that sort of power was insuffiently powerful for the occasion. The only thing that could hope to outmatch the sin of the world was, not a might that could destroy, but a love that could not be destroyed.'

My second example of spiritual victory comes from the life of a Russian woman, Julia de Beausobre, whom I met three years ago at the home of her publishers just after she had produced a remarkable book, *The Woman Who Could Not Die* (Chatto and Windus, 1938). This book, which describes the suffering and humiliation that the author endured – without bitterness or any desire for revenge – in Russia after the Revolution, should be better known than it is. The philosophy which Madame de Beausobre learned from cruel experience has been more recently distilled into a booklet entitled 'Creative Suffering'. 'The only point of her own experience which she touches upon', writes Patrick Thompson in his introduction to this booklet, 'is one which she shares with countless Russians; that of contact, face to face before a Soviet examining officer, with evil at its worst; with the infliction of pain on the innocent for pleasure; cruelty for the sake of cruelty. Those who can meet, and make something of, this may be said to know how to suffer. The author has seen it done. She tries to tell how it is done.' I commend to you both Madame de Beausobre's book and her pamphlet.

You will probably have guessed my third example. In a chapter called 'The Abysmal Hour', in *Testament of Friendship*, I battled with the sad inadequacy of words to convey not only Winifred Holtby's triumph over physical pain, but her victory over the resentful anguish that she might well have felt when faced with the premature end of a life so full, so vital and so gifted. I have space here to mention only the incident in which, during a short walk in the cold spring of 1932, she came upon a number of lambs vainly trying to drink from a frozen trough.

Recently, on her sick bed, she had listened to the St Matthew Passion coming over the wireless from York Minster, and it is clear from a chapter in *South Riding* that there was a close connection in her mind between the young lambs of that early spring, and the lamb of God 'which taketh away the sins of the world'. As she broke the ice in the trough for the lambs to drink, she heard a voice (was it beside her or within her?) clearly saying: 'Having nothing, yet possessing all things.' She told me afterwards that in a flash all her grief, her bitterness and her sense of frustration disappeared. She walked back to the cottage in which she was striving to recover some final remnant of health and strength, purged for ever from the desire for power, for comfort or for success.

You and I are crusaders today against evil, whether it be the evil committed by men, or those evils inherent in nature which man has so great a task in overcoming if he would but cease to waste his powers in fighting against his fellow. Let us remember that a head-on collision with evil, though it may produce instances of self-sacrificing heroism, will never generate the spiritual power by which alone evil is fully and finally destroyed. That spiritual power is humanity's one sure weapon, against which alone the sins of men and the gates of hell will never prevail.

The unexpected attack on Pearl Harbour on 7 December 1941 marked the declaration of war by Japan on America and Britain. Hong Kong, the Philippines and Malaya were also attacked.

On 11 December Germany and Italy declared war on the United States.

— 18 December 1941 —

*Yet when the fire of war was . . . threatening the Christian world
with disaster and desolation, I had no greater comfort than I
found in the ancient promises of God concerning the supreme
and final Light, that it should in the end put darkness to flight*
– Comenius

This third Christmas of the Second World War seems a stranger
period than even the Christmases of 1939 and 1940 in which to
be sending you the season's greetings. We remember the Prince
of Peace in a world more totally immersed in conflict than
history has ever known. Between 1914 and 1918 the Pacific
Ocean was able, with the United States, Japan and China among
the Allied and associated powers, to remain true to its name.
Today the blaze of warfare has leapt across it, lighting ominous
beacons of disaster from island to island between the Asiatic and
American continents. Even in such holiday paradises as the
Hawaiian Islands, bombs have wrought the hideous destruction
with which we in Britain are familiar, and hundreds of peace-
loving American citizens have died, caught unawares by the
treacherous cruelty of a surprise attack.

Most of us, I suppose, have some one country outside our own
to which our thoughts turn with special affection. In the nineteenth century, an Italy struggling for unification and indepen-
dence was the cherished favourite of freedom-loving statesmen
and politically-minded poets. Since the last war, many inhabitants of Britain have sought their Eldorado in Russia; a Russia in
which the totalitarian character of the Soviet regime and the
atrocities committed in its name appeared to be more than
compensated by its bold social experiments and by the astonishing change of spirit and outlook which the inheritors of the
Bolshevik Revolution have wrought within quarter of a century
in the lives of a huge illiterate population. For others France,
now a source of bewildering disillusionment, has been their land
of allegiance; they have loved the polished brilliance of her
culture and the ruthlessness of her intellectual realism. Yet
others, fewer but wiser, have looked to China, where the modern

100

political and cultural revolution of an ancient philosophical people has been interrupted by ten years of intermittent and four years of continuous warfare with an enemy whom the Chinese still refuse to hate.

For me, as you already know, the land which I love next to my own is the United States, which for nearly seventeen years has been my second home, and has shown me hospitality and friendship in over a hundred towns and cities from 41 out of the 48 states. Not only has America given me some of the best and most loyal friends that I possess; she provided sanctuary for my son and daughter – who are living half-way between the now raid-threatened coasts amid the lakes and forests of beautiful Minnesota – when I believed that I had no alternative between sending them overseas, and leaving them periodically parentless in an England perilously at war.

There is much that you and I can criticise in the United States, of course. She has still a capitalistic outlook, and is as far as most great countries from that readiness to sacrifice power and pride which is an indispensable preliminary to the practical realisation of Christianity, and to the building up of a true democracy and a lasting peace. But notwithstanding the renaissance paganism of her more materialistic ambitions, she is perhaps nearer than any country except China to the realisation of that democracy and the fulfilment of that peace. Without, as yet, any pretensions to socialism, she has created a democratic society in which the dignity of the individual, the abandonment of unequal privileges and the abolition of class-consciousness have reached a point far in advance of our own. And she has solved the problem of federating in one conscious and peaceful unity, that diversity of incompatible peoples, cultures and creeds which in Europe has created war after war, and remains a cauldron of seething animosities, now submerged beneath the false unity of repression.

For much that she is, and even more for all that she is trying to be, I deeply love America and her citizens. Japan's attack on her when she was still carrying on negotiations designed to avert a war which she did not want, gave me the same sense of shock as a hostile landing on our own island would give. The news of the raids on Hawaii and the Philippines produced a surge of emotion similar to that aroused by the scene in Lajos Biro's play, *School for Slavery*, where a Polish soldier in hiding from the Nazis suddenly announces to his fellow exiles in the Polish marshes that London has suffered and withstood the heaviest aerial mass-bombardment of September, 1940. Just as I went through that in reality, so in imagination I shared the ordeal of the American citizens in the Pacific islands, and felt in my own nerves the shocked incredulity with which the inhabitants of the lovely Californian coast must have heard the first wail of the warning siren. For the moment it was difficult to remember that Japan learnt her first lessons in imperialism from the Western powers, and that the record of predatory exploitation in India and China on the part of the leading European states during the nineteenth and twentieth centuries led the Japanese to develop and rely upon their own armed might for the maintenance of their national integrity.

But emotion, for me as for you, is not enough. It never is. We cannot help the tormented humanity of which we are part just by feeling a fierce pity for London or a passionate sympathy with San Francisco. At this Christmas season when it has become clearer than ever before that modern conflicts cannot be localised and that the race of men must choose between total peace and total war, you and I have to decide what we can usefully do in the most catastrophic hour of human history. It seems clear that there is little value now in seeking to resist the war still less in impeding those upon whom the burden of it is laid – though we retain our free right to criticise. As individuals who cannot accept a duty to kill or collaborate in the machinery of killing, we may refuse to take part in war and suffer the consequences, but to believe that any efforts of ours will check the present momentum of disaster is to inhabit a realm of fantasy in which we stop thinking at the very point where we ought to begin.

What then can we do? – pacifists as some of us still dare to call ourselves in a world where true peace cannot be resurrected for years out of the desert which man has created. It is futile now to remind the victims of collapsing societies and standards that for twenty years we challenged the vast inertia of mankind with the urgent prophesy that another great war, if allowed to begin, would mean the death of civilisation as we have known it. Are we then valueless in a society in which vital spiritual principles half obscured by lies, hypocrisy and hatred, fight for survival amid grotesque physical destruction and insidious moral deterioration?

We are not valueless. We must never permit ourselves to become defeatists with regard to that work which, as lonely missionaries, we have to fulfil in our day and generation. But to be fully valuable we must not only recognise our minority position but, in a world where the vast majority of mankind has lived by other standards than ours and now faces the logical conclusion of allegiance to those standards, we must admit that Great Britain, the United States, China and Russia have at present no alternative but to carry on their war against the Axis, either to a decisive conclusion, or through a stalemate so prolonged that the measure of suffering and loss on both sides produces a mood for negotiation.

The pacifist tries to live in accordance with the standards of a society which has not yet come. He cannot act, or expect others who do not accept his values to act, as if that society were already here. He has only one task left him – but from the standpoint of future civilisation it is the most important of all. Like the early Christians in their own totalitarian era, like medical missionaries working among the primitive races to whom hygiene and the Gospel alike seem incredible, he must point ceaselessly to the ideals of a nobler community even though he knows it is far away and that he is unlikely ever to see it.

In a situation in which manners and morals degenerate day by day, hatreds increase, facts are distorted and lies passionately disseminated, the pacifist and his fellow peace-lovers have first and foremost to keep their heads and retain their sense of perspective and detachment. Without this vital sense they cannot perform their educative task among men and women increasingly resistant to education, yet never more vitally in need of it.

As I have written you before in these letters, our job is one which with every extension of the war becomes both harder and more urgent. It is to find out and tell the truth; to remind whomsoever we can reach that truth is still the foremost of the virtues, whatever its practical inconveniences may be; to insist, as Christ on the Cross insisted, that love, not vengeance, is the only quality which will finally and permanently subdue our enemies, and that however treacherously they may behave, they are still our brothers for whom Jesus died. We shall serve no useful purpose by whitewashing, as some pacifists blindly seek to do, their sins against society, but we can take those sins upon ourselves in the sense of remembering the share of responsibility that we bear with our own country for the tide of evil which has swept over the world.

So it is not incongruous, but wholly relevant, that I should send you greetings for the birthday of the Son of Man, who taught us that our own offences and those of others can find atonement through a new way of life and an unfamiliar standard of conduct. It is not unsuitable, but wholly appropriate, that I should enclose a Christmas card with this letter, for the card will make more real to you one of those islands of civilisation in which men and women, despite many failures, are striving to live in accordance with values which mankind as a whole cannot yet accept but upon whose final establishment the future of civilisation depends. May you at least achieve, this Christmastide, the fearless security of high resolve and renewed self-dedication, and may God lead us at last through this age of strife to an era of peace on earth and goodwill among men.

Lord Vansittart, chief diplomatic adviser to the Foreign Secretary, had long been a vociferous critic of Nazism and was identified with the view, held by many, that all Germans were bad Germans.

Ah, what if some unshamed iconoclast
Crumbling old fetish raiments from the past,
Rises from dead cerements the Christ at last?
What if men take to following where He leads,
Weary of mumbling Athanasian creeds!
– Roden Noël (1834–94), *The Red Flag*

A faithful subscriber to this Letter has presented me with a difficult proposition. She wants me to answer a challenge put to her by a group of war-supporting acquaintances: 'How could pacifists have prevented this war, seeing that the Germans would never give up their ideas of conquest?'

To any possessor of quite modest historical and political knowledge, this question is not the 'poser' that those who propound it imagine. It is difficult to answer in a letter, and even more difficult at a public meeting, only because the reply depends upon an assemblage of facts which require at least the space of a book. A brief response involves a measure of excessive simplification which is, in itself, a form of inaccuracy. You might think it more timely, too, for me to comment on the loss of Singapore, the threat to Burma, India, Australia and New Zealand, or on the successful defiance by German battleships of our once unchallenged naval supremacy. Yet because, owing to these events, the prestige of this country is probably lower today than at any time throughout the history of British power politics, I feel it only right to take up the challenge and try at least to indicate an alternative policy which would certainly have produced different results.

Let me start by saying right away that the 'Vansittartism' which attributes aggressive belligerency to the Germans (or to the Japanese) as a *people* is just a form of unholy propaganda. Germany, like other nations, is composed of several politically conscious minorities and a large, politically indifferent majority. Her history for the past four centuries has tended to encourage the most aggressive of her minorities simply because her great natural energy and efficiency have been accompanied by a lack of certain specific advantages enjoyed by other leading states.

You will remember that Germany, like Italy, was one of the last European nations to achieve unification. Because she had been the starting place of the Reformation, she became, a century later, the battleground of the Wars of Religion – the subject of Aldous Huxley's latest volume, *Grey Eminence*. That Thirty Years' War, imposed upon Germany by the policy of Cardinal Richelieu and prolonged in order to keep her disunited, left her ruined, underdeveloped and chaotic. The Treaty of Westphalia in 1648 made her a mosaic of roughly three hundred backward little states. By forming the Confederation of the Rhine in 1806, Napoleon did more to unite Germany than any one before Bismarck. The Napoleonic Wars finally left the number of the German states reduced to about fifty.

Meanwhile the sixteenth-century nationalism of Britain and other European countries had grown into imperialism. By the second half of the nineteenth century, the British Empire had been built up through a combination of conquest, purchase, and that subtler method known as 'appropriation'. When young Imperial Germany, led by Bismarck who had united her, and later by Kaiser William II, desired also to join in the race for territory, she found that she could do so only at the expense of her neighbours in Europe.

The same story is approximately true of Japan, with her rapidly increasing population (now nearly 90 millions) packed into a very small territory. When she too caught the appetite for Empire from the West, the choicest Pacific territories were already occupied by the British, French, Dutch and Americans. An antiquated Nelson's Encyclopaedia, dating from my school-days just before the last war, gives the following significant figures in square miles for the territories of the chief colonial powers at that time: United Kingdom, 11,305,126; France, 4,732,100; Netherlands, 782,800; Belgium, 910,000; Portugal, 803,310; Italy, 185,200; United States, 728,330. Germany then owned 1,027,820 square miles, mainly composed of the African territories which she lost by the Treaty of Versailles. Japan, with

107

a population already numbering more than 48 million, only possessed 114,750 square miles. The annual value of the United Kingdom's exports was then £600,000,000; Germany's £375,000,000; Japan's only £42,170,000.

After their defeat in 1918, the Germans were sick of war and longed only for a period of uninterrupted peace. As I discovered for myself in 1924, they were in no mood to embark upon a new career of national conquest. According to such eye-witnesses as William L. Shirer, the American author of *Berlin Diary*, (Hamish Hamilton, 12/6) they were not in that mood even by 1939. But after the victorious Allies had seized German colonies and coal-fields, written war guilt clauses into the treaty, imposed astronomical reparations, occupied the Ruhr, admitted Germany with belated clumsiness into the League of Nations, and refused Chancellor Brüning his peaceful economic *Anschluss* with Austria, the Weimar Republic was not unnaturally discredited, and democracy associated with humiliation. Hitler came into power because the Nazis appeared to be the only alternative to perpetual dishonour and depression.

During these years between the wars, Britain and the Dominions, by means of the Ottawa Agreements and other measures, had also put up such high tariffs against German exports, that Germany could not find sufficient foreign markets. Japan had to face not only tariffs, but American and Dominion immigration laws which prevented the nationals of her overcrowded islands from emigrating to large, under-populated and convenient territories. (The population of Japan proper averages 469 to the square mile. In USA the average is 41; in Canada 3; in Northern Australia under 2.) This policy strengthened the militarist minority in Japan – a country whose Christians recently presented 7000 yen to the Christians of China for rebuilding their bombed churches.

What you ask, would pacifists have done about the German Nazis and the Japanese militarists? The first answer is that they would probably never have had to deal with them. If, by some unlikely miracle, anti-war reaction had put a pacifist British government into power in 1918, the oppressive clauses of the

Versailles Treaty would never have been written, nor the Ruhr occupied; liberal Germany would have been admitted immediately, and cordially, into the League, and Stresemann would have had many more than the 'one important concession' for which he vainly asked in order to 'save peace for this generation'.

Other opportunities for constructive reconciliation would also have occurred. In 1932, the Disarmament Conference assembled. Six years later, in February 1938, Dr Dalton, now Minister of Economic Warfare, recorded of this gathering: 'On February 10th, in the first debate of the conference, Italy proposed the abolition of all bombing aeroplanes. Germany, Russia and other states supported. The United States of America was friendly to the idea, and in June President Hoover definitely came out in favour. From the first Sir John Simon and Lord Londonderry resisted and obstructed.'

The representatives of a pacifist government would not have 'resisted and obstructed'. They would have encouraged Italy, Germany, Russia and America – just as they would have supported the similar proposal made by Japan before an official commission of jurists at The Hague in 1923 and rejected owing to French and British opposition. They would not have allowed the World Economic Conference of 1933 to become a failure owing to the operations of those sinister underground forces known as 'interests'. Nor would they have permitted the report of M. van Zeeland, drawn up a few years later to incorporate a plan of international economic reform, to be quietly pigeon-holed thanks to those self-same 'interests'. They would have used that report as the basis of an international New Deal by which the needs of the 'Have-Nots' would have been met by the 'Haves'.

Can any just, honest and rational person really maintain that a generous policy of this kind, actuated by the Christian principle of do-as-you-would-be-done-by, would not have been better for Britain, America, Russia, China and India than the present catastrophic and mismanaged war? Even some of the 'interests' themselves would have suffered less. The owners, for example,

109

of tin mines and rubber plantations in Malaya would not, by reducing or sharing their profits, have lost their possessions so completely as they have lost them now.

Yes, you may say, but surely it was no good contemplating a policy of this kind once the Nazis were in power, and much less after war had begun? My reply would be that the way to prevent Germany (or Japan) from pursuing a career of conquest is not, once again, to smash, humiliate and punish – if you can – the aggressive minority and the whole country in its name, with the inevitable consequence of a new desire for revenge and a new growth of militarism. It is to divert the course of history into new channels.

Perhaps you will argue, with Maude Royden, that you cannot do this unless you first beat the Nazis by their own type of weapon. I answer you that I do not believe that the demonism rampant today in the world, and not only in Germany and Japan, can be conquered by fire and steel. Nazism thrives, as we see repeatedly, on every policy which provokes resistance, such as bombing, blockade and threats of 'retribution'. These measures unite the despairing German people behind the oppressor within, as the only means of withstanding the enemy without.

Supposing instead – difficult as it would be at this late hour with so much of our pride already in the dust – that we were to offer, by every broadcasting device available, an immediate armistice, coupled with food for the starving and generous undertakings to reduce our arms and share the rich resources still within our control? This would not move the German and Japanese militarists, whose power flourishes on Allied ruthlessness, but it would remove from the German and Japanese people their main reason for supporting their present leaders. A large magnanimous gesture is not merely one way of ending a war, it is the *only* way to end it without sowing the seeds of another conflict.

There is not, of course, the slightest hope of obtaining such a policy from the present governments of the warring democracies. Should pacifists (as some argue) therefore cease to demand

110

it, and instead endorse the existing provocative belligerency which all history shows to be the most disastrous of courses, and the one least likely to lead to permanent peace? Are we to say that our own policy, which has never been tried, is a failure because the *opposite* of it has led the world to disaster?

In the name of truth and honesty, we cannot say so – any more than the pioneers of the early Christian Church could cease to urge the standards of the Kingdom of Heaven because these standards were unlikely to be achieved under the Roman Empire. We are still very far from that New Jerusalem, but if the early Christians had abandoned its ideals as 'impracticable' in the same way as modern pacifists are urged to repudiate their conception of a true international society as 'utopian', the teaching of the Gospels would not have survived through the ages to be a constant summons to courage and a perpetual challenge to despair.

Our function is that of voices in the wilderness, ceaselessly proclaiming the sure and certain hope that one day the peoples of the world will awaken to the true significance of the Gospel message, and learn to conduct international relations according to the standards of God's Kingdom.

Although her American publisher showed little sympathy for her views, Vera's deep affection for the United States gave her great concern about relationships between the two countries.

The following extract from a Letter written two months later summed up the problem neatly:

British unpopularity in America has two outstanding causes. The first is the responsibility for a second world war, which Americans rightly think could have been avoided, because of the series of inept British governments which prepared neither for war nor for peace. The second is our disastrous defeats in the Far East, which, among other consequences, left Australia in a perilous situation from which only the United States could rescue her.

I am not suggesting that America objects to defending Australia, for the two young civilisations have much in common. But their close alliance must inevitably lead to a fusion of anti-British resentment, which may present unforeseen complications to the post-war world.

My American readers will, I know, forgive me for recording that there are three facts which the present American critics of Britain invariably forget: first, that the inept British governments would have been less inept, and might never have been elected, if America had joined the League of Nations; secondly, that British resources, however badly distributed, were depleted by a year of solitary struggle; thirdly, that greater vigilance at Pearl Harbor might have saved Singapore.

Drawn up by Churchill and Roosevelt at Placentia Bay, Newfoundland in August 1941, the Atlantic Charter was signed by fifteen governments, including the USSR. It was the foundation stone of the United Nations. It was a broad statement of war aims: that all nations should have the right to hold free elections and to be free from foreign pressures. Noble aspirations, still unrealised half a century later.

God expects from men . . . that their Easter devotions would in some measure come up to their Easter dress
                                            – Robert South, *Sermons*

Grim as the events of the past twelve months have been, and cold as the east winds of the laggard winter still blow upon the daffodils and crocuses in parks and gardens, Eastertide brings a sense of new life and thoughts of resurrection from death and sorrow. In spite of the fact that in wartime the coming of spring means renewed campaigns and further wanton sacrifices of youth and vitality, the morning sunshine and the long light evenings renew our hopes and stimulate us to make plans for the future.

Those plans are useful both individually and socially so long as they rest upon the abiding values which alone will remain whatever may be the outcome of this war. An article by F. J. Tritton in *The Friend* for March 13th reminds us that, just at the time when the Goths sacked Rome in AD 410, St Augustine began to set down his vision of 'The City of God'. In those days men must have watched the lights of civilisation extinguished in much the same apprehensive mood as that of Sir Edward Grey who saw the lamps going out all over Europe in 1914. St Augustine could not know that the coming age of barbarism would be followed by an age of feudalism, and that in its turn by an age of industrialism, all of which in their different fashions would repudiate the Christian conception of individual souls each having unique value in the eyes of God. But he did know that the standards of the Kingdom of Heaven would outlast earthly empires, and that any new civilisation must be based upon them if it was to grow and survive.

That part of our own civilisation which is doomed – and it is not a small part – will vanish precisely because it has denied those standards, and has attempted to substitute others less difficult to fulfil and more personally profitable. In contemplating the future, therefore, you and I must beware of assuming, as the Atlantic Charter assumes, that our country will necessarily retain an initiative the right to which it has to earn all over again by new measures and great innovations.

Even if the result of the war should be as favourable to ourselves as its most ardent supporters could wish, it is still unlikely to be this country which will have the best right to draw the outlines of the future society. It is true that, left alone in the field, we kept Germany at bay for nearly a year, but China, unaided, defended herself against Japan for nearly five years. Even that achievement of ours could hardly have been maintained without support and supplies from America. If the Allied nations are indeed to be victorious, it is the United States and Russia in whose hands the shaping of the future will mainly lie. Neither of these countries is fighting to restore British imperialism in the East or the British balance-of-power policy in the West.

Not the least of our post-war problems, I suspect, will be caused by necessary adjustments in our relations with our allies. You will readily understand the difficulties of collaboration between Russia's totalitarian communism, and a Britain in process of changing (let us hope) from a tory into a socialist democracy. But if you do not happen to have read the warning articles on American opinion contributed by Alistair Cooke and Raymond Gram Swing to the *Daily Herald* and the *Sunday Express* respectively, you may not have realised that, unless our government shows a capacity for imaginative wisdom which it has yet hardly displayed, the post-war obstacles to Anglo-American friendship are likely to be even greater than those which followed 1918.

Recently I have heard one or two disturbing stories about the expression, to British visitors in the United States, of American anger and impatience with our slowness, complacency and inaction. Knowing, as I have known for so many years, the almost illimitable extent of American generosity and forbearance, I find it difficult to believe that these stories are typical. If you are one of my American readers, I hope that you will be able to reassure me on this point. But whether or not individual Britons in the USA have had to suffer for British shortcomings, the fact remains that Anglo-American (and still more Commonwealth-

American) relations are going to need a good deal of careful steering after the war by the friends of the countries concerned. For decades Canada has looked to the USA for friendship and protection; if Australia is saved from invasion, it is to General MacArthur and not to a British commander-in-chief that she will be grateful. The advocates of Anglo-American union have some difficult questions to face. Their task will not be made easier by a lack of realism here, nor by fantastic assumptions that any conceivable result of this war will put British power and prestige back on its traditional footing.

How then can you and I, with our limited knowledge and power, contribute to the future in some constructive fashion which will make it, whatever the outcome of the present struggle, a little better than the past? Apart from help to the victims of war – a form of salvage work always waiting for peace-lovers whether the period be one of bombardment, invasion or lull – our task is to maintain and strengthen the civilising respect for charity, truth and compassion which alone can produce the atmosphere conducive to a generous armistice and a lasting peace. I have said this before in these letters, I know, but it cannot be said too often. If we win the war, the need for something better than the sorry achievement of 1919 is surely obvious to everyone by now. If the result is other than the 'ultimate victory' which has become more and more 'ultimate' as time has gone by, the painful process of adaptation will not be assisted by the heightening of war passions today.

The work of maintaining civilised values is by no means limited, as some suppose, to their passive acceptance. Consider, for instance, the three qualities mentioned above – charity, truth and compassion. Each one of these, if the true peace-lover takes seriously his obligation to subscribe to them, will involve him in a definite measure of active campaigning.

Charity and its allied values – magnanimity, generosity, toleration, forgiveness – are today being undermined by one of the most evil movements which have arisen from this war. The exponents of Vansittartism have appropriately been christened 'Bitter-Enders' by the *New Statesman*, for nothing but a bitter end could come to a war conducted on their lines. I learn from the *Evening Standard* that these converts to inverted Nazism have recently formed a publishing organisation, and from other sources that the refugees in this country are now divided between the supporters and the opponents of the Vansittart campaign. Nothing could be better guaranteed than this policy of the 'Bitter-Enders' to unite Germany behind Hitler, and prevent that internal revolution which we who care for peace recognise as a far more certain and permanent method of over-coming Nazism than any military victory.

Unless some effective counterblast is made to Vansittartism, we shall be faced at the end of this war with an organised policy of calculated revenge to which the destructive but spontaneous vindictiveness of the 1918 electors will be as a pigmy to a giant. Many liberal non-pacifists have realised this; the opponents of Lord Vansittart now include Victor Gollancz – whose book *Shall Our Children Live or Die?* should be read by every peace-lover – H.J. Laski, H.N. Brailsford and G.P. Gooch. This campaign against hatred – or rather, as I prefer to put it, for constructive generosity – is one in which pacifists and non-pacifists can work together.

The support of truth is again anything but a passive proposition. It requires the 'debunking' of illusions and of 'wishful thinking', a task at which John Middleton Murry has shown himself so outstanding an expert in *Peace News*. It means the exposure of propaganda methods and the examination of atrocity stories; the clear statement of realities which the press and the BBC ignore; the recording of decent actions which indicate that our opponents, like ourselves, are human beings; and the constant presentation of the war in its historic setting.

Belief in the social importance of compassion has lately moved many of us to practical activity. It found expression before Christmas in the campaign against night-bombing, and more recently has summoned all who retain their capacity for pity to the support of the food relief campaign about which I have so often written you in these Letters. There is, indeed, no basic religious value which does not require from us some practical initiative in our daily lives.

O for a living man to lead!
That will not babble when we bleed;
O for the silent doer of the deed!
One that is happy in his height,
And one that in a nation's night
Hath solitary certitude of light
— Stephen Phillips, *A Man*

During the past fortnight you have probably read many reviews of R. Ellis Roberts' newly published biography *H.R.L. Sheppard*, if you have not actually procured the book itself. One eminent London reviewer, I noticed, called this biography 'dull'. I can only conclude that the dullness exists in the distinguished critic's mind, for though the book contains many incidents which might have been differently interpreted by other biographers, I found it absorbing. It is alive with the vitality of the man who was my friend only for the last year of his life, but whom I shall remember — as will thousands of others — more vividly than many with whom I have been intimate all my days.

With half London I had often seen and heard Dick Sheppard preach at St Martin's. He came much further into my consciousness when he conducted Winifred Holtby's funeral service there on October 1st, 1935. But the first time I actually met him was at a mass peace demonstration in a large natural amphitheatre near Dorchester on a hot summer's day of 1936. Laurence Housman took the chair, Mrs Thomas Hardy sat on the platform, and the speakers were Dick Sheppard, George Lansbury, Donald Soper, and myself. The brilliant sunshine, the enthusiastic audience of 15,000 gathered from all over Wessex, and the quality of the chief speeches made the occasion remarkable. But even more remarkable was the hilarious gaiety of the journey back to London.

The four of us returning there — Sheppard, Lansbury, Soper and I — shared a restaurant car table, and talked all the way home. The conversation was glorious but the atmosphere sweltering, and one after another we took off all the outer garments

118

which we could decently remove. The railway officials recognised Lansbury and Sheppard immediately, but the passengers did not, and Dick, as he sat in his shirt sleeves, was severely reprimanded by a sour-faced lady for laying his discarded coat on a table 'where other people have to eat'.

Soon afterwards my mother met an acquaintance of Dick's, who told her of an incident which I have always treasured. Going down to Dorchester it seemed that Dick, showing Lansbury my name as that of a fellow-speaker, had remarked with characteristic frankness: 'You know, George, I have a feeling that I shan't like that young woman.' Lansbury responded gruffly: 'So have I, Dick! So have I.' At the end of the day, when I had left them at Waterloo, Dick turned to Lansbury again. 'George, I take back everything I said about that young woman.' 'So do I, Dick! So do I.'

This generous recantation was as typical of Dick as it was undeserved. Characteristically, he gave me part of the credit for a joyous journey which owed its sparkle to him, his racy stories, and his infectious enjoyment of the disapproving lady. Certainly his reconsidered opinion could not have been due to my speech, which was one of the worst I have ever made. I am a poor open-air speaker at best; I had never before been on a pacifist, as distinct from a League of Nations Union or a vaguely 'peace', platform; and I was overwhelmed by the oratorical qualifications of my fellow speakers. But Dick evidently took a less unfavourable view of my performance than the local press and myself, for a few weeks after the Dorchester meeting he asked me to become a sponsor of his recently founded Peace Pledge Union.

This invitation was a challenge which I had to face. Like other overworked people I had long fought shy of re-thinking out my own position, but Dick's letter gave a new insistence to the far-off rumble of approaching war and compelled me to do so. That autumn I sentenced myself to speaking at a painful series of League of Nations Union meetings in order to discover whether I still believed in the 'collective security' position which I was endeavouring to maintain. Finding myself more deeply in agreement with the Peace Pledgers who turned up to question me, I took the only honest course and, for better, for worse, accepted Dick's invitation.

I can now hardly believe that it was for less than a year that I attended the sponsors' meetings in Regent Street where Dick was chairman, walked in poster parades, joined in late night deputations to Lambeth Palace, and shared platforms with Dick in many cities. Once in Manchester he made the double journey in order to appear for 15 minutes and tell his entranced audience: 'Last night I had a dream. In it George Lansbury and I were playing tennis against Hitler and Musso. George had a game leg and I was asthmatic, but we won six-love, six-love.'

Certainly I never suspected that this man who could play on the emotions of a crowd as a master plays on the strings of a violin, and dissolve with a jest the grievances of his distinguished but temperamental sponsors, was not only sick but sad, lonely, tempest-tossed, faced with the break-up of a home crushed by his own overwhelming popularity. It has remained for Ellis Roberts to tell the millions who admired and perhaps envied Dick Sheppard of the sensitive little boy terrified by an abominable grandfather, and saddled through the sarcasm of a brutal schoolmaster with a permanent inferiority complex which the final tragedy revived and reinforced.

When Dick died I was in America on a lecture tour. Towards the end of October, 1937, travelling south from Chicago, I read in a Sunday newspaper that he had been elected Rector of Glasgow University, and, getting off the train at St Louis, sent him a cable of congratulation. It was only one among hundreds of telegrams – but Dick never allowed a friend to feel that he or she was one of thousands. 'The secret', writes his biographer, 'of Dick Sheppard's greatness as a preacher and public speaker may be found in this power of talking at once to the congregation or meeting as a whole and to each man and woman in it.'

There was just time for Dick to assure me, in one of those small bright blue notes which I received weeks later, that it was because his Scottish audience had neither seen nor heard him that he 'romped home'. Through constant travelling I saw none

120

but local newspapers for several days, and the next time I caught up, in New York, with my correspondence, I found several letters from my husband telling me of Dick's death and burial. As a tribute of respect which he knew that I would be grateful for, he had walked in the funeral procession. What moved him most on that day, he said, was seeing the men on the Thames barges take off their hats and stand to attention as the cortege passed along the Embankment. Ellis Roberts relates a similar experience in a passage describing the effect of Dick's death on London:

'My wife was motoring along Upper Regent Street, her mind full of Dick, when she realised that she had passed a group of out-of-work singers. Usually one does not try to give alms from a car, another count against the internal combustion engine, but she could not pass them by while thoughts of Dick were actually in her mind. So she drew up in a side street, alighted, went back, and, on an impulse, gave the man who was collecting a ten-shilling note. He looked surprised and she found herself saying, "Take it in memory of Dick Sheppard". To her astonishment the man burst into tears.'

In the United States Dick was less well known, but I who had personally mattered to him so little set out on another series of interminable journeys feeling that the sun had gone down. Somehow his death seemed to make the approaching war more inevitable, the darkening night of the nations more fathomless now that his 'certitude of light' was gone.

In a final chapter Ellis Roberts contributes a careful assessment of Dick's work for peace. No pacifist himself, he realises that pacifism can always be defeated by logical argument, and yet be right for those who choose the pacifist road through the prophetic inspiration of an inner compulsion. 'I do not believe', he writes, 'that Dick's pacifism can be supported by the arguments which he used, and yet I believe he was gifted with rare foresight in taking the stand he did. He isolated war.'

Defined in medical terms the pacifist is a specialist, who sees that war is the deadly disease which threatens the very existence of our civilisation, and that – however unanswerable the arguments which support it – it must be overcome if that civilisation is to survive. 'Here was the chief evil, the one which, unsubdued, would render useless all other reforms.' Towards the end of his life Dick was forced to accept the terrible truth that there are men who, confronted with good, deliberately choose wickedness; but he believed, and Ellis Roberts agrees with him, that their existence only increases the need for a great company dedicated to the way of love and life.

Vera was an admirer of Mahatma Gandhi whose organisation of non-violent resistance on a large scale was of great significance to pacifists. She followed Indian affairs closely and in a Letter written the previous April, referring to the accumulation of in-equality, repression and resentment under the British Raj, she wrote:

One episode which has survived many forgotten events comes back to me from an afternoon spent eight or nine years ago with the gentle, sensitive Bengali poet who was once Tagore's secretary. Only a few weeks before, he had been refused temporary admission to a Soho club, so I deliberately took him to tea at a leading West End hotel which, to my relief, displayed more courtesy. There he recounted to me how, in his early manhood, he had been flung out of a railway carriage window by a 'pukka sahib' when he had stumbled, after a belated rush for a train, into the compartment occupied by this official and his wife. In sad dignified words which conveyed a more profound indictment than bitter invective, he described his feelings as he lay on his back in the scrub where the British overlord had thrown him.

In 1940 and 1941 Vera was invited to attend the All-India Women's Conference as the British delegate. She was keen to go and willing to undertake the journey (six weeks, via America). Travel abroad during the war was forbidden unless sanctioned by government permission; it was denied to Vera on the grounds that her presence might 'further embarrass an already tense situation'. Commenting on this decision, the President of the Conference said:

It was unfortunate. At this critical period in the relationship between the people of India and those of England, human contacts are important. Miss Vera Brittain would have forged another link in that chain of friendship between our peoples which this organisation has been slowly trying to create.

By the time the following Letter was written, Burma had fallen to the Japanese and India faced serious threat of invasion. Gandhi and the other Congress leaders were jailed in August 1942 and not released until May 1944.

Leopold Amery, as Secretary of State for India and Burma, was responsible for Indian affairs. Earlier in the year Sir Stafford Cripps was brought back from Moscow, where he was British Ambassador, to head the Cripps Mission to India in the hope of securing the co-operation of Indian nationalists.

To harmonise great enemies we must possess that which far surpasses enmity

– Lao Tze

The tragedy of India, screened from continuous public attention by the terrible and decisive battle which rages in the streets of Stalingrad, continues to typify that lack of generosity and enlightenment in high places which caused this war and has informed so much of its conduct. It endorses and underlines the failure of British statesmanship during the past two decades. At best, as the *News-Chronicle* has stated, Britain's policy is perpetuating a state of deadlock. At worst, it is driving Indian discontent underground, with consequences likely to be disastrous for ourselves if the Japanese invade India.

In his justly-criticised speech on September 10th, Mr Churchill told the House of Commons that 'it may well be that these activities by the Congress Party have been aided by Japanese Fifth Column work.' Next day the *Daily Mail* improved upon this suggestion by describing Congress as 'riddled with Fifth Columnists whose object was to work for a Japanese victory'. If this is indeed the case, it seems strange that the arrest of the Congress leaders by the government of India should have been so deeply deplored in China, which has suffered at Japanese hands far longer than any of the United Nations; and that the *News-Chronicle*'s Delhi correspondent should report, to his credit, that so far 'no documents or Japanese arms alleged to have been supplied to Indian firebrands have been produced or reported as captured.'

Seldom has one section of the British press behaved worse than in its malicious abuse of Mr Gandhi; an abuse which cannot touch the object of their emotional slanders, but does infinite harm to those who circulate and read them. These newspapers invent or 'report' most damaging allegations, and then state that Mr Churchill's 'disclosures' do nothing to 'discredit' their assertions. They out-Churchill the Prime Minister in their anxiety to lay all the blame for the situation upon the Indian leaders, and forget that the constant attribution of evil motives to others illustrates mainly the way in which the minds of the attributors work.

Amid this babel of raucous voices, it is not surprising that a reader of these letters should be anxious to receive some constructive suggestions for the pacification of India. 'Do you really think', she goes on to inquire, 'that if we gave up our share in its government now, the Moslems and Hindus would settle down peacefully together? They do not seem at present to be able to agree on the form of government they would establish, and until they do this, surely the less articulate classes must be in a far worse position than they are at present if we left India. What is the solution of this problem?'

To attempt first a reply to the specific question, there seems to be at least a possibility that the wealthy 'interests' which want Britain to maintain her hold on India are deliberately exacerbating Hindu-Moslem differences, in the same way as the rulers of this country have for centuries pursued a 'balance of power' policy in Europe on the principle of 'divide and dominate'. I should, at any rate, be interested to see what moves would be made towards Hindu-Moslem reconciliation if we announced that we would clear out of India, not at the end of the war, but as soon as the two groups had composed their differences sufficiently to make possible the formation of a national government. It is at least worth noting that on September 14th, the Delhi correspondent of *The Times* commended the *Civil and Military Gazette* of India, a newspaper critical of the Prime Minister, for a similar 'constructive suggestion'. According to *The Times* correspondent, the *Gazette* maintained that 'Mr Churchill could have fully satisfied the large bulk of sane nationalist feeling in this country if he had made an offer to transfer full power as soon as a representative national government, fitted to be a repository of that power, had been constituted.' [In that way, claims the newspaper,] Britain would have demonstrated as baseless the mass of suspicion which exists in India, and 'at the same time they would have placed on the shoulders of Indians themselves the burden of resolving the present imbroglio.'

The further proposals that follow in this letter are not merely the result of my own moderately informed cogitations, based upon the reading of books and newspapers, but of many talks with friends of India in this country, both Indian and British. In the first place, it has wisely been emphasised that India is not simply an imperial question to be solved by Britain and India alone, but a world problem intimately related to the present close of the historical epoch which began with the Renaissance, and to the replacement of oligarchical legislatures by people's governments. Hence the intervention of third parties, such as representative Americans, is to be welcomed, and not, as at present, deplored by the British government – which still adopts towards India an attitude similar to that of a feudal baron towards the villeins on his manor.

'Americans must strive sympathetically and imaginatively to get at the root of the matter before assailing Gandhi and his followers,' runs an article in the *Worldover Press* by Anup Singh, editor of *India Today* and Director of the Indian Research Bureau in New York. 'America has a great stake in India. She can no longer afford to consider India as Britain's exclusive concern.' The same article points out that when Britain, in complete disregard of India's wishes, declared India belligerent within a few hours of her own declaration of war, Gandhi could have created havoc and could have crippled the war effort in India by mass civil disobedience. But, against many protests from his followers, he refrained from doing so because, on humanitarian grounds, his sympathies were with Britain against Hitler. Mr Singh, who supports the war, makes three further suggestions: (1) The setting up now of a provisional national government in India; (2) The Viceroy should function from now on as a Governor-General does in a Dominion; (3) The military control of India, for psychological reasons, should be under a joint board, consisting of an American, an Englishman, a Russian, a Chinese, and an Indian, with a commander-in-chief of its own choice.

There seems also to be a strong case for creating an atmosphere more favourable to negotiation by announcing a successor to the present Viceroy, whose term of office, extended from 1941, is coming to an end. Indians themselves would like a man to be chosen who has genuine faith in democratic ideals, owes no definite allegiance to any political party, and is conscious of the march of historic events. As a guarantee of his democratic outlook, the new Viceroy might well be empowered to introduce an all-round reduction of salaries and expenditure. The administration of India is known to be extravagant, and to involve the payment of unnecessarily high salaries. The Delhi correspondent of the *News-Chronicle* compares the 'sacred cows and naked urchins in the decaying city of Old Delhi' with 'the vast imperial pile of pink and buff sandstone which is supposed to express the ideals of British rule in India'. According to this journalist, British officials work in huge teak-panelled offices looking on to green lawns flanked by artificial waterways. Such luxury seems, to put it mildly, unbecoming in a country whose masses, still illiterate after two centuries of British rule, live permanently upon the edge of famine.

Further suggestions for a new basis of negotiations include the abolition of the India Office, which should be placed under the Dominions Office; and an assurance, preferably by the King, that the Atlantic Charter is applicable in the case of India, and that after the war the Imperial Government, in co-operation with its allies, would assist India to gain the status of full national sovereignty. A joint statement might well be issued at once by the United Nations, declaring their recognition of India's claim to independent sovereign status and giving it their full support. Such assurances and declarations from new and respected sources might have a far-reaching psychological effect upon all political parties and groups in India, which would at least produce a change of atmosphere.

Limitations of space prevent me from expanding these proposals, but even a mere listing-up of them indicates how many possibilities for negotiation exist which have barely been mentioned officially, let alone discussed. The pronouncement of Mr Churchill, followed by the deplorable speeches of Mr Amery and Sir Stafford Cripps, that we have done all we can or will, and

128

that the initiative must now rest with the Indian Congress, is evidence not of wisdom, but of the bankruptcy of statesmanship. The time has come for you, for me, and for all who care for the future relations of Britain – not only with India, but with all other races and nations towards whom she has special responsibilities – to emphasise unceasingly that the ugly weed of hatred is the only plant that thrives in the soil of repression; and that a solution illumined by magnanimity and a gracious yielding of power has not been found wanting, but has never in fact been tried.

___ 17 December 1942 ___

Master, what of the night?-
Child, night is not at all
Anywhere, fallen or to fall,
Save in our star-stricken eyes.
Forth of our eyes it takes flight,
Look we but once nor before
Nor behind us, but straight on the skies,
Night is not then any more.
 – A. C. Swinburne, *A Watch in the Night*

As I sit down to write you at this fourth Christmas season of the Second World War, I find myself wondering in what way the Christmas spirit is most strongly alive amongst us, and how it is best able to sustain us through the war-time trials still to come.

And, while I meditate, a memory comes back which is now many years old; the memory of a morning in 1916. As a young girl whose world had been destroyed by a name on a casualty list, I asked myself a similar question. It was an Easter Day question then, formulated as I sat in St Paul's Cathedral beneath G. F. Watts' picture of Hagar in the Desert. 'Will the night soon pass? Will it ever pass? How much longer can I endure it? What will help me to endure it, if endured it must be?'

129

I was alone that morning; and I felt, perhaps, even more alone than I was. Today, in that same night which began in 1914, lifted for a moment of history, and has now descended upon us again, I am alone no longer; throughout the world I have hundreds of friends, all known to me by name, some by sight, but the great majority only by their letters. With them, of whom you are one, I want to consider a new version of that once forlorn inquiry: 'What, in a world at war, is helping us most this Christmastide to endure the night that will one day pass? Have we any abiding quality which causes us to realise more keenly the love of God who sent His Son to earth for our salvation?'

It seems to me, as I look back upon the past three years, that we have at least one spiritual hope, of which there is far more evidence than we possessed in the first Great War. This hope rests upon the underlying awareness of kinship between the common people of the world whether enemies or allies, coupled with the exercise, among the more thoughtful in all ranks of all nations, of conscious toleration based upon that awareness.

What, you may ask, is the evidence of which I write? It is difficult to define or tabulate; it consists of a story here, an incident there, of which the significance, emerging through the fog of war propaganda, seems to point with the clearness of a Star of Bethlehem to the love and pity of man for man. I have written, for instance, about the noble sermon preached by Pastor von Bodelschwingh after the bombing of his hospital at Bethel-bei-Bielefeld; and others have related the brave words of forgiveness recently spoken by another German pastor at the grave of two women parishioners after the RAF had passed over his parish. Today we know that in a Sussex village, at the burial service of twenty-nine children and their teachers, the Bishop of Chichester (and, he tells us, the bereaved parents too) rose to the same high opportunity, and spoke words not of hate, but of sorrow crowned by faith.

But bishops and pastors, you may say, are men of lofty character, specially chosen to lead others into the way of the Cross. What of the more ordinary people like you and me? Are they really showing patience, humanity, toleration?

Let me give you two examples of fellowship taken from the fighting forces. We learned not long ago from the *Evening Standard* that when General Ritter von Thoma, Commander of the Afrika Korps, was captured in the Battle of Egypt, General Montgomery entertained him to a dinner at which the two men discussed the battle, and marked out the strategy on the table-cloth. But generals, perhaps, are not the common people; they come into a special category? Here, then, in a press-cutting from the Johannesburg *Sunday Times* sent to me by a reader, is a letter from a South African woman which recalls one member of our fellowship who voluntarily tended the neglected graves of three German airmen at a cemetery in Kent. Under the heading 'Desert Graves', the first two paragraphs run as follows: 'My husband is "up North" and I recently had a letter from him enclosing negatives and snaps of a grave in which three South African Air Force officers are buried. He came across the grave in an old German camp, and was surprised at the trouble which they had taken with it. The head-stone is formed with the wing-tip of a Messerschmitt machine, and in front of it is a cross bearing their names.'

But soldiers, you may object, are comrades in misfortune. What evidence have we of toleration among civilians at home? I have reason to believe in a growing volume of evidence, even though much of it is negative in expression. Did you see, I wonder, the beautiful article called *All Souls' Day*, contributed by H. N. Brailsford, to the *New Statesman* of November 14th? In this article, the writer reminds us that Johannes Brahms called his famous Requiem "*Ein Deutsches Requiem*" because its words were taken, not from the Latin, but from the homely German of Luther's Bible. Brailsford goes on to ask what, in the name of pity, we and the German singers of the Requiem are doing today, and to plead that even in the midst of battle we should remember the 'communion of saints' from many nations.

Much moved by his theme I wrote to thank him, and because I was an old friend he replied, telling me that the article had brought him a shoal of letters too numerous to answer. They were all of thanks, and he 'had expected abuse'. In circumstances far more provocative to the majority than Brailsford's memorable essay, I, too, have 'expected abuse'. Week after week, year after year, I have written books, letters, articles, expressing minority opinions which are anathema to many. Yet I can count the letters of abuse on my ten fingers, while those written in friendship fill several files. Are we to suppose that British people write letters only when they approve, and refrain when they disagree? If so, it is a pleasing trait; but I suspect that the explanation lies deeper.

From the days of Wycliffe and earlier, British domestic history has been largely a story of conflicts in which the minority saw more clearly than the majority, and ultimately won the day. Though a sense of historical perspective is still comparatively rare, the citizens of this country appear to cherish an inherited suspicion that the minority may well prove to be right. To this is now added the growing perception that minority views on war must ultimately be accepted if civilisation may hope to survive. Although, therefore, Britain officially disapproves of her contemporary rebels, they become a source of pride the moment that they are part of history. This peculiarity of ours finds expression in a recent addition, entitled *British Rebels and Reformers*, to the propagandist series *Britain in Pictures*. The author, Harry Roberts, quotes with approval a distinguished Christian minister who stated that 'all our liberties are due to men who, when their conscience has compelled them, have broken the laws of the land.'

In this attitude of toleration towards pioneers exploring the undeveloped territories of human fellowship, I see reflected a deep if still inarticulate desire among the people of many nations to know and understand their counterparts. The realisation is becoming clearer that international grievances are largely of political manufacture; that beneath these much propagated differences lies the fundamental unity of humanity, with its loves, sorrows, and aspirations. Thus the individual who rejects war as a solution of international dilemmas, and refuses to admit that for rational beings there can ever be 'no alternative', is

132

voicing a hope which is part of the stuff of man's dreams and desires, however explicit his external rejection.

To get on the road to that common understanding, we have only to picture the preoccupations of all 'small people' and particularly of their women during this Christmas week. The wives and mothers from a million broken families, waiting in suspense for news of their men or grateful, perhaps, for good tidings lately received, are searching depleted shops for toys now rare, or for trifles to put in the Christmas stockings of children whose fathers are far away.

When these children light their Yule-tree candles and say their Christmas prayers, it is in the same spirit and to the same God – for whom they are all His sons and daughters, whether we call them German, French, Italian, British or American. Let us think kindly of them this week, wherever they may be, and, forgetting those differences which cannot obliterate the essential unity of mankind, remember the Child who took upon himself the likeness of our fragile human flesh, and whose mercy is big enough to redeem us all.

P.S. Amid the comparative plenty of our own Christmas, we shall recall especially those families in occupied countries who are deprived of everything that gives Christmas celebrations their life and colour. You will be glad at least to know that, according to a statement by Mr Dingle Foot on November 17th, the despatch of 100 tons of Canadian dried milk to Greece is now to be permitted. At that date, the first 30 tons had already been loaded for shipment in Montreal. There seems little doubt that this response to the request of the Neutral Commission operating in Greece has been expedited by the demands of the public conscience here. I am proud and grateful for the contribution made by the readers of these letters to the expression of that conscience. This preliminary concession is not, of course, adequate to the Greek children's need, and it is important that we should continue to make known our concern.

In a previous letter, discussing again the case for an armistice, Vera referred to the plight of the thousands of starving people in various parts of Europe and to the Jews, reporting that according to the Inter-Allied Information Committee, five million were in danger of extermination. She then turned to the dilemma with which she, and others like her, were constantly preoccupied. She wrote:

That brings me to the consideration involved by the feeling of some of my peace-loving friends that, evil though the war is, our moral obligation to the victims of Nazidom compels us to continue it. Have those who feel this moral obligation (which every decent person must share) really decided wherein it lies? Are they more deeply concerned to rescue the five million who can still be saved, or to exact retribution at some distant date from the executioners of the two million who have already died? Surely, from every consideration of humanity, what matters is to rescue those who are threatened. If you were a Jewish mother whose brother had been put to death by the Nazis, would you be more anxious to track down his murderer, or to save your terrified children from a similar fate?

I do not see how any rational person can doubt the answer to this question. But it is the termination or interruption of the war, and not its increasingly bitter continuation, which is the more likely to save these children. The war itself, its length and its geographical vastness, are the

134

factors responsible for the deaths of the majority. According to a provisional census taken in May, 1939, and quoted by the Royal Institute of International Affairs, the total number of Jews in the pre-war Reich was no more than 339,892. If the war had not occurred, this number would have represented the limit of the potential Jewish victims. The statement of the Inter-Allied Information Committee itself implicitly acknowledges the extent to which Jewish suffering arises from the length of the war and the increasing moral deterioration which this has involved.

'Persecution of the Jews in the enemy-occupied countries of Europe began, in general, soon after Axis invasion,' runs the summary in *The Times*. 'At first the persecution took the form mainly of depriving Jews of their civil rights. Then the pace and intensity of persecution grew. Many Jews were arrested and thrown into concentration camps. Deportations became more frequent . . . In the middle of 1942 there was a general intensification of measures against the Jews.'

What indication could be clearer that, the longer the war continues, the worse the plight of the Jewish victims will be? A pause in the fury of hostilities would at least make possible their removal to neutral or allied countries. Such measures will be difficult, if not impossible, so long as the fighting goes on.

___ 28 January 1943 ___

Teach me to feel another's woe,
To hide the fault I see;
That mercy I to others show,
That mercy show to me.
   – Alexander Pope, *Universal Prayer*

In a previous letter, I mentioned Hitler's persecution of the Jews, and in this connection made two main points: first, that many who protested seemed to be more interested in punishing the Nazi executioners than in saving their victims; secondly, that the longer the war continued, the worse the position of these victims was likely to become.

Today I want to draw your urgent attention to the very moving and remarkably restrained pamphlet by Victor Gollancz, *Let My People Go*, which describes the present plight of the Jewish race in Europe, and suggests useful forms of immediate action. This pamphlet bears out my own contention that the sufferings of the Jews appear to have been publicised less with the purpose of saving them, than with that of stirring up anti-German hatred. This hatred in its turn provokes new demands for 'retribution', which thus tends to become, in the words of Stephen Hobhouse, 'a refuge for those who don't want to spend thought or substance in helping the victims.'

Victor Gollancz also shows that even during war a good deal can and should be done to help these victims of Nazi cruelty. I urge you to purchase or borrow his pamphlet at once (it only costs 3d, and can be obtained from any large bookshop), read the Summary in Section 1, and act upon some or all of the suggestions on page 9.

Where help on the largest possible scale is so vitally demanded, we need not waste time questioning whether every story of Nazi atrocities is well-founded. The moment that a government or people is faced with a grave moral responsibility, the path to action is liable to become slippery with red herrings, and controversy about the accuracy of information can easily be used as one of these. Victor Gollancz himself does not maintain that every word of the Polish White Paper is 'unquestionably true'. All that we need now remember is that millions of Jews are in peril and that thousands could be saved – and by *us*. We should not seek to lay the responsibility for taking them into safety upon the Americans, Russians, South Americans, Spanish, Turkish, Swedes or Portuguese, until *we*, the citizens of a rich, vast and under-populated Commonwealth, have done everything that is in our power.

As I pointed out there is a tragic parallel between the plight of the hunted Jews and that of the starving peoples of Europe (who are often, of course, themselves Jews, and victims of both Nazi persecution and British blockade). To suggest that post-war 'retribution' will save an interned Jewish baby from extermination is as futile as arguing that 'liberation' two or three years hence will rescue a starving Belgian child from slow and horrible death. The pains of all these pitiful victims can only too easily be used to fan the flames of warlike passion; yet questions in the House of Commons, deputations to the appropriate Ministers, and letters to the press from uneasy correspondents, too often receive a mere blank negation.

'If even a very few of Hitler's victims have a chance of escape but are refused sanctuary by us,' writes the younger Josiah Wedgwood in a letter to the *News-Chronicle* for December 22nd, 'then, however much we may protest or threaten retribution to their persecutors, their blood is on our hands also.'

What, you will ask, could this country do? Victor Gollancz's pamphlet will give you details; in my limited space I can call your attention only to two steps that we could take at once, and to a third that might have been taken. On page 6, Gollancz quotes an extract from a letter written to *The Times* of December 22nd by Sir Neill Malcolm, stating that 4,000–5,000 Jewish refugees are waiting in Spain and Portugal for a chance to go overseas. This fact was not only confirmed to me personally by a relief worker recently in France, but my informant indicated that unless these refugees were rescued quickly they would be sent back (presumably because Spain is one of the countries afflicted by famine) into Nazi-controlled territory. We could urge our government to admit this small number of refugees immediately, and whenever possible add personal offers of hospitality.

Secondly, there are homes waiting for thousands of refugees in Palestine. On my desk lies the copy of a telegram received a few days ago by the Women's International Zionist Organisation (75 Great Russell Street, WC1) from Jewish Women's Organisations in Palestine. The most important section of this long telegram runs as follows: 'Ways could be found to stop torture of innocent and rescue remnant Jewish people Europe stop open arms and homes await them in Palestine stop if authorities will create conditions Jewish women in Palestine pledge themselves to do all in their power help in absorption in Palestine of children all ages stop WIZO in addition regards its concern help refugee women rebuild new life here stop pray that urgent appeal of women will go out to Allied governments awake free world conscience.'

Here again is a practical solution. I cannot enter in this letter into explanations of why and how the pro-Arab (i.e. pro-Moslem) policy of our government has limited the immigration of Jews into Palestine. I only ask you to urge that, when life and death are at stake for millions, this policy should be relaxed at least until these victims are safe from their tormentors.

A third and numerically quite small chance of service which this country could have taken has apparently already been lost. According to a question asked in the House by Mr Shinwell on January 20th, 2,000 French-Jewish children to whom visas were refused here have since been deported to Germany. I reproduce the first part of this discreditable episode as given by Claude Cockburn's news-sheet *The Week* for January 7th, 1943:

'The *Daily Telegraph* on January 6th published as its principal correspondence a letter from Sir Andrew McFadyean, former General Secretary to the Reparation Commission and of the Dawes Committee.

'Sir Andrew fully confirmed the facts as stated by *The Week*, revealing also a fact which could not be published at the outset, that the representations to which *The Week* referred took the form of a deputation to Mr Morrison, which appealed for permission for the entry of 2,000 children from Vichy France.

' "The request", says Sir Andrew, "was unconditionally refused, partly on the ground that it might cause an outburst of
anti-Semitism here. That is a slander on the British people. News
had just been received that of 2,000 children, from two years of
age upwards, deported from Vichy France in cattle trucks, half
were dead on arrival at their destination and the rest were
dying."

'The deputation included the Archbishop of Canterbury,
Cardinal Hinsley, the Moderator of the Church of Scotland, Mr
Harold Nicolson, Major Victor Cazalet, Mr Wilfred Roberts,
the Honourable William Astor, and Mrs Corbett Ashby.

'All were moved to intense indignation by the remarks of Mr
Morrison. The young Astor was in naval officer's uniform, and
in a fury of indignation remarked afterwards that he had seen his
own men sharing their rations with Greek refugee children and
would be very sorry to have to report to them on the Home
Office attitude.'

What, you may well ask is the 'anti-Semitism' of which the
Home Office spoke, and does it, in any case, apply to young and
helpless children? Is it not another red herring, and one of a
peculiarly slimy and offensive variety? We know, of course, that
there is a good deal of semi-underground, semi-fascist, anti-
Jewish propaganda, and fairly numerous instances of prejudice
against individual Jews. Recently I discussed this subject with
a very intelligent university woman, Christian by religion but
Jewish by birth. She herself had been asked by an organisation to
which she belonged to investigate cases of anti-Semitism, and
had invariably discovered that individual grievances of a kind
which might be caused by any citizen of any country had been
given a racial animus by propaganda. She added rather drily that
Jewish minds were apt to work quicker than British minds,
thereby causing considerable jealousy in cities with large Jewish
populations.

But it is, as Sir Andrew McFadyean stated, a slander on the
British people to suggest that personal and psychological difficulties of this kind would be allowed, even by the few who felt
them, to interfere with the rescue of children from torture and

139

death. Even according to the rough justice of 'making the punishment fit the crime' (which is not really justice at all, since psychological research tends to prove ever more clearly that crime is not cured or eliminated by punishment), massacre is hardly an appropriate payment for instances of personal self-glorification or even for the large-scale provocation of commercial jealousy.

We British are kindly people; we should prove by our actions that we possess sanity and perspective as well. Even though the Jewish community is able to care for Hitler's victims, let us (and especially those of us who have no Jewish blood or connections) scotch the bogey of anti-Semitism by our own generosity and initiative. And let us do it *now*, before many thousands of individuals who love, hope and suffer exactly as we do, are dead and beyond recall.

The reference to the Beveridge Report was prompted by the publication, three months earlier, of the report of the Inter-Departmental Committee on Social Insurance and Allied Services, of which Sir William Beveridge, Master of University College, Oxford (and Liberal MP for Berwick-on-Tweed 1944–5), was chairman. It was the blueprint for the welfare state and its proposals included, for the first time, compulsory sickness and unemployment insurance and the setting up of a Ministry of Social Security. It seemed at the time to be a pipe-dream, but most of its provisions were implemented within two years of the end of the war. Beveridge lost his seat in 1945 and was ennobled a year later.

We would be one in hatred of all wrong,
One in our love of all things sweet and fair,
One with the joy that breaketh into song,
One with the grief that trembleth into prayer,
One in the power that makes the children free,
To follow truth, and thus to follow thee.

From a hymn sung at the Service of Prayer for India
at St Martin-in-the-Fields, 25 February 1943

In these letters I have often written you about the vital importance of a true perspective. It seems to me that the need to keep our sense of proportion becomes greater, not less, as the years of war go by. We become tired more quickly, our private anxieties grow greater, our emotions are more easily aroused. The result is that some domestic problem or business controversy is apt to loom disproportionately in our minds. What should be a limited question swells until it looks like a major issue, blotting out the horizon at the very moment when we should be trying to see beyond it.

Not long ago, when I thought that my son might be returning from America immediately, instead of (as I hope) during the summer, I wrote to a Quaker friend in whose spiritual power I have great confidence, and asked if he would pray for me and for the boy when he was on the sea. In reply came a kindly and well-justified rebuke. 'I'm not good at systematic prayer, and often wonder how far it can be directed on a particuar object. . . . I seem to feel I can do most good to anyone in need by lifting up the whole world, all life, with my heart to God.'

This timely admonition brought back to me some lines on another subject by a very different non-Quaker writer, which I quoted in a book about the last war ten years ago. 'A man of adequate vitality and zest', wrote Bertrand Russell in *The Conquest of Happiness*, 'will surmount all misfortunes by the emergence after each blow of an interest in life and the world which cannot be narrowed down so much as to make one loss fatal. To be defeated by one loss or even by several is not something to be admired as a proof of sensibility, but something to be deplored as a failure in vitality. All our affections are at the mercy of death, which may strike down those whom we love at any moment. It is therefore necessary that our lives should not have that narrow intensity which puts the whole meaning and purpose of our life at the mercy of accident.'

I know clearly enough that neither Bertrand Russell nor my Quaker friend intended to underrate the value of human affections. As an eminent Catholic priest, long dead, told my husband and myself in the short sermon which he delivered at our marriage service, 'We cannot understand the love of God until we have known the love of man.' What the two writers meant, I believe, is that human affections are themselves circumscribed and poorer than they should be if we limit them to individuals, instead of regarding them as contributory to the universal sum of love and ourselves as part of that whole creation which groaneth and travaileth together in its struggle towards higher standards and finer values.

I felt additionally rebuked for the measure of my mental concentration on private problems when I recently attended the service of intercession for India and Gandhi at St Martin's-in-the-Fields. The congregation which prayed there was part of a vast underground movement (since most forms of true spiritual life have been driven 'underground' for the time being) which is working in many unpublicised but persistent ways for the end of deadlock not only in India, but in the whole international world. The profound struggle for a nobler interpretation of 'retribution' than that of the politicians and some of the bishops; the campaign in favour of mercy for the Jews of Europe rather than vengeance upon their persecutors; the attempt to modify the blockade policy of the British government in time to save the lives of millions of Europe's children – all these are one with the endeavour to bring a new vision and a greater power of imagination to bear upon the tragedy by which saints and leaders remain shut in prison by authorities which were never more in need of spiritual grace than now.

How urgently, I thought, as we prayed and sang in that most famous of London's churches which the air raids so miraculously spared, the energetic aggressive West requires the patient contemplative insight of the East to guide it through its present quarrels to a truer perspective! Only recently a friend had compared the attitude of the Viceroy towards Gandhi's fast with that of Pilate washing his hands at the trial of Jesus. It seemed to me too that when the history of our time comes to be assessed from the standpoint of the centuries, the part played by the Viceroy may appear not dissimilar from that of the Procurator of Judea, and the total consequences of the present situation in India may be comparable in their long-range effects to those of the drama staged in Galilee two thousand years ago.

From contemplating the Indian dilemma I went on to think of some immense questions which loom upon the skyline: the future of the Beveridge Report, the threatened deterioration of Anglo-American relations, due (so I am convinced) very largely to the fact that so many of the wrong people are now sitting in official seats, as well as going over to the United States themselves; the military victories on the eastern front and the certainty that Russia will have a predominating influence upon the peace; and began to feel ashamed of ever becoming preoccupied with personal troubles. But if we are to contribute usefully by our thinking to all these problems (and certainly we can achieve no ultimate effectiveness unless we begin to think now), we surely need super-strength from some source or another to help us to put our own anxieties in their proper place.

One or two readers have lately written to say that they find these letters less useful than they were because my attitude has become 'more religious' in the course of three and a half years. To be able to 'stand alone' used, I admit, to be an ideal of my youth; but in finding my way through the long dark tunnel of this Second World War, I have come to feel closer than ever before to the spirit of the Collect for the second Sunday in Lent which begins with the words: 'Almighty God, who seest that we have no power of ourselves to help ourselves. . . .'

If we are not today believers in God, then we must surely

believe in the power communicated to other men and women by those who serve their fellows whether in large ways or small. It is not necessary to be a Gandhi, or a Henry Wallace, or a William Beveridge, in order to contribute to the sum of spiritual strength which is available for those who need it. Only yesterday, a letter from a stranger reminded me of the lasting effects of such a personal victory as that of Winifred Holtby in her struggle with death.

Winifred's response to the medical verdict that she had only two or three more years to live, was an immediate plunge into the writing of *Mandoa, Mandoa!*, her brilliant satire on British imperialism, and an increase of her efforts for the education and liberation of African natives. She had achieved the detachment and perspective that most of us lack – detachment from her own pain and bitter regret for the years that she would miss, perspective which showed her that the problems of imperialism and the needs of the Africans would still be there when she was gone. The result has been that – whether or not you believe that the immortal part of her experiences *conscious* survival – she has become (even more, perhaps, than she would have done if she had lived to be old) a symbol and an inspiration to many souls reluctantly facing the valley of the shadow.

My correspondent yesterday wrote that she was dying of an incurable disease, and felt (as so many of us would feel in the circumstances) that she lacked the courage to confront what lay before her. Because she believed that the story of Winifred's final years would help, she had tried to buy my biography of her, only to be told by the booksellers that the book was reprinting and unobtainable. Could I help her to procure a copy? Fortunately I could; some time may elapse before the new edition is ready, but my co-operative publishers agreed to put together and bind a copy for my correspondent within ten days. But the incident started me thinking about the secret of Winifred's power over so many who know no more of her than that she wrote *South Riding*, and died young, over seven years ago.

And I came to the conclusion that the secret perhaps lay in her ability to achieve a perspective which saw her own life, with

145

its peculiar tragedy of early death and the apparent premature end of her work, in its right relation to the great purposes for which, while she could, she lived. For in the last resort perspective is a spiritual quality, which sees time in the light of eternity, and ourselves and our anxieties in relation to the whole panorama of our own age and the years to be.

It is curious that Vera did not mention the title of her book *Testament of Youth*; first published in 1933. Fifty years later it was being studied by thousands of A-level students.

Victor Gollancz published the war-time edition. He also contributed a Foreword to *Above All Nations* when it was published in 1945. It included contributions from many readers of the Letters.

The figure Vera quotes for civilian casualties was not far out. By the end of the war it had increased to 60,595. The number killed in the British forces totalled 264,443. Another 30,000 died in the Merchant Navy.

The centenary party referred to in the postscript was to celebrate the 100th issue of the *Letter to Peace Lovers*.

*Everyone must have noticed during the war the contrast
between the ferocity of our civilians, and the reasonableness and
compunction of our soldiers from the front. . . . The civilian
called the German the Hun, and, in the comparative safety of
home, clamoured for his extermination with a full mouth. The
soldier called him Jerry, meaning 'companion in misfortune'. . . .
This does not mean that the British civilian is one sort of person
and the British soldier another. It means that the civilian neither
sees nor knows what he is doing, and that the soldier sees it and
has to do it*

— George Bernard Shaw, *Prefaces*

Recently a book of mine telling the story of youth caught up into
the machinery of the last war was re-issued in a new war-time
edition. This book was written and first published at a period
when post-war reaction was at its height, and the information,
therefore, that the new edition of 16,000 copies had sold out
before publication moved me to hopeful astonishment. It seemed
worthwhile to write to my American publishers, informing them
of the strange phenomenon, and suggesting that the book's
republication in the United States might have the same result. So
I did so, enclosing a paragraph from a letter which one of my
readers had received from her fiancé, a young political officer in
the Sudan, and had sent on to me. This paragraph described how
he had to clear a battlefield 'somewhere in Abyssinia', and
within the shadow of a wall found a British soldier lying dead
with my book in his hand, open at a poem beginning 'Violets
from Plug Street Wood. . . .'

The response from America arrived a few days ago. It stated,
benevolently but firmly, that the head of the 'Sales Department'
had gone away to think the matter over, but that his first reaction had been No, the market wouldn't be ready for such a
republication. 'My guess', added the writer, 'is that he is right.
We have to get a long way further in this war before the people
here would be ready to read that book anew.'

I wonder how far you would agree with my reply to this letter?

Within recent months quite a number of young American soldiers and nurses have spontaneously got into touch with me because they have read my books, and it seems to me that their attitude towards the problems which these books discuss is very much the same as that of the young people in the British forces. So I wrote my publisher that the reactions of American civilians and Americans in the forces might well be quite different, and that America was, in effect, confronting the same great gulf in feeling and experience between the people at home and those on active service abroad, that England knew in the last war. The Shaw quotation at the head of this letter describes in a few sentences those contrasting reactions.

Today in Britain, as I told my publisher, that particular gulf has ceased to exist, owing to the fact that the suffering of the civilian population has been, up to date, as great as that of the troops. It was recently announced in the press that the number of civilians killed in air-raids in Britain now amount to between forty and fifty thousand, with a somewhat larger number of injured. For security reasons we are not told the total number of casualties in the British forces, but I doubt whether they amount to more than this (though the opening of a Second Front would certainly alter the balance).

This situation of being 'all in it together', and sharing the war's worst consequences, has completely changed the attitude of the civilian population at home from that which I certainly remember between 1914 and 1919. Today, as Bernard Shaw wrote of the last war's soldiers, we are 'companions in misfortune' at home as well as abroad. Many people who would never accept the description 'pacifist' go even further, and quite openly express their sympathy for civilian sufferers in Cologne, Berlin, Essen, and other burnt and battered cities of the now much-raided Reich. 'I wouldn't wish this trouble on any other woman,' says the young Lancashire mother in Burton Cooper's play *We are The People* after her small boy has been killed in an air raid.

Although from some quarters the cries for 'reprisals' have been noisy and are often loudly publicised by certain organs of the press, the air raids here have shown to a remarkable degree that, with the ordinary decent human being, suffering produces tolerance rather than the reverse. As I have often reminded you, when a Gallup poll was taken on reprisals at the height of the raids, less than half the inhabitants of inner London asked for retaliation. The voices most vehemently raised in favour of it came from Cumberland, Westmorland and the North Riding.

The greater toleration grows, the more frequently to be found in the midst of war are those acts of humanity which, if they became characteristic not even of a majority but only of a large minority in every nation, would quickly make war impossible. When the inability to hate not only reaches a certain point but is generally recognised as having reached it, fighting and slaughtering cannot be carried on, since quite a negligible proportion of mankind is naturally adapted to cold-blooded deliberate killing.

Hence the acts of humanity daily performed by soldiers and civilians who have suffered are not 'played-up' by the wartime press. When you find them in national newspapers they are seldom printed on the main pages – though the *Daily Herald* of April 22nd did carry on its front page the story of the Italian prisoners on the Northumberland moors who dragged an RAF pilot from the wreckage of his crashed aeroplane at great risk to their own lives. More often such items are tucked into the bottom of an inside column, or quoted in magazines run by relatively small pacifist or near-pacifist groups. Seldom indeed do they come to the knowledge of the general public.

For this reason my husband, George Catlin, and I are now jointly preparing an anthology of stories, incidents, letters and poems designed to illustrate the survival of human tolerance and compassion in the midst of war. The title is to be *Above All Nations*, taken from an inscription on the campus of my husband's American university, Cornell: 'Above all nations is humanity'. We believe that the publication of such a book, and the evidence within its covers, will contribute their small quota to the mood which will ultimately make war impossible.

If the readers of this letter would care to collaborate with us in this enterprise, we shall be pleased and grateful. We know, from our own contacts and correspondence, that in private letters, local newspapers, parish magazines, etc., there is almost certainly a wealth of just the material we need. But such material is normally inaccessible because the anthologist does not know where to find it, and cannot set out on the infinite task of searching the files of every local paper. Should you, therefore, in your daily life come across incidents or stories which will help us in our endeavour to compass 'humanity' within the covers of a book, the value of this volume would be greatly increased and its scope enlarged. From time to time many letter-readers have sent me such examples from their own experience, and I have nearly always been able to make good use of them either in the letter itself or in other publications. If you have an opportunity of doing this and would kindly mark the envelope *Anthology*, it can be forwarded direct to me, without having to be opened and read.

Here from *The Times* of April 22nd, are two verses of just the kind that we hope to include in the section devoted to poems. They are entitled *Written After Dunkirk*, and are the work of Commander H. M. Darrell Brown, who lost his life when in command of HMS *Ibis* off Algiers.

> A hundred thousand heroes
> With banners flying high
> Are marching down the ages
> To show us how to die.
>
> One man, disgraced and lonely,
> Yet whispering still 'forgive',
> Cross-hung and dying slowly
> Still shows us how to live.

These lines seem more appropriate to this Easter-tide than the jubilant sound of church bells to which I have just been listening.

P.S. Although the chaos of books and papers in our Chelsea house, to which we have just returned, threatens to engulf us for two or three weeks, it is now possible to fix the date of the Centenary Party. I shall, therefore, be delighted to welcome those of you who can come to 2 Cheyne Walk, Chelsea, on Saturday, June 5th, from 3.0–6.0. As over 200 readers have signified their intention of coming, I am reluctantly obliged to ask each of you to bring a small quantity of tea and milk (with just enough sugar for yourself if you take it) and a few sandwiches or cakes. When you arrive, these contributions will be received by our helpers and 'pooled' so that the resultant buffet will, I hope, provide a good meal with plenty of variety! If you are only staying temporarily in London and have no access to rations, I shall not, of course, expect you to contribute, as those of us who come from our own homes will probably provide between us enough for everybody. Tea will be preceded by a short conference on the purpose of the Letter and methods of making it more widely known. Any provisions left over will be given away.

— 17 June 1943 —

Let everyone, then, who thinks with pain on all these great evils, so horrible, so ruthless, acknowledge this is misery. And if anyone either endures or thinks of them without mental pain, this is a more miserable plight still, for he thinks himself happy because he has lost human feeling

— St Augustine, *The City of God*

While travelling to a lecture on Sunday, June 6th, I happened to read the leading article in the *Sunday Express*. It was entitled 'NO PITY! NO MERCY!' If you too saw it, you will probably remember the following paragraphs:

'Three years ago we stood alone. . . . Now we attack, and the beast – apparently very strong, formidable and ferocious, yet possibly nearer the point of cracking than we think – is caged.

'If we are to succeed we must not harbour cant and humbug. Voices are already heard, crying that mercy must temper justice, that vengeance belongs alone to God, not to His instruments,

152

that bombs on women and children are wicked, that the destruction of dams and the release of floods is not clean warfare, that we must not sink to the level of the Germans . . . As the doom of Germany becomes more certain the voices may grow louder. They may well have a sinister inspiration. The sincere and well-meaning voices are probably encouraged by the sound of the voices made in Germany. . . .

'All these sentimental appeals are bunkum and hypocrisy in effect, whether they come from a familiar prelate or some unsuspected Quisling. . . . We must show no mercy till the deed is done. If we do we shall be traitors to humanity.'

I am obviously one of the voices selected for condemnation by the *Sunday Express*. Mine is only a small voice, speaking through these letters and in a few other places. But if I were the only voice left in England to say it, and were to be shot tomorrow for saying it, I should still maintain that by every civilised standard, Christian or otherwise, it is brutal and wicked to attempt to win a war by burning and starving to death the young and helpless, and by letting loose overwhelming floods upon unsuspecting mothers and their innocent children in the small crowded homesteads of an industrial area. And judging by the conversations that I hear in trains and shops, I believe that the great majority of England's population agree with me, though most of them dare not say so.

Twenty-five years ago, in the spring of 1918, I was nursing in a military hospital at Étaples. At that time the main line to Paris had been protected from air attack for nearly four years by the long chain of army hospitals dividing the road and the railway between Étaples and Camiers. For several weeks during that spring, it was reported to the nurses that German reconnaissance planes had been over the camp dropping leaflets: 'Move your railway line or move your hospitals!' Needless to say, nothing was done – not even when a small preliminary raid on Étaples village put the bridge over the River Canche out of action for twelve hours. Finally the Germans came over, bombed the line, and killed a number of nurses and patients in the adjacent hospitals. From England went up a howl of indignation which drowned whatever apologetic mention might have been made about the warning leaflets. They had been dropped none the less, as we knew who were there. Could not our rulers who pride themselves on their superiority to German brutality have done at least as much for the women and their children in the Ruhr valleys, before they were swept away with no chance of escape when the dams were broken?

I need hardly explain to you, I think, that I am not a 'Quisling.' I do not know, and never have known, a single member of the Nazi Party. I listen neither to Lord Haw-Haw nor to the BBC and I take my views even less, if that were possible, from Dr Goebbels than from the *Sunday Express*. I only know that if I were one of the airmen who broke the dams, I should be haunted by the thought of those drowned floating faces for the rest of my life. In the *News-Chronicle* of June 11th, an eye-witness quoted from Stockholm reports the scenes in the grave-yards where the German people buried their families, as 'indescribable'. But it is not, I know, with the young pilots, but with those who give them their orders, that responsibility really lies. One can only pray that God's mercy may be with them, and with all other war-makers to whom in varying degrees, belated realisation will come. As I sit here writing above the Thames in our much-blitzed borough, I know that, whether I live to see it or not, the time will arrive when a flood-tide of reaction against hate will sweep the present false standards away, and horrify the men and women who temporarily subscribed to them.

In that day not honour but execration will be the portion of those who adopted from the Nazi leaders the standards of unrestricted cruelty against which they profess to be fighting. After all, people sometimes say to me: the Germans began it, why always blame the British? My reply is that I am not responsible for cruel deeds done by the Nazis in the name of the Germans, and much as I deplore them I cannot prevent them. But so long as the breath is in me I shall protest against abominations done by my government in the name of the British, of whom I am one. The mercilessness of others does not release us from the obligation to control ourselves.

154

Looking round for a congenial explanation of such 'senti-mentalists' as myself, the *Sunday Express* suggests that we are moved by 'sinister inspiration', 'encouraged by the sound of the voices made in Germany'. Does this editorial writer really dare to imply that the Gospels are of German origin, or the Epistles of Paul, or such masterpieces of meekness and truth as Bunyan's *Pilgrim's Progress*? Have we reached a stage at which our editors are so frightened of the eternal verities and their implications, that the only escape from them is a dishonest attempt to identify them with German propaganda? It is not my voice, but the voice of the *Sunday Express*, which carries a sound reminiscent of those German and Italian teachers whose work laid the founda-tions of the Nazi philosophy. 'It is better', wrote Machiavelli in *Arte della Guerra*, 'to conquer an enemy by hunger than by fighting, in which last victory fortune has more share than virtue or courage.' And it was Heinrich von Treitschke, the German historian, who wrote: 'We live in a warlike age; the over-sentimental philanthropic fashion of judging things has passed into the background. . . . The greatness of war is just what at first sight seems to be its horror – that for the sake of their country men will overcome the natural feelings of humanity.'

Britain, as we are so often reminded, is still a democratic country. You and I and the rest of our fellow nationals are free, as the *Sunday Express* editorial writer urges, to bomb, burn, drown and starve our enemies (and sometimes, in the attempt, our friends as well) without that compunction or those mis-givings which distinguish the human being from the beast of prey. But let us make no mistake about whose company we join when we do these things – or whose we repudiate.

Think what a world we could make if we put into our peace endeavours the same self-sacrifice, the same energy and the same co-operation as we use in the wastefulness of war
> – Sir Archibald Wavell in a message to the
> Ladies' Committee of the War Gifts Fund, quoted by
> the *Daily Telegraph*, 23 October 1941

This month India – so long discreetly banished from the front pages of our censored press – is again in the news owing to the appointment of Field-Marshal Sir Archibald Wavell as the new Viceroy of India.

Most of the various friends to whom I have put the question: 'What do you think of Wavell's appointment?' have replied cautiously, 'Well, it might be worse.' Personally, after reading the quotation which appears at the head of this letter and one or two similar utterances, I feel that it might be a great deal worse. In all my writings, as I think you know, I have maintained (on the solid basis of four years' experience of fighting men in the last war) that the real enemy of peace is not the soldier who knows war's cost, but the belligerent civilian. This is especially true of the civilian who wages war from an editorial chair or a ministerial office, and allows himself to be photographed smiling complacently beside the 'hero' of the moment – usually some young man who at the behest of his superior has carried out a deed responsible for the deaths of hundreds of helpless children.

Suffering is one of the deep well-springs of compassion. Because the soldier suffers, he pities. It was the British Tommies in the occupied Rhineland of 1919 who shared their rations with the starving population during the Allies' post-war blockade of central Europe. It was General Smuts who exclaimed at Versailles: 'God is writing a very different treaty from this!' and General Sir Ian Hamilton, the great soldier of Gallipoli, who supported his protest. It was Field-Marshal Sir William Robertson, Chief of the Imperial General Staff during the last war, who asked to be buried without military honours because a life of war-making had taught him the futility of war as a policy.

So let us preserve an open mind about Sir Archibald Wavell, and hope that, like the Duke of Wellington at the Congress of Vienna in 1815, he may prove a wiser diplomat than the professional politicians.

P.S. You will be interested to know that we had over 200 guests at the Centenary Party, including friends from as far away as Doncaster and Pembrokeshire. (Incidentally, they left unconsumed quite a goodly store of provisions, which we presented to the Hungerford Club, run by the Anglican Pacifist Fellowship for society's poorest victims, the 'down-and-outs' of the Embankment, in a shelter near Charing Cross.)

___ 12 August 1943 ___

It was a distinguished Christian minister who said that 'all our liberties are due to men who, when their conscience has compelled them, have broken the laws of the land'; and Emerson pronounced the profound caveat *that 'good men must not obey the laws too well.' Some of the wisest, bravest and noblest of our race have been rebels*
                    – Harry Roberts, *British Rebels and Reformers*

On August 3rd, as I came out of St Margaret's, Westminster, from the memorial service for my old friend, Lord Wedgwood of Barlaston, I began to meditate on the dominant part played by courageous individualism in the moulding of British history. During these days which have witnessed so marked a decline of the individual, who has been conscripted, registered, and classified in large and ever-growing categories by the totalitarian state, the unrepentant individualist has a value and a significance never surpassed throughout the long chronicle of our country.

Colonel Josiah Wedgwood (I never became quite accustomed to the 'Baron') was one of the political champions upon whom I had come to rely in crises, and, like many other recipients of official disfavour, I shall miss him greatly. He was also part of

157

the Staffordshire tradition which belongs to my own background, being the appropriate descendant of a twelfth-century
rebel, and great-great-grandson of the Josiah Wedgwood who
founded the world-famous pottery. His family and mine lived in
the same district for two hundred years and probably longer,
since our own humbler and less adventurous records go back
only so far as the Richard Brittain who was Mayor of
Newcastle-under-Lyme in 1741.

But 'Jos' was far more than the most vivid modern member of
his colourful family. I first came to know him personally at a
Chelsea party which Winifred Holtby gave a dozen or so years
ago for African natives and their friends. It was the kind of party
at which one would expect to find him, for he was a consistent
and irrepressible Don Quixote, the unrepentant supporter of
suffragettes, Jews, refugees, conscientious objectors, and other
oppressed and struggling minorities. Though anything but
pacifist himself he married a pacifist as his second wife, and lived
with her for nearly twenty-five years of loving comradeship
which ended only with his death. His innate heterodoxy prevented him, for all his popularity, from rising to high political
office, but his life followed the great precedent set by Pym and
Hampden, John Wilkes and Mary Wollstonecraft, Tom Paine
and Francis Place, William Wilberforce and Emmeline Pankhurst. In the history of our country, such names as these are apt
to be longer remembered than the names of cabinet ministers.

That is why, in these dark days when the lanterns lit by the
human spirit are few, Josiah Wedgwood, though dead, will live
on as a symbol. He symbolises not only the fearless individualism of British rebels and reformers, but the hard core of resistance to regimentation which lies at the heart of the British
people. Fortunately for the future of our society, there comes a
point at which even the British slow worm turns, and his
characteristic inertia changes to a mute indignation which
expresses itself in a quiet but determined revolt. One such point
was reached at the beginning of the blitz on London, when the
bombed and menaced population, inadequately provided with
shelters and rest-centres, resolutely took possession of the

158

Underground despite official prohibitions and protests. Another emerged at the end of last month with the mass opposition to the 'holidays at home' policy which the Ministry of Transport sought to impose upon workers jaded by four years of unremitting toil and monotony. It would be interesting to know how many members of that Ministry possess country cottages and are accustomed to enjoy golfing weekends.

Though the Ministry's failure to understand and consider human and particularly feminine needs is deplorable, the revolt itself has been a hopeful sign. It means that individualism – the consciousness, that is, of individual rights and the realisation of a just limit to human endurance – cannot be wholly destroyed in this country even by totalitarian war and those who make it. So long as England produces her Josiah Wedgwoods, and her patient but ultimately resistant workers, she possesses a better guarantee against fascist regimentation than any 'unconditional surrender' by contemporary dictators.

___ 9 September 1943 ___

Whatever attitude the Christian Church was later to adopt towards women, there is no question that its Founder recognised them as human beings, and treated their spiritual individuality as of greater importance than their sex
— Winifred Holtby, *Women and a Changing Civilisation*

If you live in or near London, you probably heard of a mass meeting at the Central Hall, Westminster, on Saturday last, organised by the Women's Publicity Planning Association. The purpose of this crowded and enthusiastic gathering was to press for the adoption of an Equal Citizenship (Blanket) Bill to clear our laws and regulations of all discriminations based upon sex.

It is hardly necessary for me to remind you that the destructive unbiological society in which we are living is not so much a man-made world (though it is this too), as a world in which what may be called masculine values have dominated life and habit.

From the beginning of human history, mankind has been confronted by a conflict between two mutually exclusive principles which, for convenience of terminology, are frequently described as the masculine and the feminine. The former, which has hitherto prevailed, expresses itself through the rule of power and the tyranny of the strong. The latter involves the reign of love, the triumph of co-operation, and the estimate of individual human souls as ends rather than means.

Up to date the majority of women, moulded by tradition and education, have accepted masculine values as a matter of course, and a conspicuous few – such as Catherine of Russia and Maria Theresa of Austria – have outstripped men of comparable status in the application of those values. On the other hand, a minority of great men – whose ranks include Socrates, Buddha, Christ, Francis of Assisi, Erasmus, and Gandhi – have been guided by the feminine principle which seeks to create and to save.

In our own day, you and I have seen an exaggerated development of the masculine principle in that form of moral and spiritual bankruptcy which we know as fascism. The purposeless confusion of the present war becomes the more apparent as events show us ever more clearly that this fungoid growth is by no means confined to the totalitarian states which are fighting both with and against us. 'It is mere hypocrisy on the part of democratic propagandists', writes Herbert Read in *The Politics of the Unpolitical*, 'to pretend that Great Britain or the United States enjoy some mythical happiness or freedom which is denied to the Germans, the Russians or the Italians.' In the destructive fascist world of power-politics, it is inevitable that women – like Jews and other subject races – should be relegated to an auxiliary rôle. In the creative world of individual human values, it is just as inevitable that women should occupy an equal place as citizens. Let us make no mistake: mere military victory will never rid us of fascism unless we are also victorious over the power principle by which fascism is inspired. The chief evidence of such a victory will be the restoration of the individual to the spiritual status of which fascism has deprived him.

When the opponents of equal citizenship point out that the use of their vote by women has not led to the end of economic exploitation or to the outlawry of war, they demand a result which equal franchise alone could never have achieved. In itself the vote represented only one limited form of equality; it was a symbol of the power to achieve equal citizenship rather than the fact. The advance in status attained by women during the past thirty years has made them more effective citizens in a world dominated by masculine values. It is still far from bringing about the change from a destructive to a creative principle of life which we must achieve or perish.

Equal citizenship itself is only one factor in the transformation of power-politics into welfare-politics; but it is an important factor. The Equal Citizenship (Blanket) Bill, if passed into law, would represent a significant move in the right direction. We cannot abolish tradition by legislation, or expect an Act of Parliament to eliminate the deep-rooted prejudice of centuries. But the automatic removal of certain reactionary precedents could not help but have a speedy effect upon the position of women as a whole.

In a newly published book on the Blanket Bill, Dorothy Evans, organiser of the Women for Westminster movement, shows how equal rights of pay in the Civil Service, in local government offices, and in public corporations such as the London Passenger Transport Board, would profoundly influence the rates offered by private employers for similar types of work. To prove the likelihood of this, we have only to compare the status of women in the limited number of occupations where equal rates do prevail with their status where rates are still unequal. In my own profession, for instance, and in the allied fields of painting, music, and drama where individual initiative has always been estimated far higher than tradition, a publisher who offered his women writers a lower scale of royalties on account of their sex would receive short shrift from the Society of Authors and other literary organisations.

The speakers at last Saturday's meeting – Mrs Sieff in the Chair, Mrs Corbett-Ashby, Dr Edith Summerskill, MP,

Constance Colwill, Dorothy Evans, Alderman Emil Davies and myself – explained the various changes which would occur if the Blanket Bill became law. My own speech dealt with equal pay and the position of the married woman, for it is in the sphere of marriage that women's subjection lingers longest in practice, and the women's movement has made least apparent headway. This, I believe, is largely due to a traditional identification of wifehood and motherhood with domestic work. The ultimate consequence of such a confusion is to deny marriage and children to women with outstanding gifts, without stopping to ask whether a mother serves her offspring best by darning their socks or by passing on to them her energy and talents. The race must suffer in quality if fundamental human relationships are bound up with a form of occupation unlikely to be congenial to women with special powers or qualifications, or if certain professions in which she may be skilled are barred to her because she has a husband. Marriage and motherhood can hardly bring happiness to any member of the resulting family if they become symbols of frustration to the woman who enters into them.

The artificial character of customs and regulations which deprive married women of the right to paid work is made apparent by the readiness with which they are abandoned the moment that some national need or crisis makes them inconvenient. When a large proportion of the fathers of young children are overseas and in many cases will never return; when juvenile delinquency is on the increase; when shopping is infinitely slow and tedious; when the preparation of rationed food requires great care if a child is to receive a balanced diet; when dangers of unusual kinds, such as fire and bombs, threaten the very existence of the family: then there is some reason to argue that a mother's place is in the home. But it is precisely at the time when these perils and problems occur that she is asked to leave it. War propaganda is even subtly designed to make her feel unpatriotic if she puts the permanent welfare of her family before the temporary and abnormal needs of the state.

Today our government is grimly unimpressed by the hoary argument that woman's place is the home. A Blanket Bill to clear

162

our laws of sex discriminations would prevent our rulers from reviving the old shibboleths to women's disadvantage when the war is over.

The Kellogg Pact was negotiated in 1928 by Frank Kellogg, then US Secretary of State, and M. Aristide Briand, the French Foreign Minister. It condemned war as a means of settling disputes and was eventually signed by forty-five nations.

The improbably named Equal Citizenship (Blanket) Bill about which Vera wrote in her last letter appears to have suffered an early demise. It did not get to the floor of the House of Commons let alone the Statute Book. Women had to wait until 1970 for the Equal Pay Act and 1975 for the Sex Discrimination Act.

Among all my patients in the second half of life – that is to say,
over thirty-five – there has not been one whose problem in the
last resort was not that of finding a religious outlook on life. It is
safe to say that every one of them felt ill because he had lost that
which living religions of every age have given their followers,
and none of them has been really healed who did not regain his
religious outlook
                                    – C.G. Jung, *Modern Man in Search of a Soul*

I hope you will forgive me if this week I write you an entirely
personal letter, for I want to reply in this way to a question
which many friends and readers have recently asked me. Why,
they inquire, do I subscribe in these Letters and other recent
writings, to a 'Christian' point of view which was previously
absent? Once or twice there has even been the suggestion
(though not, of course, put so crudely as I am putting it) that in
these dark days Christianity perhaps 'pays' better than agnosticism. Both to you and to myself, therefore, I am anxious to
answer this real challenge to my faith and sincerity, for I believe I
can explain them in terms which may make articulate the similar
experiences of others.

My explanation begins with the last war. Though this broke
out soon after I left school, I had time in the intervening period
to read much of the rationalist literature, known as 'the Higher
Criticism', which was then so widely discussed. Amongst this
literature, the book which most deeply influenced my own and
other immature minds was Mrs Humphry Ward's *Robert
Elsmere*, that famous story of an Anglican cleric who turned
agnostic. Although it is nearly thirty years since I read it, I can
still quote from memory the four-line verse with which, I believe,
the book concludes – 'Far hence he lies,/In the lorn Syrian
town,/And on his grave with shining eyes/The Syrian stars look
down.' Except as a memory and an example, Christ, according
to this school of thought, was buried and finished.

This early agnosticism was soon reinforced by the first Great
War. The present younger generation, mostly cynical or resigned

in its attitude towards war and conscription, cannot even imagine the votive idealism of the eager volunteers who were their own age in 1914. But after three years our victimisation by elderly self-interest had become plain, and patriotism 'wore threadbare'. Those who survived – a much smaller proportion than, so far, of this war – saw our guileless idealism trampled in the dust. The hearts of our rulers were ruthless, and there seemed to be no God to say them nay.

By the end of the war, however, some of us had not only recognised our real enemy, but had perceived a goal. There might be no God, but there was still an ideal – though a different ideal from the false one which had been used to persuade us to accept the war. At the time it seemed to be an ideal to which man could strive unaided by divine power. We struggled towards it, seeing the possibility of realising it through the League of Nations, the Kellogg Pact, the aspirations of the Labour governments of 1924 and 1929, and the writings of eminent authors who then appeared to share our convictions. But as 1939 came nearer, we who had first thrown ourselves into war and then into peace, realised that we were again going to be outwitted. This time, however, there was a difference. It no longer seemed to us that we had been tricked into serving a false ideal. The ideal remained true; it merely appeared more difficult of realisation because our leaders were pursuing, by the senseless method of weak provocation, ends which appeared to us to be utterly vain.

'During those twenty years,' writes Robert M. Rayner in *The Twenty Years' Truce*, 'the governments and peoples of Europe have provided shocking examples of how public affairs should not be conducted. If we do not now make stepping-stones of our dead selves we are doomed. It seems we are to have a second chance; nobody can suppose that we shall have a third.'

I cannot remember at exactly what stage I began to perceive the connection between the catastrophe of a second world war and the existence of God, but it must have been as recently as 1939. Two elements contributed to a new and growing conviction. The first was this impersonal crescendo of

166

Europe's tragedy; the second arose from a more individual experience.

Partly through reading, partly through watching the downward sequence of world events, I came to realise that much of the evidence for the existence of God lies in the inevitability with which causes produce their effects. If the self-interested, provocative policies which some of us strove to avert during the twenty years' armistice had led to disaster less surely than they did, the proof of God's existence would, I felt, have been less clear. The fact that unchristian values had driven mankind to the edge of the abyss seemed to supply incontrovertible testimony that an opposite policy – the way of God, the road of the Cross – would produce an opposite result.

I have tried to explain the other aspect of my changed attitude in a little book called '*Humiliation With Honour*' which was published some months ago. For to me the war brought a new experience of humiliation – not indeed comparable to that which so many others have suffered in prison and elsewhere, but notable by contrast with the period immediately before it.

In the seven years between 1933 and 1940, I had enjoyed a considerable measure of worldly success. Seven years is not, perhaps, long compared with the years of publicity enjoyed or endured by some of our longest-lived authors, but it was sufficient to get me into the habit of expecting to exercise authority and command respect. When I achieved that position after years of struggling obscurity, it did not occur to me that anything but my own death or disability could end it.

But I reckoned without the panic period of threatened invasion in 1940. My unorthodox opinions had been well-known when I had been given an exit permit to fulfil a normal series of periodic professional engagements in the United States at the end of 1939, and even though I returned just in time for the beginning of troubles which I had foreseen, I did not imagine that I could ever be suspected of disloyalty or treasonable intrigue. I soon learnt differently when, in the autumn of 1940, I went to the Passport Office to inquire about the fate of an application for permission to fulfil another series of American

167

engagements some months later, and observed the mild but uncomplimentary sensation which the inquiry produced.

Since that time I have had three further invitations to visit America, two to visit India as British delegate to the All-India Women's Congress in successive years, and one to lecture in Sweden; but I have been permitted to fulfil none of them. An existence once as widely international as the world itself has been compulsorily narrowed and rendered almost parochial. Many other manifestations, too numerous to mention, of official and literary disapproval, arrived on the heels of the first rebuff to quench my erstwhile confidence and self-esteem.

One day in that autmn of 1940 I went out alone for a country walk, smitten with despair due to the loss of my son and daughter, who had been sent overseas in the expectation of periodic American visits, but were now parted from me for a period which then seemed incalculable. (One is now home again, and the other expected daily.) The bright afternoon shone with that peculiar radiance which all nature wears after a respite from death, such as the citizens of London and other bombarded towns repeatedly experienced during the blitz. How or why it happened I cannot tell, but on that walk the realisation suddenly came to me that my grief and humiliation were indeed a spiritual experience, which brought me nearer to the heart of religious conviction than I could ever have come in the previous years of triumph. Just as an earlier sense of God's reality had reached me through the disastrous consequences of international failure, so I now perceived that God is to be found more readily in the depths than upon the heights.

Ever since then I have believed that a severe blow to pride and prestige, whether isolated or repeated, just or unjust, is a source of that type of revelation by which the individual becomes united with all those men and women who, through sin, sorrow, poverty, or sickness, have descended into the abyss of suffering. Never again, I think, after such an experience, would it be possible to ask a fellow creature to pay the price of wrong-doing while standing self-righteously aside oneself, since the main test of a Christian community is surely its readiness to carry

168

vicariously the Cross of shame. So, at last, I began dimly to understand the doctrine of atonement, and to realise why love is prepared to suffer long and be kind.

By such diverse yet interconnected routes, I have become convinced of the existence of God. If you ask me what I mean by God, I shall find your question more difficult to answer, but perhaps the conception to which I have come closest is expressed by the late Thomas R. Kelly: 'Some, like Meister Eckhart and Jacob Boehme, the greatest mystics of the West, have asserted an *Urgrund*, a Godhead, a more basic view of Reality underlying all the variety of divine forms that are conceivable.'

But I am only at the beginning of religious experience, while you, perhaps, like many others, have been conscious of the presence of God for years. Some day I may be able to see and express more clearly my own vision of that 'far off, divine event' towards which I grow daily more convinced that 'the whole creation moves'.

Defence Regulation 18B gave the Home Secretary power to imprison without trial anybody he believed likely to endanger the safety of the realm. It was used extensively.

Confinement of the person by secretly hurrying him to gaol where his sufferings are unknown and forgotten, is a less public and less striking, and, therefore, a more dangerous form of arbitrary government

— Sir William Blackstone (1723–1780)

Not long ago the Prison Reform Council invited me to contribute an Introduction to the third of their publications, shortly to be issued under the title of *Prisoners' Circle*.

I had only just completed this Introduction, which I called 'The Forgotten Prisoner', when I received by post within a few days of each other two pamphlets which reminded me that not the least cruelly forgotten and neglected amongst the prisoners of whom I had written are the men and women still interned under Regulation 18B. The longer of these two pamphlets, 'In Search of Justice', is produced at 6d by the 18B Publicity Council, 15 Woburn Square, WC1. The other, 'It Can't Happen Here', was more recently published by the Petition of Right Council (whose sponsors include Laurence Housman, Corder Catchpool and Douglas Reed), which has been formed to organise an appeal to Parliament for revision of the administration of Regulation 18B. This leaflet quotes a number of opinions, adverse to the present exercise of the regulation, expressed by various MPs, who include members of such different groups and parties as Earl Winterton, Sir Irving Albery, James Maxton, Commander Bower, R.R. Stokes, Aneurin Bevan, and Major Lyons.

The famous *Commentaries* of Sir William Blackstone, the great writer on English law, make clear that British justice is founded upon three basic principles and enactments – Habeas Corpus, Magna Carta, and the Bill of Rights. Within recent history these principles have been seriously menaced only during periods of war, in which the state takes more than normal control over the lives of its citizens. The unpopularity of 'DORA' (Defence of the Realm Act) during the last war showed the fear and suspicion immediately aroused among the British people by any departure, for whatever reason, from the historic lines along which our legislation has developed.

The present war began with an almost universal expression of respect by our legislators for the rights of minorities and individuals. But nothing undermines basic principles so effectively as fear; and though the people of Britain kept their heads during the invasion scare of 1940, many of their rulers gave way to panic. While the citizens of London philosophically awaited Hitler's next instalment of frightfulness to the summer music of brass bands in Trafalgar Square, their legislators a few hundred yards away were hastily imposing that blockade of the Continent which has already cost the lives of thousands of innocent children, and passing the Emergency Powers Act which gave to the government a sweeping authority difficult to distinguish in some of its aspects from the powers possessed by the Gestapo and Ogpu of the totalitarian states.

At that time a long war seemed improbable, and few people realised that after more than three years, several hundred British citizens would still be detained, often in circumstances of misery and hardship, merely on the suspicion of a Home Secretary who is not required either to bring them to trial, confront them with their accusers, produce the evidence which has led to their imprisonment, or even to take the advice of an advisory committee appointed by himself. The prophecies of certain famous novels which foretold the advent of fascism in the Anglo-Saxon democracies – such as Naomi Mitchison's *You Have Been Warned* and Sinclair Lewis's *It Can't Happen Here* – are daily being fulfilled in terms of this modern Star Chamber, with its secret and sinister procedures of which the public know and hear so little.

Nearly 2,000 men and women have already suffered imprisonment under this regulation. Some have been released, after periods of one, two or three years, without explanation but over 400 still remain in prison or camp. These people have already suffered the equivalent of a five years' sentence; yet have never been charged, tried, or accused of any wrong-doing. Meanwhile, they and their husbands, wives and children suffer

172

those desolate accompaniments of imprisonment which often punish the innocent more harshly than the guilty where guilt exists – broken homes, sacrificed youth, destitution, illness and death. Here is only one of several tragedies recorded by the 18B Publicity Council:

'Case No. 11. Mr and Mrs W.E.B. .... Mr B, a builder by trade, had married a German woman. She was arrested in May, 1940, as of 'hostile origin'. Mr B, British by birth and descent, was also arrested as having 'hostile association'. Mrs B was taken to Holloway with her little boy, aged only 15 months, where they were placed in a damp, unheated cell. After a fortnight, the child was sent to a public institution and was not seen again by either of his parents until nearly a year later, when he was returned to his mother in Holloway. Mrs B was pregnant, but was subjected to the same deprivations and hardships as her fellow-detainees. After Christmas, she was removed to the prison hospital, where she was left to fend for herself during her twenty-four hours labour. She gave birth to a girl on January 27th, 1941. Three weeks later, mother and child were back in the prison cell under usual prison conditions. When the little boy was sent back to his mother, the three lived together in the cell until transported to the Isle of Man. Both children were ill and Mrs B prostrate with fatigue and anxiety.

'The boy, originally a strong, healthy child, came back from the institution stunted and emaciated. The journey to the island proved a severe trial. Weary hours of waiting, hardly any food, no help in carrying their baggage, this poor young mother had a terrible ordeal with her two baby children. During the voyage no food was provided, and Mrs B, who was breast-feeding the baby, was terribly seasick and collapsed. She was even denied fresh air and only permitted to sit in the lavatory. At last those who had money (and many had none) were allowed to buy a cup of tea at fourpence. Those who had no money could not even obtain a drink of water except from the tap in the washbasin. Upon arrival, Mrs B, carrying her baby, and with the other child clinging to her skirt, was ordered to march to the railway station and to carry her luggage. As this was obviously impossible she was at last taken to her destination in a 'Black Maria' and reached her quarters at Port Erin at 9.15 p.m. They had left Fleetwood after travelling all night by train at 5.30 that morning!

'At Port Erin, Mrs B and her children were given a room without any heating facilities – even hot-water bottles for the children were refused. Naturally they caught cold, and eventually the boy developed whooping cough. The baby caught this complaint – and died on November 15th. Imagine the poor father's anguish – a prisoner himself – unable to do anything to alleviate his dear ones' suffering. Mr B asked that he might be allowed to bury his baby daughter in his home town. This request was granted by the Home Office, but only on condition that he bore the entire expense. As detention for over 18 months had deprived him of his livelihood, he had to arrange to sell the last remains of his small property. Thus a "Christian" country treats little children!'

Today, after nearly half a decade of such grief and misery for many 'small men' while the heads of states build historic reputations, no early end to the war seems to be visualised or even desired by the Allied leaders. The 'Second Front', we are told by the press, is now unlikely to be developed before next spring or summer. Every year, as the half-starved French complain, our 'victory' is put off for another year; and meanwhile the world's supply of food and raw materials gets smaller, more emaciated children perish from starvation, more broken families see no end to their tragic separations, more young men and women face the disastrous postponement of their trainings and careers. And the victims of Regulation 18B remain in prison. Some – like Sir Oswald Mosley and his anti-semitic fascists – once truculently occupied the limelight; but today they too are almost forgotten. Few things in our democracy are more sinister than the fact that they have been, and could be so effectively 'put away' – out of sight and out of mind.

We are deliberately left with the impression that the less conspicuous detainees are also potential enemies of this country. But how do we know that some of them are not, rather,

174

possessed of information more valuable to the community than creditable to the government? How many, again, are suspected for good reasons, and how many are the victims of gossiping neighbours, jealous busybodies, or political opponents?

Perhaps you and I, the citizens of a war-making state, can do little or nothing to initiate those discussions which will ultimately lead the world back to peace – though to be over-convinced of our powerlessness is the worst form of defeatism. But at least we can begin the restoration of peace-time sanity by demanding traditional British justice for the victims of Regulation 18B, and by urging renewed efforts on their behalf upon our Members of Parliament.

From the beginning of the war Vera used such influence as she had to persuade the authorities to confine their bombing to military targets 'whatever Germany might do to us'.

In November 1941 she circulated a petition against night bombing. Among her co-signatories were the Bishop of Chichester, C.E.M. Joad, John Middleton Murry and Sybil Thorndike.

By now the limitation of bombing had become a forlorn hope, but she kept the pressure up and in April 1944 her book *Seeds of Chaos*, which was largely a protest against the saturation policy of 'Bomber' Sir Arthur Harris, produced, according to Dorothy Thompson in the *Sunday Chronicle*, 'fury' in America.

However, Harris's policy clearly had the Prime Minister's support. In a memo to General Ismay (Chief of Staff) he wrote: 'In the last war the bombing of open cities was regarded as forbidden. Now everybody does it as a matter of course. It is simply a question of fashion changing as she does between long and short skirts for women.'

As Vera reported in a later letter, her book was supported by a protest against mass bombing in *Fellowship* (New York) which was signed by Oswald Garrison Villard, H.E. Fosdick and twenty-eight Protestant clergymen.

Were they ashamed when they had committed abomination?
                                                    – Jeremiah, VI, 15.

The conditional release of Sir Oswald Mosley – who ought to have been tried in 1940, and should be tried now in order to establish the exact nature of the charges against him – has served to distract public attention from our terrible raids on Berlin and other German cities, and to side-step uneasy calculations regarding their present and future consequences. The crowds which gathered in Whitehall to protest against Mosley's removal from Holloway might more usefully have raised their voices against the employment of young British airmen to commit abominations of ruthlessness characteristic of that very fascism of which Sir Oswald is the symbol.

Describing a recent air-raid on the small city of Münster – whose bishop has made so many courageous criticisms of the Nazis – Noel Panter, Zurich correspondent of the *Daily Telegraph*, commented on Oct. 13th that 'the territory of the Reich is being battered and laid waste as never before in the history of modern warfare.' It was in the town hall at Münster, the capital of Westphalia, that the treaty which concluded the Thirty Years' War was signed on Oct. 14th, 1648. Of that war James Harvey Robinson, American author of *The History of Western Europe*, wrote in this standard school text book, first published in 1902:

'The accounts of the misery and depopulation of Germany caused by the Thirty Years' War are well-nigh incredible. Thousands of villages were wiped out altogether; in some regions the population was reduced by one half; in others to a third, or even less, of what it had been at the opening of the conflict. The flourishing city of Augsburg was left with but sixteen thousand souls instead of eighty thousand. *The people were fearfully barbarised by privation and suffering and by the atrocities of the soldiers of all the various nations. Until the end of the 18th century [i.e. 150 years] Germany was too exhausted and impoverished to make any considerable contribution to the culture of Europe.*' (Italics mine)

The *Daily Telegraph* correspondent, however, boasts that the territory of the Reich is being laid waste as never before in the history of modern warfare; in other words, that the 'atrocities' of its enemies exceed even those of the Thirty Years' War. Inevitably, therefore, the after-effects in terms of privation and barbarism will be still graver and more prolonged. Is this a prospect to which even the least thoughtful among the British and American peoples look forward with enthusiasm?

Stars and Stripes, the newspaper read by the US armed forces, reports that air warfare observers see the Berlin raids as 'one of the most terrible experiments in military history, namely, an attempt to wipe out a great enemy capital from the air'. The United Press reckons that another 20 to 25 raids would be required 'to finish the job'. And Germany is by no means the only victim. The following brief quotations from recent newspapers give us a faint idea of the sufferings of Italy and German-occupied Europe: 'Three heavy air-raids have rendered Turin practically uninhabitable, according to reports reaching Chiasso' (*Daily Herald*, Nov. 13th). 'The German-controlled Paris radio, quoting reports from Italy, said yesterday that the town of Frascati, location of the German GHQ near Rome, had been flattened out by Anglo-American bombers. There were more than 5,000 victims' (*Sunday Express*, Sept. 19th). 'About 900 were killed, and 1,900 injured, in the Allied raids on France on Wednesday night and Thursday, said Vichy radio yesterday.' (*Sunday Express*, Sept. 19th). 'The French town of Modane-Foureaux was completely destroyed in the latest RAF raid on Modane and surrounding districts,' says the Swiss newspaper, *Tribune de Genève*, quoted by Reuter, Nov. 13th. This newspaper added: 'The latest air-raid lasted nearly two hours. The alarm could not be given in time because the sirens did not function.'

The change from the 'precision' bombing of military objectives to the present 'obliteration' bombing of whole areas, with their churches, libraries, schools, hospitals, museums, and vulnerable human beings, came with the appointment of Sir Arthur Harris to the control of Bomber Command on March

178

3rd, 1942. Speaking in New York on March 29th, 1943, Air Marshal Billy Bishop, VC, described Sir Arthur as 'a tiger with no mercy in his heart' towards the enemy. To the pitiless policy of this man – reinforced, of course, by the determination of his political leaders to 'bomb, burn, and ruthlessly destroy' – millions of Germans, Italians and French owe the devastation of their beautiful towns, and thousands of enemy and ex-Allied families the death, injury or mental derangement of young, helpless and cherished members. These memories alone, of grief and unspeakable horror, are likely to prove an implacable obstacle to the building of a better world.

According to the American news-magazine *Time* for June 7th, 1943, Sir Arthur Harris, between the wars, 'developed the "pacification by bombing" policy which kept unruly Indian tribes more or less under control.' This policy was, you may remember, a main reason why Sir John Simon and Lord Londonderry, at the Disarmament Conference of 1932, opposed the abolition of the bombing aeroplane which Germany, Russia, Italy and the United States supported. To the efforts of these men to preserve a diabolical instrument of death, the world's innocent civilians (including thousands of children born since the outbreak of war) owe their present indescribable sufferings. We should remember this when we discuss post-war 'retribution' for war criminals. Germany, Italy and Japan are not the only countries which have names to contribute.

A further comment in *Time* added: 'The air offensive against Germany is suffering from understatement.' Is this perhaps due to a recognition, by those who are conducting the RAF onslaught, that the ordinary decent British citizen would not endorse this type of bombing if he were given full details, and realised what these attacks mean for human flesh and blood? Here is one account of the condition of Western Germany by a Swiss correspondent – who also records, in *Das Volksrecht*, (Zurich), for Oct 2nd, 1943, that 'the whole of Nuremberg is one great ruin, whereas the Siemens-Schuckert works which were probably the object of the bombardment, received no damage':

'Over 70 per cent of the big western towns have been destroyed. A comparison with the French territories destroyed during the first World War is impossible; the destruction in western Germany today is already many times greater than that of the last war in France. It is characteristic that the destruction is greatest in the centre of the cities, whereas certain industrial establishments which the British reported as destroyed showed, as I witnessed myself repeatedly, no damage whatever. . . . The cities which our train passed presented a frightful sight. Dortmund, Gelsenkirchen, Oberhausen and Duisberg are great heaps of rubble from which ghostly mineshafts protrude. The heaps of ruins are sometimes so enormous that one often wonders whither they must ultimately be transported.

'I did not at first have the feeling that there was enormous destruction in Essen, as all the buildings round the station square were intact. Behind them, however, the terror began. The entire centre of the town and the old part are one pile of rubble from which rise up only a few isolated houses. . . .

'Düsseldorf made the most frightful impression of all the western German cities. This once beautiful city is today a heap of ruins. The gaiety of its population has vanished. There are sad faces to be seen everywhere. The new railway station is completely destroyed. The station square with its great hotels and the main post office is covered with ruins. The centre, north and south of the city have suffered most. All the entertainment buildings have disappeared; the Municipal Theatre, the Concert House, the Jaegerhof Castle, the Apollo Theatre, and all the great cinemas and department stores. . . . A high police official told me that 2,500 people were killed during one night of heavy bombardment and that the Provincial Fire Insurance building still covers its victims. Eighteen thousand dwelling houses have been destroyed in Düsseldorf and 350,000 people rendered homeless.

'These figures do not include the destruction in the [industrial] suburbs of Gerresheim and Benrath. According to the police officer, frightful scenes occurred in Wuppertal, as the city is situated in a valley and possessed narrow streets which made any flight impossible. Numerous victims ran around aimlessly like burning torches until they died. One thousand eight hundred people were killed by the bombardment.'

According to an article by Group Captain Hugh Edwards, VC, in the *Daily Mail* for Oct. 13th, 1943: 'Crews have no time to dwell on the terrible nature of the attack being carried out down below; they are intent on carrying out their mission and preserving themselves.' But what is likely to be the effect of their deeds upon the more sensitive of these young flyers when in future years they come to know what 'the terrible nature of the attack' really meant, and have time to think about it? Some of their victims – those who are still there – may perhaps forgive them, but will they ever forgive themselves? What aftermath of nightmare and breakdown will come? Has any nation the right to make its young men the instruments of such a policy?

These are the questions that you and I should be asking ourselves today. Thousands of mothers of young airmen must already be asking them in their hearts. There is no need to wait for the end of the war before we consider exactly what we are doing as a nation, and decide whether we desire the government which we elected to continue to carry out, through its Bomber Command, a policy of murder and massacre in the name of the British people.

Churchill, Roosevelt and Stalin had their first meeting, at Teheran, on 28 November 1943.

The decision to invade Western Europe was confirmed and there were far-reaching discussions about the drawing of new boundaries in Eastern Europe, including the partitioning of Germany and Poland (which country, the cynic may recall, Britain went to war to save).

'Vercors' was the pseudonym of Jean-Marcel Bruller (born 1902), a printer and engineer. He was a supporter of the Resistance and, with Pierre de Lescure, founded *Les Editions de Minuit* for publishing the work of underground authors. *Le Silence de la Mer* was written in 1942, smuggled out of France, translated into English by Cyril Connolly and published by Macmillan, from whom the French edition is still available.

National hatred is something peculiar. You will find it strongest and most violent when there is the lowest degree of culture. But there is a degree where it vanishes altogether, and where a person stands to a certain extent above nations, and feels the weal or woe of a neighbouring people as if it had happened to his own

– Johann Wolfgang von Goethe,
Conversation with Eckermann, 1830

This week I write to you at a season never before experienced by any person now living – a fifth wartime Christmas. In the last war, as you will remember, the Christmas which ended the final year of fighting came just after the cessation of hostilities (at any rate those of a military character). We who survived when so much of our contemporary youth had vanished looked forward to peace, though we now know that there was no peace in the hearts of the men who could have saved mankind from its present disasters, but in fear, obstinacy, and blindness threw away the greatest opportunity of all time.

At this fifth Christmas, hostilities still bitterly continue, and their end seems far away despite Mr Herbert Morrison's [the Home Secretary's] reference to 'the last' parliamentary session of wartime, and Mr Oliver Lyttelton's [the Minister of Production's] mention of 'imminent victory' – whatever that may mean for our nation to which the conclusion of fighting will reveal nothing but an immense panorama of suffering in all its pity and terror. We know – as the last issue of this letter reminded you – that our bombs are turning large parts of Europe into heaps of ruins; that diseases may follow which will make the present much-publicised epidemic of mild influenza seem like an era of rude health; and that the world is threatened with a total food shortage which may bring catastrophe greater even than war to enormous areas, unless the reluctance of such fortunate countries as the United States to reduce their comfortable standard of living for the benefit of others can be drastically overcome. And, seeking the bread of consolation, we are handed instead the opaque stone of the Teheran Declaration, to whose studied vagueness not even the officially inspired press can impart positive concreteness. If you are a student of history, your mind will inevitably turn back to 1815 and that equally vague though more pious document, the Holy Alliance – which Metternich described as mere 'verbiage', and Canning called 'a loud-sounding nothing'.

This Christmas letter which I write you in our still more troubled times might well be entitled 'I sit and think and remember'. It is too easy for all of us, in moments of depression, to add the years of one war to those of the other which now exceeds the first in length, and consider how much creative energy the total has absorbed. For me that energy has been diverted from the work of imagination which I love best of all occupations, to the practical service, in the first war, of the wounded and dying and in the second to the service of peace with its invisible weapons of the mind and spirit. Those hospital Christmases now seem very far away but for most of us the four which began in 1939 will haunt such celebrations as our diminishing stocks and facilities can achieve this year.

The present Christmas, which officially finds our nation on the highroad to 'victory', means for me the return home of my children after three years of unintended separation. This much of comfort (and how much it is!) I know too well is withheld from many, still separated from their nearest and dearest by the dire chances of war.

What consolation, then, is common to all of us, whether we have a family with whom to spend Christmas, or must face it alone? I believe we shall find our consolation (and how infinite it is!) in that deep human unity which will survive and finally overcome the ambitious scheming of political leaders – so insignificant, for all the noise that surrounds them, in the universal plan – whose horizon is bounded by national frontiers. I wrote you last Christmas of this human kinship, which both transcends and underlies the artificial antagonisms of war. Today I am moved to emphasise it again, for I have just been reading (in a somewhat literal abridged translation, published by the

184

American magazine *Life,* because the French original is temporarily out of print) the most remarkable piece of literature to come out of oppressed Europe during this war, *Le Silence de la Mer.*

You may already have heard of this long-short story, written in occupied France by a French author who signs himself 'Vercors' but whose real name is kept secret. We do not know whether he is an established writer whose books were familiar to lovers of literature before the war, or a new author whose genius has flowered under the stress of suffering and peril. In either case, he is a master both of literary expression and of human understanding. The book itself was printed on underground presses and published by an underground house called *Editions de Minuit.* The proofs of the story were smuggled out of France to London, where Hachette republished it in French. Macmillan are shortly to issue an English translation in Britain and America. If you cannot get this little book in time for Christmas, I recommend it as 'required reading' for 1944.

The theme of the story is very simple. A young German officer – a musician and a man of culture – is billeted from the autumn of 1940 to the summer of 1941 at the house of an old Frenchman and his niece. Every evening after the first few days, the officer comes into the room where the old man and the girl are sitting, and talks to them of Germany, of his love for France, and of his hope of a 'marriage' between their two countries. He speaks of his admiration for French literature; he compares the beauty of Chartres with the loveliness of Nuremberg – since bombed into ruins by warmaking vandalism. ('For a German, that is the city that makes his heart swell, because there he finds the phantoms dear to his heart, the memory, in every stone, of those who made the nobility of ancient Germany.') But throughout these regular monologues the old man and his niece keep silence. That silence is never broken in front of the officer until one word – one only – is spoken by the girl at the end.

The editors of *Life* advertise this story as a symbol of the resistance of France. They emphasise the fact that the writer, and all those who helped him to publication, thereby put a price on their own heads. They point to the book as evidence that men of letters are standing beside the workers who commit sabotage and the chiefs who prepare an army of insurrection. They fail to see – or perhaps deliberately refrain from seeing – the deeper significance of the story as an epic of human unity and a final argument against all war.

As the evenings repeat themselves from winter to summer, we see, hear and feel the fundamental sympathy between these three cultured and sensitive people breaking through the self-imposed barrier of silence. Then comes the day when the officer goes to Paris on leave – and returns to avoid for a time the company of his host and hostess, because he has at last realised the true intentions of Nazi barbarism towards France. We share the tense, disappointed expectancy of the old man and his niece, until the officer finally comes in to tell them of the anguish caused him by his discoveries in Paris, and his decision to volunteer for the Russian front.

' "I have exercised my right," he said simply. "I have asked to join a field division . . ." His arm was raised toward the east – toward those immense plains where the future wheat will be fertilised with corpses.'

And we realise then what we have gradually perceived all along – the despairing love which has arisen between the German officer and his silent young hostess. Her final half-spoken answering word – 'Goodbye' – is a perfect expression, more moving than the loveliest lamentation in literature, of the illimitable suffering brought to the individual by war. But it is also a symbol of the hope which lives for us in the unextinguishable human spirit, and its power to love and understand.

The author's supreme achievement lies in the fact that, as the story closes, it is the German whose tragedy stirs us most deeply to pity and sorrow. Throughout the book his courtesy and gentleness have never failed; not once in all the evenings of unanswered discourse has he uttered a word which, by requiring a reply, could embarrass his host and hostess in the maintenance of their silence. And this character has been created by a Frenchman who is himself a victim of the Nazi terror, and who thereby demonstrates that Lord Vansittart, and the *Sunday Express* editorial writer who on December 5th assured us for the hundredth time that 'the people of Germany are vile', and the rest who deny to all Germans the standards and values of civilised living, are just plain wrong. They are wrong in terms of that undying human fellowship which will prevail when they and their feverish hate-mongering are clean forgotten.

Le Silence de la Mer embodies in its pages the permanent conflict between the beast and the angel in man. When the Sunday newspapers persuade us that the beast is dominant, a book such as this comes to prove that the angel will triumph by means of those spiritual qualities over which alone the principalities and powers of this world can exercise no control. In the sure and certain hope of that ultimate triumph, and in deep gratitude for your loyalty to the faith in mankind which we share, I send you my greetings for this fifth Christmas of war.

— 23 March 1944 —

Lord, give to men who are old and rougher
The things that little children suffer,
And let keep bright and undefiled
The young years of the little child
— John Masefield, *The Everlasting Mercy*

You may remember that the daily press of March 11th gave much space to the refusal by Eire to abandon her neutrality and sever diplomatic relations with the Axis at the bidding of the United States supported by Britain. Possibly you may feel, especially in view of subsequent 'sanctions', that had this attempt by a great power to compel a small one to act against its own interests and wishes been made by a member of the Axis, our politicians and press would have been the first to protest against the exercise of 'aggression' by superior forces.

It is, of course, true, as the Allies maintain, that Eire benefited from the protection of the British Navy and Air Force during the dangerous early years of the war. But Eire does not share the view of her would-be allies that but for their help she would have been an ill-treated victim of Axis policy. The war was not of her making nor of her seeking; and those who made it (for a heavy measure of responsibility lies on *both* sides) have at least some moral obligation to protect countries which are unwillingly endangered. Eire, at any rate, is a typical example of the truth uttered by Landquist, a character in one of Ibsen's plays – 'It all comes back in the end.' No doubt the British statesmen who mishandled the problem of Irish affairs during the last war never dreamed that, in a quarter of a century, and still within the lifetime of some who then carried great responsibility, they would require Irish help. In the case of Ireland as of Germany, they sowed the wind, and are now reaping the whirlwind as clearly in terms of Irish non-co-operation as of Nazi aggression.

This problem occupied so much newspaper space on March 11th, that you may easily have missed another quite different item which to me, as perhaps to you, signifies one more triumphant milestone reached in a long and patient campaign. I refer to the promise made by the Minister of Education, with the support of the House of Commons, that the ban so obstinately imposed upon the employment of married women teachers will be removed by the new Education Bill. 'Married women teachers', said Mr Butler, according to *The Times*, 'in difficult years had literally saved the situation in the schools, and their fine example had caused the Government to make the change he had just indicated.'

This significant and far-reaching victory for the cause of equal rights and opportunities between the sexes is slipping on to the statute book almost as unobtrusively as the first instalment of the Parliamentary franchise for women slipped on to it in the dark early spring of 1918. Now, as then, this new concession is advertised as a 'reward' for the effective and self-sacrificing services of women during war. Actually, it owes far more to the political and educational campaigns which preceded the wars in each case. War, by removing male competition and by demonstrating the completely unrealistic character of masculine

188

prejudice regarding women's capacity, has simply provided a final proof of the justice of claims made by women during previous decades.

Ever since I have had any pretentions to take part in 'public life', I have written and spoken in favour of the employment of married women – whose ability to combine their work with the care of a husband and children has long been demonstrated in all the artistic professions. During the hopeful years of the nineteen-twenties, Winifred Holtby and I stood on rostrums in Hyde Park or Hampstead Heath to emphasise the unjust and artificial inequality imposed by the ban upon married women, which perforce made a woman an unreliable employee however keen she might be on her work, and caused her, whatever her gifts, to be less worth the expenditure of public money upon grants and scholarships than a man.

Now that the ban on married women teachers has been removed, there seems little doubt that other barriers against the employment of married women – in the Civil Service, for example, and, with some local authorities, against the use of married women doctors – will shortly disappear. The removal of the ban was probably more urgent in the teaching profession than in any other, for the time has come when the influence and understanding of wives and mothers in the schools of this and other countries is more urgently needed than it has ever been.

Writing eight weeks before D-Day and four days after the Russians entered Rumania, Vera was not to know that some of the senior German officers, notably Field Marshal von Witzleben (West Europe C-in-C), were plotting (not for the first time) to overthrow Hitler. They had doubts about getting the necessary support partly because of Churchill's insistence on unconditional surrender.

It was not until 20 July that Colonel Count von Stauffenberg planted the bomb which resulted in his own, Witzleben's and many others' execution but left Hitler shaken but not seriously hurt. It did however make him less stable and more unpredictable.

Yes, we are going to suffer, now; the sky
Throbs like a feverish forehead; pain is real:
The groping searchlights suddenly reveal
The little natures that will make us cry

— W.H. Auden

For the past four years my background of war has been almost exclusively London. War for me, as perhaps for you, has meant noisy nights interspersed with periods of unreliable silence; dark fiery skies; the growing shabbiness of houses and streets; the gradual extension of air-raid damage, with its accompanying dust and debris, and its smells of sulphur and charred wood. The symbol of the last war always seemed to me, after I returned from France, to be a candle stuck in the neck of a bottle. The symbol of this one, at any rate for dwellers in raided cities, will surely be a broken window.

But during these Easter days, owing to the recovery of a cottage bought for my children before the war and let during their absence in USA, I have renewed my acquaintance with a country district which I last saw in the late spring of 1940. Only eight miles from the coast, it was then expecting paratroops and early invasion; the signposts had been removed from the winding lanes, and concrete blocks hastily assembled at crossroads. Today the signposts are back again and the concrete blocks have been rolled into the woods. The stretch of rare and lovely country which surrounds our cottage has just been declared a 'prohibited area', for like many other coastal districts it is now expecting, not invasion, but a share in the Second Front.

From such an area one sees the war in a totally different perspective. The noisy nights (though we get them occasionally) give place to noisy days; to the sound of frequent sirens and gunfire from the coast, the clatter of heavy traffic passing to unknown destinations, the uneasy roar from the skies of combatant aeroplanes (surely a sound which mankind will spare itself for ever when these terrible days are over?). Instead of damaged roofs and piles of rubble, the children and I look out

191

upon the illusive tranquillity of rural England, late-budding after many weeks of cold dry winds, but none the less heart-breaking and incongruous in the loveliness of the early spring sunshine.

The contrast between the awakening beauty of which man in his sin and folly denies himself enjoyment, and the avoidable tragedy for which the United Nations are so loudly preparing, brings an atmosphere of indescribable tension to this whole countryside. How many of the uniformed young men who look casually upon the bare branches of oak and beech against the cloudless blue, will be dead before those boughs are heavy with summer foliage? Into my mind comes a letter, long forgotten, but all too appropriate, which I wrote in 1915 during my first spring as a college student to a boy in the Territorials who was dead by the end of the year:

'I think it is harder now the spring days are beginning to come to keep the thought of war before one's mind . . . and during the calm and beautiful days we have had lately it seems so much more appropriate to imagine that you and E are actually enjoying the spring than to think that before long you may be in the trenches fighting men you do not really hate. In the churches at Oxford, where so many of the congregation are soldiers, we are always having it impressed upon us that "the call of our country is the call of God." Is it? I wish I could feel sure that it was. At this time of the year it seems that everything ought to be creative, not destructive, and that we should encourage things to live and not die.'

It is against our background of sea and moor and woodland that I have just been reading a remarkable article in the *Christian Century* (Chicago) for Feb. 2nd, 1944, called 'Last Plea for Europe', by Oswald Garrison Villard. Mr Villard, formerly the editor of the New York *Nation*, is known to many English readers through his books and his American News-Letter circulated by the National Peace Council. In the last war he was, I believe, a pacifist; in this he did not adopt the full pacifist position owing to the vehemence of the anti-Nazi sentiments which he expressed in a little volume entitled *Inside Germany*, published during the first year of the war after a visit to Central

Europe. But recently, in common with 28 Protestant clergymen, he signed a protest against the 'obliteration bombing' of Germany and Occupied Europe by the Anglo-American air forces. In this article he makes a final plea to whatever remnants of humanity and commonsense the leaders of the United Nations may still possess, in the hope that America and England may be spared the deliberate mass slaughter which a Second Front must involve.

'Once more', writes Mr Villard, 'I appeal for dying Europe – and for America too. I dare not suppose that my plea will carry far, but I must make it. My conscience will give me no peace until I do. Just because the voices of my fellow-countrymen are still, I must cry out on behalf of millions who are now condemned to die. I appeal from Caesar to the court of public opinion on behalf of those 400,000 or 500,000 American youths who, according to James Byrnes, the "assistant president", to Secretary Stimson and to other high officials, are bound to fall in the assault on Europe now scheduled for early spring.

'Nothing in all my lifetime has seemed to me so incredible as the silence which has followed this announcement. No man in high position, no group of Americans, no society and no church has said one word in an effort to save the flower of our youth from the fate that awaits them. "We trust our generals. . . . We must believe the President when he declares that this will shorten the war and save the loss of more lives. . . . After all it isn't our fault. The Germans began it and we have got to teach them not to do it again." So run the acquiescences and avoidances of those who refuse to face the facts. Their hearts are too dulled by slaughter to make a single protest, even though their own families and friends may well pay the price. It is incredible.'

It is incredible indeed. Every word that Mr Villard utters about American acquiescences and American evasions is equally true of Britain. The mothers whose sons have reached, or are reaching, military age, all remember 'the war to end war', and recall, during the years which followed, the utter defeat of every idealistic aim for which their own generation died. Why, then, are they silent now? What makes them think that the results of this war – of which the aims as yet, have hardly been stated – will justify the sacrifice of a generation, any more than those of the last? I contemplate my own sixteen-year-old boy, and thank God that for him the period of choice, of decision, is still eighteen months ahead. Whatever may happen to him then, at least he will escape the mass-suicide of the current Second Front. What should I feel and do if he were just about to be involved in it? Again I ask: Why are the mothers of Britain, like the mothers of America, acquiescent and silent? Have they learnt nothing from the example of Cassino; from the fact that – as Aneurin Bevan said in Parliament– the 'soft belly of the Axis' has turned out to be its hard backbone? This silence of English mothers – and of English fathers too – seems to me to be the most deathly example of the herd instinct that I have yet encountered in a lifetime of war and international disaster.

But Mr Villard deserves further quotation. 'I plead', he says, 'not only for Europe. I plead for England. For England cannot survive the destruction of Europe upon which it depended for so large a proportion of its trade, for its intellectual stimulus and for its inspiration in art and music. It is widely reported that the reason why Winston Churchill, to his lasting credit, fought against Mr Stalin and Mr Roosevelt at Teheran in the matter of the second front, was that among other things he feared that England would pay too horrible a price at the hands of the Germans when the final struggle came. This report may be apocryphal. I have no means of vouching for it. I can only say that it ought to be true for the threat is there, whether the Germans have secret weapons or not. Unless they are totally prostrate and without an air force, they can be relied on to make their most desperate effort to prevent defeat from the moment that the invasion forces begin to assemble. So I plead for the British boys who are destined for immolation. Their country suffers deeply today because of the generation lost in the first World War. I plead for the England that I love more than any other country save my own – that it may yet be saved.

'I plead for the Lowlands, as I pray that the responsibility for the destruction of what is left of their civilisation shall not be laid

194

at our doors. If veteran soldiers are nauseated by what they see after two armies have fought over a territory, what will happen to our invaders as they sweep through the wrecks of the Dutch and Belgian cities? What will these raw troops of ours say when they see the effect of the German invasion, of the hunger blockade and the continual bombing?'

He finally concludes with some constructive suggestions for avoiding the holocaust of young men for which so many towns and villages of our lovely Easter countryside are sedulously preparing. 'Many competent civilians and military people think we could go far towards breaking down German morale by abandoning our stupid unconditional surrender policy and returning to our own policy in the last war by giving the Germans the just peace points to which we shall ask their submission. Why can't we at least try to forestall the second front by taking this step? ... Why does not American public opinion, why, in heaven's name, do not the churches of America demand this simple step which may save a half million of our young men? Can the clergy of this country not see where their duty lies? Can they not respond to the simplest humanitarian motives? Will they not take the lead now in demanding in the name of Christ himself that no single stone be left unturned to save Europe and save America from the horror that lies before us?'

I suggest that each one of us makes Mr Villard's plea our own. It is our democratic right to express ourselves on such matters of life and death to the Prime Minister, the Service Ministers, and our MPs. So long as the period of calamity has not yet begun, there is still time to act. A few groups – the Women's International League, for example, in both Britain and America – have already given a lead. Let it not be said that, once again, the flower of British youth perished because, even on behalf of their own sons, the mothers and fathers of England lacked the courage to speak.

Shortly after Vera wrote this Letter, Churchill issued a secret memorandum, of which this is an extract:

6 July 1944
It may be several weeks or even months before I shall ask you to drench Germany with poison gas, and if we do it, let us do it 100 per cent.

In the meanwhile I want the matter studied in cold blood by sensible people and not by that particular set of psalm-singing, uniformed defeatists which one runs across now here and there. . . . I shall, of course, have to square Uncle Joe and the President.

Churchill's military advisers counselled otherwise.

We rise by things that are under our feet;
By what we have mastered of good and gain;
By the pride deposed and the passion slain,
And the vanquished ills that we hourly meet
                  – J.G. Holland, *Graduation*

You will be interested to hear that the cause of Food Relief has gained a new and powerful advocate in the person of Clare Boothe Luce, who in mid-April contributed to the New York *Herald-Tribune* a vigorous double-column letter summarising all the familiar arguments in favour of relief at once, and introducing several new ones.

In case you do not realise the significance of this intervention, I should explain that Mrs Luce is an American Congresswoman, the writer of several successful plays such as *The Women* and *Margin For Error*, and the wife of Henry Luce, the proprietor of *Time, Life*, and *Fortune*. Her reputation in America suggests a combination of Lady Astor and J.B. Priestley, and though she is not always as wise as she is brilliant, she and her husband are probably the most influential couple in the United States, apart from the Roosevelts. I am hoping that the Food Relief Campaign may be able to reproduce Mrs Luce's letter as a leaflet.

There is now no doubt that the blockade of Occupied Europe, and the obliteration bombing of German and ex-Allied cities, are the two aspects of the war about which the conscience of mankind, wherever it is still sensitive, feels the most unhappy. They are, as it were, the cracks in the armour of Juggernaut, the soft spots into which the arrows of misgiving can still penetrate. It may well be that, after the war is over, the controversies which gather round these questions will be seen as the starting-point of the final revulsion which, in one country or another, will bring the fighting to an end.

But underlying these controversies is another and deeper problem, which raises its head wherever they are discussed. It is one on which the pacifist, though from a totally different angle, often joins issue with as much vehemence as the militarist. This

197

problem is the old dilemma about 'humanising' war; the doubt whether an evil, once let loose upon the world, can be curbed, limited and restrained. That it should be is denied alike by German generals, and by the uncompromising 'absolutists' at Peace Pledge Union annual general meetings.

'All idea of philanthropy in war is a pernicious error,' wrote Karl von Clausewitz. 'He who employs physical force to its full extent without sparing blood, always gains the preponderance over the adversary who will not act in the same way, and he will dictate the law to the latter. . . . War knows of only one method: force.' 'What have we to do with food relief or the limitation of bombing?' cries the uncompromising pacifist. 'These are not pacifist issues. Our job is to stop war.' In similar mood, I have heard the critics of prison reform insist: 'There's no use in trying to ameliorate conditions. It's the *system* we've got to get rid of!'

No one could agree more profoundly than myself that war, like the existence of a vindictive penal code, is the fundamental evil. 'War is not a humanitarian undertaking,' writes one of my American critics, and I can only reply: 'Exactly. That is why it should not be undertaken.' With full conviction I endorse the words of the Chicago *Christian Century* in a fine article on obliteration bombing, published on March 22nd and recently circulated by the International Fellowship of Reconciliation: 'It is *war* that is the atrocity, and there is no reason to expect that its barbarous nature can be held in check. The responsibility of the Christian is to oppose war by opposing and helping to cure the conditions that breed it. Nevertheless . . . admitting that the insane logic of war requires all things to be done which are necessary to win victory, yet millions of Christians find themselves tormented with the question: "Is such horror as this indiscriminate slaughter of civilians necessary?" When Mr Churchill says, "There are no lengths in violence to which we will not go," such Christians cry out from the depths of their shaken souls, "not *any*"?'

It is true that when war comes, the pacifist has admittedly failed for the time being in his main purpose, but this does not thereafter exonerate him from any attempt to mitigate war's worst excesses. On the contrary his very failure to prevent war makes its excesses his direct responsibility, which he would be evading indeed if he were to sit back self-righteously refusing 'salvage work', and excusing himself from the difficult endeavour to restrain the growth of barbarousness in his own community, on the ground that these efforts will not fulfil his deepest purpose. It is here that the pacifist can work with the more humanitarian supporters of 'legitimate' war, such as the Bishop of Chichester and Professor Stanley Jevons. It is not for him to refuse co-operation with these men on the ground that their position seems to him self-contradictory. He is not the dictator of another man's logic or another man's conviction, for logic and conviction are essentially the products of individual mental conflict. His concern is with results, even if those results fall far short of his total endeavour.

It is, however, at least questionable whether in the long run this piece-by-piece method will not carry him to his goal more quickly than the direct means which he would prefer. Arthur Hugh Clough's familiar line, which describes the main tide 'through creeks and inlets making', symbolises the fashion in which minor attacks at many points may undermine a tradition or conquer an evil more completely than a head-on assault. The difference, I suppose, is that between the evolutionary and the revolutionary method of progress. Revolution is obviously the more speedy, but within a comparatively short time it may end – as in Russia – by creating a society dominated by principles diametrically opposed to those which inspired the revolutionaries, and bearing a character not dissimilar in essence, though different in externals, from the regime which has been overthrown.

The historically recent past, at any rate, has shown that, while spectacular renunciations of war have never yet succeeded, the less ambitious attempts to limit its worst evils have not only been effective over long periods, but have sometimes come near to producing the kind of international atmosphere in which war's abolition has at least appeared conceivable. The Kellogg Pact has followed the Holy Alliance into the limbo of political hallucinations, but the humbler endeavours of Grotius and his followers to build a science of international law took full advantage of the revulsion which followed the cruel wars of the seventeenth century. When George Orwell, writing recently in *The Tribune*, airily dismissed 'all talk of "humanising" war' as 'sheer humbug', he was simply and crudely unhistorical. In *What Acts of War are Justifiable*, Professor A.L. Goodhart, Professor of Jurisprudence in the University of Oxford, after paying tribute to the pioneer work of Grotius, goes on to state: 'Further progress was made during the eighteenth century, with the result that the unrestrained cruelty of former wars was in large part absent from the Napoleonic Wars. It was, however, after 1850 that the most striking advance was made by means of various treaties and conventions, in which the rules relating to warfare were partially formulated.'

Even in the present war, there are depths to which the combatants have not yet descended – such as a general massacre of all prisoners, bacteriological warfare, and the use of poison gas. Although gas, as George Orwell alleges, may be ineffective in a war of movement, and according to him has been avoided for this reason alone, certain American voices have already asserted its potential value in dislodging the Japanese invaders of Pacific islands. In *Fellowship* for March, 1944, John Nevin Sayre quoted an article from the American journal *Newsweek* for December 20th, 1943, by a well-known Washington columnist, Ernest K. Lindley, entitled 'Thoughts on the Use of Gas in Warfare'. It opened, Dr Sayre tells us, with these ominous paragraphs:

'A week ago Admiral Pratt wrote on the lessons of Tarawa. To his conclusion this lay reporter feels impelled, after extensive inquiry, to add one assertion: that the use of gas would have enabled us to capture Tarawa almost without a casualty. If the tons of bombs dropped on Tarawa from the air had been heavy gas, of the mustard type, the island would have been so thoroughly drenched that in all probability not a defender would have survived. . . . In a drive across the Central Pacific, the use of gas would expedite our progress and diminish our casualties.

Any area that can be segregated is ideal for the use of gas. The small islands of the Pacific fit the prescription. We have the transportation capacity in planes – supplemented if necessary by naval bombardment – to smother most of these island outposts of Japan with gas.'

A similar opinion was quoted from a dispatch by Major-General William N. Porter, chief of the US chemical warfare service, in the Montreal *Daily Star* on December 23rd. These sinister suggestions may well have been officially inspired 'feelers'. The fact that they have not been carried out means that up to date the USA has not yet wholly abandoned its wartime standards to the advocates of unrestricted cruelty.

The question of war's 'humanisation', not as an alternative but as a preliminary to its abolition, is one of the greatest philosophic and practical problems which confront us today. I hope to examine it more fully in the near future in both a long article (in the July *Christian Pacifist*), and a pamphlet. But though we live in a period of moral and spiritual setback never paralleled since the grim days of the Thirty Years' War, for me at least, encouragement lies in the belief that our smallest endeavours to check this setback are contributing to that upward swing of the pendulum which the future will see.

The arrival of the first of Hitler's 'secret weapons', the V1s, on 13 June came as a great disappointment for those who thought the invasion of the Continent was the beginning of the end.

By the time this Letter was written many flying bombs had fallen, mostly on London, although the BBC never went beyond saying 'Southern England'. Vera's comparison, in the Letter after this, with shells and whizz bangs hardly does the V1s justice. They were very difficult to intercept, travelled faster than most of our fighters and were extremely destructive. One bomb was capable of destroying a whole row of houses. Altogether there were 2,419 V1s and they killed 6,184 civilians. The last fell in March 1945 at Datchworth, Hertfordshire.

Hitler was boasting of more horrors to follow and in this respect was as good as his word.

Faith is the bird that feels the light when the dawn is still dark

— Rabindranath Tagore

As I begin this letter to you from our cottage garden during a few days in 'Southern England', the fight for Cherbourg is going on opposite us on the other side of the Channel. Sometimes the noise of the guns from the sea – or even perhaps from France – seems to be carried to my ears on the wind, reminding me of the strange shudder, half sound and half sensation, which penetrated to the base hospitals at Étaples from the front line during the last war.

At Easter, when we came back here for the first time after more than three years, I wrote you of the waiting tension which even then lay over the villages and woodlands of this lovely coastal county. You will realise now that the landings in Normandy, though I expected them long before they came, were no surprise to me. Never, to borrow the Prime Minister's phraseology, have I had to keep silence about so much for so long. The fact that the preparations which I witnessed filled me with grief, rather than with the hope and joy which the first press announcements appeared to take for granted among this country's much-enduring citizens, seemed sometimes to make that silence harder.

It is still too early to attempt any general assessment of this new phase of the war, but if our experience in Italy can be regarded as a guide, military progress is likely for a long time to be slow and costly. The initial attempts by politicians and BBC commentators to inject us with a heady excitement seemed singularly incongruous when compared with the mute acceptance, barely finding expression in a comment, with which the population of London received the news. Neither the occupants of the bus nor the driver of the taxi in which I travelled across town on the morning of June 6th so much as mentioned the invasion. That evening, the terminus from which I left to give three lectures in Lincolnshire was quiet and deserted, and though there were few trains leaving the station, my own was half empty. Nowhere did I see demonstrations or a hint of jubilation. London has known many crises during the past five years, and this was just one more.

For those who possess imagination and are not submerged in that timeless anxiety for husband, son, or brother which links the waiting women of this war with those who watched and prayed in the last, it is inevitable that the further suffering that this new campaign must bring to Europe and especially to France should rouse our deepest compassion. Thinking first, as we cannot help but think, of the death of that youth – British, American, German – which is so sorely needed for the rebuilding of shattered civilisation, we who are civilians in this war remember the civilians of northern France, who now for the third time in a generation see their lands devastated and their homes destroyed by battle.

Similar ordeals will doubtless follow for other parts of Europe, unless some miracle – some 'act of God' in very truth – arrests the momentum of war which (as some of us prophesied in 1939) seems incapable of being stopped by the hands that started it. A careful reading of the newspapers reveals the hardening, demoralising effect of continued chaos and insecurity upon the populations of battle areas, and especially upon their younger members. During the second week of the invasion, a correspondent sent me a cutting from that day's *Evening News* containing only two headlines: 'Children See Germans Die. "C'est bon", they say: "C'est bon"'. Comment appears unnecessary. But it is obvious that the most difficult function which will fall to the relief workers now preparing in their thousands to enter Europe will be, not to feed the hungry or comfort the suffering, but to transform into civilised beings the young people brutalised by years of privation and peril.

'Of the 22,000 inhabitants of Tivoli', reports *The Times* correspondent in Italy, describing the heavy bomb damage which has reduced to 'a piteous state' this little pleasure resort in the Alban hills near Rome, 'about 15,000 have now returned from their refuges in the hills and installed themselves as best they can among the remaining houses. The British civil affairs officer who is ministering to their needs so far as he is able told me that the inhabitants met the allied troops with black looks when they first entered the town, but that they soon changed their attitude when they realised that something was being done for them.' His experience suggests that some elementary lessons in psychology are an essential part of the preliminary equipment of all would-be relief workers.

To England the invasion, and the months of 'saturation' bombing which preceded it, have brought in the shape of 'pilotless' planes, a form of retaliation which has caused devastation and suffering in a number of southern cities, and in the country lying between. Once more the dwellers in these districts have to remind themselves, in their struggle to overcome the disturbing effect of a new peril upon their powers of concentration, that civilisation will not be rebuilt by those who have sought immunity from danger and fear, but by the men and women who have shared in paying the price of sin, even though they foresaw its consequences and endeavoured to prevent them. But after listening in country and town to the frequent sirens (which the editor of the *Sunday Express*, on the Sunday following the invasion, optimistically told us that the majority of British people would probably never hear again!), and waiting for the sinister explosions which follow them, I cannot help but reflect upon our own share of responsibility for this nightmare weapon of haphazard destruction – which causes, as always, the greatest anguish to the 'poor plain people' who are least to blame for war and its excesses. The next step down from the criminality of 'saturation' bombing, with its indiscriminate massacre of civilians, is the utter insanity of mechanical bombing directed against areas even larger than those demolished in Germany by the Anglo-American air forces.

To expect the Nazis to refrain from taking this next step in the downward sequence of scientific brutalities against civilians in which we have become their successful rivals, would have been to expect from them a degree of moral restraint which we have little evidence that they possess (though we must not join with

The Times in refusing them credit for treating Rome, like Paris, as an open city). Wars will perhaps cease when some nation – let us hope that it may be ours – reaches a moral level at which it is able to repudiate the temptation to go one better than its enemy in the use of mechanised atrocities.

Meanwhile the Nazi attempt to justify the employment of their abominable weapon has a similar ring to the statement made in the House of Commons by Sir Archibald Sinclair on March 31st, 1943, in reply to Mr R. R. Stokes, who asked whether on any occasion instructions had been given to British airmen to engage in area bombing rather than limit their attention to purely military targets. 'The targets of Bomber Command are always military', said Sir Archibald, 'but night bombing of military objectives necessarily involves bombing the area in which they are situated.' In comparable mood George Schroeder, the special correspondent of the German News Agency, wrote on June 17th: 'The pilotless bomb is being applied for military exigencies only since London houses Eisenhower's General Staff HQ, and Southern England is the hinterland of the present invasion battle in Normandy.' (*The Observer*, June 18th, 1944.)

On this excuse I can only comment – as I have similarly commented on equally bland excuses by our own politicians – that indiscriminate winged bombs are at least as likely to hit Westminster Abbey as Eisenhower's Headquarters, and even more likely to destroy the humble homes of war-weary workers whose genuine interests are the same among all nations.

Now that this new period of the war has started, defeating the faint hope that some creative inspiration among the statesmen of the world might save the youth of many peoples, those who care for peace are faced with alternative probabilities which appear equally unlikely to lead to the type of outcome that we desire. The United Nations may win a speedy victory under leaders committed to a policy of 'unconditional surrender', and, dictating their terms to a people still physically vigorous and spiritually undefeated, bequeath to our children the military recrudescence of Germany and a third World War. Or a prolonged stalemate may ensue between the Allies and a Germany that cannot win but refuses to surrender, involving years of relatively stagnant warfare, and the perpetuation of suffering in bombed and famished Europe.

No lover of peace can wish for either result. All history teaches us that no *great* nation can be permanently crushed, and that the treaties that endure are those which leave the defeated enemy without a grievance, such as the Duke of Wellington helped to make at the Congress of Vienna, and the victorious British drew up with the Boers after the South African War. Yet none of us can hope for a prolongation of Europe's agony, and the slow or violent deaths of yet more children. We can but work and press for the reconciliation in which our faith is entire, and pray that the Lord will shorten these days before another young generation has utterly perished.

___ 13 July 1944 ___

Life is not that which we know and plan for, but that which we believe and dare

– Martin Niemoller

If you happen to be an inhabitant of 'Southern England', you doubtless share my impression that the pilotless plane has ousted the Second Front as a popular topic of conversation. Judging by my own reactions and by the conversations that I hear in households, shops, cafés and shelters, there are three main reasons why even the most convinced of the war's supporters are unable to confront this new peril with the spirited determination which marked their endurance of the 1940-41 blitz.

The first – and largely unacknowledged – reason is, I believe, an instinctive realisation that our rulers, by their blind and obstinate policy of 'saturation' bombing, have wantonly brought further unnecessary misery upon the heads of their own people. Behind the government-inspired press rejoicings of the past two years over each German city 'wiped out', the semi-articulate

207

public was shocked and revolted by such atrocities as the breach of the Eder and Mohne dams and the 'obliteration' of Hamburg. They now perceive, from the opening of the Second Front, that the Allies are relying for their victory neither upon strategic bombing nor implacable blockade, but mainly upon ordinary military tactics; and that therefore the suffering of civilians upon both sides is largely incidental, and could easily have been avoided by less callous leadership amongst all the belligerents.

Secondly, it is obvious that after five years of war, rationing, and general insecurity, people have less resistance both physically and psychologically than they possessed in 1940. The power to endure depends not only upon personal heroism, but upon such purely physical constituents as calcium and fat, which we all now lack in varying degrees. Psychologically, the persistent propaganda about 'victory' and 'liberation', which has been imposed upon us ever since the preparations for the Second Front began, has decreased rather than strengthened resistance by creating the impression that the end of the war was just round the corner, and that the worst of our trials were over, whatever woes might still be inflicted upon France, Italy, Belgium, Holland, Norway and Germany. People have long exhausted their capacity for excitement; danger today is merely tedious to oneself and a source of anxiety on behalf of others. Each man and woman is close to the mood which I once described as characteristic of the closing stages of an earlier conflict: 'I had no further experience to gain from the war; nothing remained except to endure it.'

The growing effect of war weariness is probably felt most acutely by the parents of young children, whose homes have been broken up and whose families, in the endeavour to find relative security and some measure of continuous education, have been repeatedly pushed from district to district and even from country to country, and are now undergoing the process all over again. In the *New Statesman and Nation* for July 1st, the editor – who is not, I believe, a father – complacently invites his readers to resist the new robot by reflecting that 'Southern England is a part of the same battlefield as Normandy and that the toughest part of the war is still to come.' This consideration fails, I am afraid, to reconcile me to the realisation that ever since my son and daughter were twelve and nine, I have sought in vain, year after year, to provide them with those conditions of undisturbed development which are the birthright of childhood. The fact that the children of Stalingrad have had no education does not persuade me that it is a good idea that mine should have none either. There are, I am sure, thousands of other parents in this country whose reactions are precisely the same as my own.

A third and less rational objection to the pilotless plane lies in the sense of being afflicted by something uncanny and super-natural which it appears to give to some of its victims. The explanation is probably due to the fact that, despite the hostile overhead throb, the scream of the descending bomb and the final roar of the explosion, so much of its progress is silent, and in heavy traffic cannot be heard at all. This is, of course, especially characteristic of the bombs which glide for some distance after the engine cuts out, leaving the population below with the con-tinuous impression that destruction may fall upon them from any part of the skies at any moment. To many people, the thunder of guns and rockets which accompanied the former type of air-raid brought reassurance, particularly at night. When explosions occurred, it was then always possible to console one-self with the reflection that 'it's only our guns'. Today the relief which accompanies the knowledge that once more the robot has passed over, is negatived by the remorse-making probability that death or agony has come to someone else. For the imaginative, it is particularly difficult to subdue that reflection in the quest for necessary sleep. Personally, I have found it most stabilising to discard all the old reactions to a 'raid', and instead reflect that I am living in an area which is liable to continuous and persistent shelling, of a type frequently experienced in Dover, and endured by Paris from 'Big Bertha' at the end of the last war. The 'doodlebug', it is true, is a peculiarly noisy and obnoxious kind of shell, but up to date it is at least a shell which can be intercepted, and there is no essential difference between its objectionable buzz and the whine of a 'whizz-bang'.

In spite of the above analysis of negative reactions, I am still moved to admiration by the equable endurance of the great mass of humanity – an endurance which is none the less meritorious because it should never have been required. At the end of June, for instance, it was my duty to take the chair at a meeting in a large church situated in one of the areas most subject to robot bombing. Had no audience appeared we should not have been surprised, but quite a large gathering arrived, and serenely awaited our appearance beneath the unprotected brick roof of the church. During the meeting we had two alerts and a number of relatively near explosions, but hardly a member of the audience left, and neither of the speakers, both German refugees, moved so much as a muscle or curtailed their speeches by a sentence. The questions put to them at the end were unhurried, well-considered and intelligent in their quest for the unusual information which these speakers could give. I was reminded by the whole experience of Martin Niemoller's words, quoted at the head of this letter.

The press of June 29th contained one encouraging item which, owing to the stresses arising from robots and the Second Front, you may possibly have missed. This was the judgment given by Mr Justice Birkett in favour of Learie Constantine, the West Indian cricketer and civil servant, who brought an action against the Imperial London Hotels, Ltd, for refusing to receive and lodge him on the ground of his colour. Awarding him £5 5s. 0d. damages, the judge said that he was bound by the form in which the action was brought to award nominal damages only. He went on to comment: 'Mr Constantine bore himself with modesty and dignity and dealt with questions with intelligence and truth. He was not concerned to be vindictive or malicious, but was obviously affected by the indignity and humiliation which had been put upon him.'

This case, in addition to General Eisenhower's disapproval of the findings of the court-martial which recently condemned an American Negro soldier to death for a sexual offence, suggests that in Britain, at any rate, we are reaching a position in which coloured men and women will be able to count upon a fair

210

measure of decency and justice. Much progress has evidently been made since Winifred Holtby tramped the streets of London vainly seeking a lodging for Clements Kadalie, the native secretary of the South African Industrial and Commercial Workers' Union. Despite bombardment and invasion, we can still describe some aspects of our civilisation in the words which the astronomer Galileo is said to have whispered to a friend as he rose from signing the official recantation of his discovery that the earth moves round the sun: '*E pur si muove!*' ('It moves, nevertheless!')

Among the servicemen who shared Vera's feelings about the suffering of French civilians was Captain William Douglas Home, now well known as a play-wright, whose elder brother was to become Prime Minister. On 8 September 1944 Douglas Home, with great courage, refused to order the bombardment of Le Havre which was packed with civilians. This was after a request by the German Commander to be given three days to evacuate all civilians was refused, even though, four days later, the battle still had not started. Home wrote home saying that he was convinced that 'unconditional surrender is costing thousands of un-necessarily expended lives'. He was court-martialed and sentenced to a year's imprisonment with hard labour. The incident is described in his book *Sins of Commission* (Michael Russell, 1985).

(Shortly before we went to press, William Douglas Home made moves to obtain a pardon. He was prompted by the controversy surrounding Kurt Wald-heim's alleged war crimes whose investigators referred to the Nuremburg trials and the 'long established tradition of soldiers not being punished for disobeying certain orders'. Home was quoted in *The Times* as saying 'I felt if I'd obeyed orders at Le Havre I would have been party to what we now call war crimes.')

By the time this Letter was written the Russians were advancing steadily. Cherbourg was captured and, after much bitter fighting involving massive air sup-port, Caen and St Lo had fallen. On 26 August Ameri-can troops marched up the Champs Elysées. The British led the way into Belgium early in September.

The disproportion between the quarrels of nations and the suffering which fighting out those quarrels involves; the poor and barren prizes which reward sublime endeavour on the battlefield; the fleeting triumphs of war; the long, slow rebuilding; the awful risks so hardily run; the doom missed by a hair's breadth, by the spin of a coin, by the accident of an accident — all this should make the prevention of another great war the main preoccupation of mankind

— Winston Churchill, *The World Crisis*
(pub. 1929 and dedicated 'To All Who Hope')

Since I wrote your last letter, the swiftness of events in France and Belgium has changed the whole character and outlook of the war. Whatever the nature of the coming struggle in Germany — and it may well be tough and prolonged — there is now no question that Holland, Denmark and Norway will shortly be delivered from Nazi occupation. According to Jersey-born Lord Justice du Parcq, as reported in the *Sunday Express* of Sept. 10th the German garrisons in the Channel Islands may hold out right to the end of the European war, 'because an Allied softening up process with shells and bombs would kill our own subjects as well as the Germans'. These words must have made wry reading for refugee French citizens of Brest and Le Havre, whose compatriots have had to endure the Anglo-American 'softening up' which British subjects are spared.

For England the chief effect of the Allied *Blitzkrieg* has been the 'liberation' from flying bombs of London and the 'bomb alleys' of the south. One interesting comment on the last-moment appearance of the flying bomb in the European war was recently made at a Friends International conference by Professor Norman Bentwich, who believes that the 'doodlebug' may prove a blessing in disguise if it makes more real to public imagination the potential terrors of another war. One reason, he reminded his audience, why wars recur is that the generation which makes them invariably assumes that the methods of the new war will be similar to those of its predecessor. Like the French who poured

213

so much of their national wealth into the ineffective Maginot Line, nations become satisfied with their power to strike or to defend themselves in terms of outdated weapons.

The flying bomb, arriving after high explosives, incendiaries, butterfly bombs, anti-personnel bombs, and all the rest of the bomb family which have visited London during the past half-decade, provides a clear warning of the mechanically controlled weapons by which whole populations will be done to death in circumstances of unimaginable horror if a third World War is allowed to occur. Then indeed will be fulfilled, even more dreadfully than in this war, Winston Churchill's famous prophecy in *The World Crisis*: 'No more may Alexander, Cæsar and Napoleon lead armies to victory, ride their horses on the field of battle sharing the perils of their soldiers and deciding the fate of empires by the resolves and gestures of a few intense hours. For the future they will sit surrounded by clerks in offices, as safe, as quiet and as dreary as Government departments, while the fighting men in scores of thousands are slaughtered or stifled over the telephone by machinery. . . . Next time the competition may be to kill women and children and the civil population generally, and victory will give herself in sorry nuptials to the spectacled hero who organises it on the largest scale.'

Such a degree of mental and moral lunacy would have to be reached before the deliberate endorsement of massacres far exceeding the mass slaughters of this war, that even the 'Big Four' who are now preparing to take the world's destinies in their hands may well agree with the Winston Churchill of 1929 that the prevention of another great war should be 'the main preoccupation of mankind'.

After five years of menace and four of constant bombardment, London has been through too much suffering to be any more jubilant over its present release from 'the terror by night' and 'the arrow that flieth by day' than it became when the long-anticipated invasion started. Its rejoicing is subdued, though relief is visible in the faces and manners of its much-tried population. On Sunday, September 10th, the first Sunday that London felt as consciously free from flying bombs as the coming official relaxation of Civil Defence and black-out regulations could make it, I noticed more people in the West End than I had seen there since the early summer. Elsewhere it was still an empty city, but in Piccadilly and Leicester Square the holiday atmosphere seemed almost to suggest a normal peace-time Sunday. For all my awareness of terrible things still happening overseas, it was impossible to avoid sharing that mood. So much of it arises from the conscious thankfulness with which (despite the lurking threat of 'V2') we can see the members of our families go out for long periods without the perpetual fear of never seeing them alive again – a fear alas! fulfilled for so many during these years of heavy anxieties and grave responsibilities.

Though the sense of corporate experience adds so much to the capacity for personal endurance, these anxieties have not been less acute because millions have shared them. Each family is a private world; each individual has only one life to live and one death to die. The sense of freedom that has come with the rolling away of this burden means that we in London and the south will require self-discipline in order constantly to remember the misery that the war is still causing to so many others. I have met quite a number of people lately whose sole interest in the Allied advance centred upon the early occupation of the Pas de Calais and the capture of the flying-bomb sites. Such an egotistical attitude is in itself an obstacle to the education of public opinion regarding plans for a constructive peace and the impartial relief of all who are needy and starving in Europe.

The removal of the flying-bomb menace from London and the liberation of large parts of France may well indicate the piecemeal fashion in which this war will end. The expectation that history will repeat itself in a way that seldom occurs has fixed so firm an anticipation of another Armistice Day in the minds of those who remember the first, that many British citizens are looking for a sudden German capitulation and some specific occasion on which they can throw off the weight of the war and physically fling its restraints behind them. But such a day may never come. As *The Observer* of Sept. 10th pointed out, 'The Nazi policy in 1944 is the precise reverse of the policy of

215

Ludendorff and the Kaiser in 1918. So far from abdicating, they are in every way intensifying their terror, and taking a firmer grip on the German population.'

The surrender of Germany may come here and there, and by slow degrees, until German resistance is finally at an end. It would surely be best for us all that this should happen; that no psychological 'D-Day' should give *carte blanche* to the invading forces of selfishness and greed. If the war ends gradually, the sudden violent reaction against war preoccupations and the deliberate forgetfulness of war-created problems, characteristic of 1919, may not occur at all. We shall thus both keep our war consciousness and carry our vigilance with us into a new era, ushered in without the preliminary frenzy which set the survivors of 1914–1918 hysterically dancing in the Grafton Galleries with pictures of the Canadian dead on the walls.

The V2s were extremely destructive rocket-propelled bombs which travelled faster than the speed of sound so that there was no warning of their approach. The first arrived in London on 8 September 1944 and the last only six weeks before the end of the war. A total of 1,115 V2s fell on London, killing 2,754 people.

There had been widespread hopes that the war would be ended before Christmas by the Arnhem campaign, in which Montgomery's forces would enter the Ruhr through Holland and Belgium. But the plan failed and there were heavy casualties.

The Lord gets his best soldiers out of the highlands of affliction
— C.H. Spurgeon, Sorrow's Discipline

A few days ago I received two letters from the United States, written in early September. One confidently prophesied that the war in Europe would be over by November 1st; the other described the preparations being made in New York for the celebration of 'V-Day'. I put them away uncertain whether I most wanted to laugh or to weep.

Nothing could have brought home to me more forcibly than these delayed letters the change of mood wrought in a warring world by the passage of two months. One obvious fact that emerges is the extent to which the Americans have under-estimated German tenacity — a misjudgment for which we can hardly criticise them, since with longer and closer opportunities for knowledge we have repeatedly been guilty of it ourselves. There was, nevertheless, a moment during the Nazi retreat from France when American confidence might have been justified; a moment at which some more inspired gesture of leadership than the obstinate parrot-cry of 'unconditional surrender' might have interrupted the costly and purposeless 'fight to a finish', and saved Allied lives on a scale unattainable by any claim made for the still 'experimental' mass slaughters of obliteration bombing.

That opportunity passed unseized, leaving Germany uncon-quered and the disillusioned peoples of the United Nations in the deep trough of reaction after the triumphant 'October, 1918' feeling of the late summer. In London the brief hope of freedom from attack after four years of bombardment departed with the arrival of 'V2', leaving a flat sense of fatigue and disappoint-ment. The other day, buying early Christmas cards for American friends in one of London's finest stores, I was the chance means of terminating a sharp uncharacteristic quarrel between two of the well-educated girls who serve the counters. Frayed tempers and melancholy faces have succeeded the over-sanguine expecta-tion of an early victory as, in the metropolis which has known war at closer quarters during the past five years than any part of

218

Britain except the south-east coast, ten million people face a sixth wartime winter.

You may remember that in these letters I have often written on the importance of attaining a wide perspective as part of the necessary technique of endurance. Sharing, as no one can help but share, in the prevailing consciousness of anti-climax I look upon the dark panorama of a world in chaos as a prelude to recovering a sense of proportion. As I write, journalistic comments on the re-election of President Roosevelt echo from the American scene, still overshadowed by the recent death of Wendell Willkie – an untimely tragedy, comparable to our own loss of Archbishop Temple, which may well make more ultimate difference to America's part in world affairs than the new choice of President.

But it is not to the United States that I look in the quest for a self-forgetting perspective. Except for the members of those families whose husbands and sons have gone overseas, America, in this war as in the last, has enjoyed the doubtful blessing of immunity in a society of stricken nations. She has known no real shortages of food or clothing, and for this reason has made a greater imaginative effort to understand the problems of under-nourished European countries than we who stand closer to them and share a few of their lesser deprivations. She has experienced no continuous threat of danger and death to vast numbers of her citizens, and hence has tended to exaggerate the actual perils which fret our nerves and sustain our apprehensions as consistently as she has under-estimated the resolute strength of Germany.

In seeking the sense of balance that may be conveyed to the less unfortunate by the spectacle of suffering beyond estimation, my mind goes back to ten days in the late spring of 1936 which left behind a memory of unexpected enchantment. A lecture tour of less than two weeks in America would result in no more than a superficial impression of three or four States, linked by railroads and highways covering the prairie-filled immensities of a sub-continent. But in Holland ten days was sufficient for a relatively comprehensive knowledge of a tiny country whose

219

vivid charm, scintillating cleanliness and warm-hearted hospitality I had not previously encountered.

With a clarity seldom surpassed in my rich experience, I remember the broad dignified boulevards and incomparable flower-shops of The Hague; the incredible patchwork-quilts of colour in the bulb-fields near Haarlem, and the salt tang of the air above that flat reclaimed land arched by its unimpeded vista of open sky; the unexpected pines and sand-dunes near Apeldoorn; the wide sweep of the River Yssel at Deventer; the modern streamlined radio station at Hilversum; the library filled with patiently collected treasures of international literature belonging to the Jewish university professor who entertained me at Gröningen. And finally, in a museum surrounded by the old streets and canals of Amsterdam, I found the spirit of the Dutch people embodied in the genius of Rembrandt and stood longer spell-bound by 'The Anatomy Lesson' than by any picture since Leonardo da Vinci's 'The Last Supper' in the Chapel of Santa Maria delle Gracie outside Milan.

Where are they now? – the cultured Jewish household; the cheerful bourgeois family who invited me to their pleasant home in the suburbs of Amsterdam; the young mothers of small children with whom I stayed at Haarlem and The Hague; the editors, doctors and school-teachers who could then discuss, with a detachment now unbelievable, the Nazi celebrations of the Rhineland re-occupation which I had just witnessed at Cologne. In the last war, neutral Holland emerged with her prestige enhanced and her land unimpaired. Today, thanks to the terrible paradox by which the 'liberation' of a people is achieved at the cost of their homes, the economic life of their country, and their civilisation itself that past fortune is no more than a wistful memory of 'happier things'.

According to an article by Zoë Farmar, entitled 'The Waters Are Rising', in the *News-Chronicle* for October 31st, no nation in Western Europe has undergone what Holland is now suffering. 'So many and heavy have been the blows to mind and body', she writes, 'it is perhaps difficult even to appreciate a new disaster which may disable a nation of nine million people for years to come – more years than even the hard and labour-hungry work of rebuilding houses and schools, ships and churches in our own nation. For already one quarter of Holland is under salt water, and to recover fertility for the growing of food crops may take up to seven years, depending upon the salt-cleansing rainfalls. And if the Germans carry out the total threat of their present blackmail against the Dutch, as so far they are steadily continuing to do, 45 per cent – nearly one half of the whole country – will be inundated.'

Perhaps we have read or listened to accounts of the RAF dam-breaking operations which brought the sea-waves pouring over the low-lying island of Walcheren without fully realising what these exploits mean to a country whose national life has been built upon the control of the waters, perseveringly achieved yard by yard, in the course of the centuries. They mean that the Dutch must look back to the bitter but swift process of conquest as almost idyllic compared with the agonising experience of deliverance.

'Holland', continues Zoë Farmar, 'is fast approaching some-thing of the degree of suffering that has been wrought upon parts of Eastern Europe and the Balkans. In terms of immediate conflict it may not be so long drawn out. In terms of reconstruc-tion, it is awful to consider. Just now something like seven millions of people are without heat with which to warm, cook and see at night, for their coal mines in the Limburg district, which is a fighting zone, cannot produce or transport the coal. They are hungry – in some districts to the point where life cannot be maintained, in others to the level where children become afflicted for life and the weak die. This year's losses through flooding amount to some 657,000 acres of arable land, and 327,500 acres of pasture, or milk-making fields, 17 per cent of their food production area. The little food which is available cannot be got to those who need it.'

'What', she finally asks, 'can the individual do when made aware of such catastrophe?' We can only echo: 'What indeed?' But we can, at any rate, more truly estimate our own dis-appointments and exasperations against the shadow of that monumental suffering, and have the grace to feel ashamed of the sharpened tempers, the defeatist impatience, the self-interested satisfaction in the dried fruits and Christmas turkeys which a dozen other nations need more urgently than ourselves. We can but be silent before the dimensions, grown beyond human control, of mankind's greatest of all catastrophies; and seek in the affliction of others that sense of proportion which may help us to help them, and at least enable us to emerge courageously from our smaller tribulations.

The effects of the Allied blockade on the food supplies of Europe were constantly on Vera's mind. In October 1942 she was protesting because although shipments of wheat had been permitted, the Ministry of Economic Warfare was refusing navicerts (permitting neutral ships through the blockade) for dried milk awaiting shipment from Argentina and desperately needed by thousands of Greek children.

The following February, after acting as a judge in a 'Britain's Bonniest Baby' competition, she wrote:

Suddenly, with the baby competition in my mind and the famine reports before me, I had as clear a call as I have ever received to drop everything I was doing and make an urgent appeal to other parents to help in saving at least a few of Europe's children. It was just as though a voice within had said to me, Write. So I put aside the absorbing war novel which is now half finished, and started then and there on the pamphlet. Unless I wrote it quickly, I knew that I could never get it published before the Archbishop made his appeal and the country's conscience became, perhaps, more sensitive to Europe's tragedy. So I wrote the pamphlet all that evening and the whole of the next day.

The pamphlet was entitled 'One of These Little Ones' and was widely circulated. She published it at her own expense.

Our capacity exceeds our will-power: and it is often only to excuse ourselves that we hug the belief that things are impossible
– La Rochefoucauld, Maxims (No. 30)

Recently two Bournemouth mothers wrote to the *Sunday Express* asking that the 'fruits of victory' should be made 'edible and tangible – quickly!'

It was doubtless in response to this type of unthinking demand that Colonel Llewellin, Minister of Food, recently announced the allocation of extra Christmas rations for the citizens of this country. Those of us who protested at the time against a clamour for luxuries while neighbouring peoples still lacked necessities, have observed with relief the degree of public concern aroused by the government's Christmas proposals. According to Mr A.J. Cummings, the *News-Chronicle* alone received 70 letters questioning the propriety of increased rations for Britons while French, Belgians, Dutch, Norwegians, Poles and Italians still went hungry. Here at least is some concrete evidence that the years of educative work done by the Food Relief Campaign and the Famine Relief Committee have had their effect upon the public conscience.

One letter which appeared in *The Times* on November 14th summed up the position so truthfully and authoritatively that it is worth quoting in full. Written by Sir Charles J. Martin and two other members of the Lister Institute of Preventive Medicine (Division of Nutrition), it ran as follows:

'Sir, It has been a surprise to many that, notwithstanding the tragic food shortage in many countries of Europe, the Food Minister should propose to increase the rations for the British people at Christmas and that his proposals should have evoked relatively little public criticism. It is clear that many usually well-informed people are not really alive to the state of affairs in Europe, or lack the spiritual vitality which would make them ashamed to receive an increase of their own comparative plenty while others are looking starvation in the face. There can be no doubt of the facts. Although in certain agricultural districts there

224

may be comparative plenty owing to the accumulations caused by breakdown of transport, the reports of severe food shortage have been confirmed by eye-witnesses who have recently visited large towns in Belgium, Holland and Italy. The situation is known to be serious also in many districts of Greece and Yugoslavia and districts of France. There is not only a shortage of special foods which could be met by more adequate distribution and by provision of special synthetic vitamins. The deficiency is of food, of any food and especially of bread and fats. Authentic stories are told of the children of even well-to-do families picking over the garbage bins near Allied camps to relieve the pangs of hunger with any scraps of food they can find.

'We have been and still are the best fed country of Europe, thanks to the efforts of the Royal and Merchant Navies, and to the enlightened policy of our Food Ministry, which would be the first to acknowledge its debt to its scientific advisers and to the Government Committee on Scientific Food Policy. Thanks to these, we have been provided with an adequate ration of fats and a national bread of good quality which has remained unrationed. The same is true of our abundant potato supply, and no one need go hungry. Specially imported foods such as milk, eggs, cheese, cod liver oil, and orange juice have been partially reserved for the priority classes that need them most. Our population has not suffered in health from its wartime diet and one important class – the children – has improved in general health, stamina, growth, and development. Should we not, therefore, as a professedly Christian country, continue to restrict ourselves to a diet that is adequate and healthy, and be willing to forgo any extra luxuries until our neighbours have enough plain food to nourish their bodies?'

In reply to this type of protest, the Minister of Food replies that the difficulty is 'largely a matter of internal distribution and of a shortage of port intake capacity'; in other words, military needs are represented as exhausting the few existing facilities, and hungry Europeans must wait. Non-experts have no alternative but to accept this information, though it is difficult to believe that small ports and harbours, unsuitable for the landing

225

of heavy weapons and large quantities of military supplies, could not be sufficiently rehabilitated for the reception of comparatively small allocations of food-stuffs. 'Far more food', Colonel Llewellin tells us, 'has been set aside here for the relief of the liberated areas than the very small amount needed for the British extra fare at Christmas. . . . Let no one think that we have neglected our European allies, or that we have not set food aside for them. In fact the food for them and the food for our extra fare at Christmas are separate: and we are going to supply both. People in this country can take up their Christmas bonuses, which they have well deserved, without in any way feeling that they are doing so at the expense of the people of Europe.'

For those who are anxious to enjoy their luxuries without any sense of remorse, this statement is doubtless consoling. The *Manchester Guardian*, in a leading article on Nov. 15th entitled 'Fair Share For Christmas', estimated that the total amount of extras involved no more than 2,000 tons of basic food-stuffs. But among these extras are meat and margarine; and on Nov. 16th, at the first press conference held in London by ex-Governor Lehman, the Director General of UNRRA [United Nations Relief and Rehabilitation Administration], a Food Relief Campaign reporter ascertained in response to his questions that, although supplies of food-stuffs for UNRRA's relief work are sufficient in certain categories, there are serious deficiencies in some of the most vital needs, such as meat and fats. It is therefore significant that the Food Minister failed to satisfy Miss Rathbone's request for an assurance that the extra Christmas rations would not mean less food available for Europe.

But even if the food supplies now accumulated were adequate in every category, it is – to put the matter at its lowest moral level – extremely bad propaganda to indulge in luxuries while our neighbours in Europe (to say nothing of our political dependents in India) lack the necessities of life. And of the persistent shortage abundant evidence, both public and private, continues to pour in. On November 3rd, at a press conference held by the United Nations Information Organisation to correct misapprehensions about the needs of Europe, it was emphasised that France was suffering from prolonged malnutrition, particularly among the working classes. This was borne out in a private letter written to me on Oct. 18th by a friend who is a leading aircraftsman in the RAF, and was recently in the South of France. He had, he said, made friends with some French people in a large city, which I judged from internal evidence to be Lyons, and related that when, in exchange for a bottle of beer, he brought them some coffee and bully beef, 'they sat down and cried.' They thought that the troops were silly, he continued, to let such things go, for they themselves had not tasted coffee for four years, and their meat ration was about a quarter of a pound per month. 'Where it came from was doubtful, as I saw very few cattle.'

In Belgium, it was stated at the press conference, 40 per cent of the infantile population is undernourished, the main shortages being milk, butter and meat. The Belgians are asking UNRRA for special baby foods and medical supplies as well as linen for its hospitals. In Holland, according to the Netherlands Information Bureau, reported by the *Manchester Guardian* on Nov. 4th, the diet in the larger western towns has diminished to less than 1,000 calories a day. 'Margarine and butter supplies were completely exhausted by Nov. 1st. Bread grain was no longer available in Amsterdam after Oct. 23rd and in Haarlem after Oct. 30th. Sugar, where available in small quantities, is reserved for children up to four years.'

In view of this situation, the Food Relief Campaign of which I am chairman proposes to find out, by Parliamentary questions or alternative methods, whether it is a fact that civilian food reserves of five and a half million tons (as against the normal one and a half million tons) have been accumulated in Britain; whether we are still importing large quantities of food stuffs from overseas; and whether United Nations merchant shipping as well as British shipping is being used for this purpose. If so, we intend to ask whether the government will consider diverting the greater part of these supplies and shipping to Europe for three months to expedite the urgent task of relief, irrespective of the possibility that such a decision might curtail the rations available for civilian consumption in Britain.

If the reply is unsatisfactory, we believe that some gesture of renunciation, accompanied by an explanatory public statement, is called for with regard to our Christmas rations. Since (in view of official insistence that sufficient port accommodation and transport are not available) it would probably be useless to ask for the extra rations to be sent to Europe, one suggestion is that they should be given away as 'conscience gifts' to individuals especially in need of them, such as children, the aged, or patients in hospitals. These gifts would receive added significance if their purpose were explained to the shop where they were purchased, to the local Food Control Committee, to the Ministry of Food and to the Foreign Secretary. Already one children's hospital in London has expressed its willingness to receive gifts for its young patients offered on this basis.

As the *Times* letter which I have quoted points out, it is spiritually inappropriate to accept a national increase of rations while our allies starve. Already the British troops in Greece have gone on half rations in order to improve supplies for the Greek population. If men in the forces are forgoing luxuries so that their hungry neighbours may receive more necessities, civilians at home can hardly do less.

—— 28 December 1944 ——

No arts, no letters, no society, and which is worst of all, continuall fear and danger of violent death, and the life of man solitary, poore, nasty, brutish and short

— Thomas Hobbes, *Leviathan*, Chap. 18

The curtain descends upon 1944. After the brief flickering hopes of the early autumn, the prospect for the New Year answers more closely to Hobbes' famous description of primitive anarchy than any which Europe has known throughout its centuries of historic strife. Tragic chaos coupled with starvation confronts

228

the citizens of Greece and Poland; political unrest, under-nourishment and the destructive sway of military combat make life hideous in Italy and Belgium. Revolutionary conflicts following hard upon economic distress threaten every country which still awaits the appalling process of 'liberation'. In Germany, putting her last offensive energies into resistance to the bitter end, forced upon her by Allied policy, the conditions produced by three years of massacre bombing defy our imagination. If ever an international panorama justified those who maintained five and a half years ago that any alternative approach to outstanding dilemmas was better than modern war with its trail of gigantic devastation, this justification is provided by the European scene today.

The coming year, with its terrifying range of problems presented to puny man by the Nemesis of events which have passed beyond his control, demands of us that we take stock of the situation and try to understand its larger implications. What, for instance, has actually been happening in Greece? And how far does the condition of Europe as a whole relate to the chronological sequence of events in this storm centre of man's history?

Looking back upon that long and complex story, we see the perpetual conflict of the two major forces which shape human nature; the struggle of dominant power, enthroned privilege and entrenched reaction, against freedom, toleration, individuality and love. The farther we travel from our own day, the easier the recognition of these forces becomes. Hence we are accustomed to think, correctly, of Imperial Rome as embodying the one tendency, and of the early Christian Church as inspired by the other. But if we contemplate a period no more remote than the last century and a half, we can still clearly perceive the forces which we now call liberalism, struggling, despite setbacks, incongruities and Napoleonic imperialism, to express themselves through the French Revolution. Notwithstanding his personal autocracy, Napoleon carried so much of the revolution's ideology into the countries he conquered that it is debatable whether, in frustrating his attempt to unify Europe, Britain was not guilty of a major crime against European society. The

229

perpetuation of disunity meant that the revolutionary liberalism which dominated the nineteenth century was imperfectly realised, and therefore gave way before the growth of that counter-revolution against which Britain went to war in 1939.

If the counter-revolution had been represented solely by Nazi Germany and her satellites, our present ideological problem would still be as simple as it then appeared. Actually, the counter-revolutionary forces operate through every government or other authority which restricts the freedom of the individual to live, love, worship, meet, travel and communicate with his fellows as his conscience and aspirations dictate. This freedom is threatened by every totalitarian institution, and not least by the powerful government of Soviet Russia and the policies of her 'fellow travellers'.

Is there any part of the world, you may ask, in which liberal values still retain any real authority? They are probably strongest in the more progressive areas of the United States and, in spite of temporary German domination, in the Scandinavian countries. Liberalism is capable of early resurrection (though not necessarily in the shape of a political party) in Britain and in France; and it might ultimately be revived in Germany and Italy *provided that* material destruction followed by political chaos does not reach a point where all civilised standards are obliterated, as they were after the Thirty Years' War. 'Unconditional surrender' is a criminal demand because it first creates and then prolongs that condition of anarchy in which mental and spiritual re-creation becomes impossible.

Where liberalism is weak – either permanently as in the Balkans, or temporarily as in Britain – it tends to ally itself with the counter-revolutionary totalitarianism of the Left rather than with that of the Right. The reason is obvious; despotic power on the Left is embodied in tyrants who have arisen from the once oppressed masses while on the Right it perpetuates the older type of privilege which finds its symbolic figures in reactionary monarchs, aristocrats and oligarchs. This explains why the leaders of resistance movements have been so susceptible, especially in the Balkans, to the propaganda from Moscow, and

230

indicates why such normally honest and progressive British journals as the *News-Chronicle* and the *New Statesman* begin to suppress facts and excuse tyrannies as soon as they discuss the policy of the Soviet Union. Neither the one paper nor the other is likely to denounce the political cynicism of the 'deal' which gives Russia a free hand in Poland (for the defence of whose integrity the war nominally began) in return for similar advantages for Britain in Greece (which dominates the naval 'lifeline' cherished by traditional British imperialism).

Unfortunately for Britain, the bargain is unequal in so far as the British Right had little power to influence events in Poland, while the Russian Left (without saying or doing anything diplomatically 'incorrect') definitely influences large sections of the Greek population. The petulance displayed by Mr. Churchill in his unfortunate speech in the debate on Greece may well have been due to his consciousness of this inequality, to which his own dependence upon Stalin leaves him powerless to object.

One of the most disturbing features of this war has been the widespread popular forgetfulness of Mr Churchill's long political record, combined with equally widespread public dismay when, in crises such as that of the Greek uprising, he reveals himself as the personality that he has always been. Except for the followers of Lord Vansittart, who voluntarily delude themselves with an over-simple explanation of enormously complicated problems, the ordinary intelligent man knows that neither he nor, probably, anyone else can grasp the total moral and material implications of this total war. In five years he has learnt to recognise the half-truths and deceptive silences of the press and radio, but he knows that he has not sufficient information to pronounce accurate judgments on major issues. Sometimes, however, his insight and imagination atone for this inadequate knowledge, enabling him to formulate a dim but basically truthful idea of the apocalyptic character of this violent age.

Judging Mr Churchill solely by his record and his own utterances, it appears that he has not only failed to understand the deeper meaning of these days, but unlike the ordinary humble

231

man or woman, he is not even aware of his failure. With un-limited information at his disposal, he tends to mistake informa-tion for insight and military knowledge for wisdom. When the situation appears to demand it he can produce fine academic definitions of democracy, but his own attitude is closer to that of the so-called 'enlightened despots' of eighteenth century Europe, who were often more despotic than enlightened. Throughout this war he has been accepted by an admiring nation as the champion of the anti-fascist forces, but during the pre-war decade he was too closely and admittedly sympathetic to fascist leaders to be permanently mistaken for their natural opponent. He opposes only those forms of fascism which threaten his personal authority and that of the old-style British imperialism with which he has identified himself; and in this struggle for power he is ready to co-operate with the neo-imperialism of the Soviet Union, which in the necessarily short remainder of his lifetime is unlikely to threaten the out-dated Britain of his loyalties in the direct sense that Hitler's empire has threatened it. A lonely anachronistic figure perched on a mammoth pedestal from which unperceived by him, the tide of human progress has receded, he neither understands nor wishes to understand the character of the new forces pushing their way all over Europe from underground darkness into the light. He knows no more about the lives, loves, homes, hopes, aspirations and agonies of the 'poor plain people' than you and I know about the occupa-tional emotions of a termite.

In the recent elections to their National Executive by the Labour Party Conference, you may have perceived the begin-nings of a more rationally critical attitude towards Britain's wartime premier on the part of this hero-worshipping nation. Mr Churchill's most persistent and irreverent opponent, Aneurin Bevan, MP for Ebbw Vale, became one of the newly elected members of the Executive, while a profounder critic, Reginald Sorensen, the consistently pacifist Member for West Leyton and one of the best Christians in the House, came within two places of election.

We need not waste time and energy in condemning Mr

Churchill's misplaced flippancies and characteristic blindnesses; that task can safely be left to the inexorable long-range judgement of history. Our primary obligation is to interpret correctly the omens of our age, and to recognise and identify ourselves with every movement which will re-create at long last the status of human affections and the sacredness of individual life.

On 16 December 1944, when Allied victory seemed imminent, Field Marshal von Runstedt, having amassed twenty-four German divisions, launched an attack in the Ardennes between Monschau and Trier. The weather was bad and the Allies were taken completely by surprise. The Germans got as far as Dinant and the lost ground was not recovered until the end of January.

Meanwhile, the Russians were in Poland, East Prussia, and on the Oder, within fifty miles of Berlin.

In August 1944 delegates from UK, USA, USSR and the Republic of China met at Dumbarton Oaks Mansion, Georgetown, USA. They produced a hopeful document outlining an international organisation for the maintenance of peace and security after the war. It was a further step towards the formation of the United Nations Organisation.

Unless the positive inducements to peace predominate in the settlement, the outcome is much more likely to be war than peace. Peace-making is not a single act but a process, and if its goal is the establishment of a true security against war, its practical aim should be, not the stabilisation of non-war, but the creation of a co-operative human society from which the dispositions to war and aggression have been removed. . . . The paramount business of peace is the building up of the common life of the world.

– Peace Aims Leaflet No. 4 of the National Peace Council

The vast and dramatic sweep of the campaign on the Eastern front seems again to have precipitated this warring world on to the threshold of major conclusive events. Many people besides myself have doubted whether Mr Churchill and President Roosevelt – whose power is a wartime authority which is bound progressively to decline with the immediate change in the psychological atmosphere that the conclusion of hostilities in Europe will bring – really desire to see an early end to the war. But that Stalin wishes, and has always wished, for a conclusion as swift as it is decisive can hardly be questioned.

The continuation of Stalin's authority within the Soviet Union is one of those factors in the total situation upon which we can count. His enormous, under-developed empire has an unlimited future, and whatever plans he may have for ultimate Russian domination over Europe or any other part of the earth, he wants to get on with the great task of re-creating the political and economic life of the USSR. Hence, after careful and prolonged preparation, he is putting the whole of Russia's gigantic military strength into an effort to end the war against Germany.

Here in the West, where von Rundstedt's judiciously-timed offensive so long deprived the Allies of initiative, we await the outcome of events with little temptation to indulge in the too easy optimism of last autumn. Even without Hitler's vehement exhortations to resistance in his short speech of January 30th, we know now that the Nazi Reich, offered only the bankrupt

235

expedient of 'unconditional surrender', is unlikely to collapse in similar fashion to the Kaiser's Germany, which hopefully believed in the Fourteen Points as the basis of peace. Somehow, too, the conditions of this coldest of our six wartime winters have added to our scepticism. A victory mood is not induced by the persistent crashing of V-bombs on 'southern England', nor by the burst pipes, frozen drains and fireless hearths of a snow-bound countryside.

No doubt you will agree that these discomforts, in spite of their temporarily destructive effect upon work and concentration, have nevertheless their creative aspect. It is, for the most part, only through personal experience of hardship that our kindly but unimaginative people can enter with some measure of understanding into the present sufferings of famished, ill-clad, half-frozen Europe. As we read of those forty-mile columns of hungry refugees, bereft of homes and possessions, making their desperate way westward through bitter cold from the battle areas of Eastern Germany, and note the press reports which state that the German Red Cross cannot cope with all the resulting cases of frost-bite and exposure, it is difficult to believe that even in the hardest war-embittered hearts, compassion will not arise for the millions of suffering human beings included amongst our enemies.

'The refugees set out village by village and try to keep together as best they can,' runs one account given by the German Overseas News Agency and quoted by the *News-Chronicle* on Jan. 31st. 'They vary in size from small groups comprising only a few carts to giant queues stretching for 30 to 40 miles, straggling along with many thousands of vehicles. Grim winter weather is making things very difficult for them. Women, children, and aged persons are walking for hundreds of miles with scarcely a rest. Food for the horses is hard to find and the animals grow weaker every day. . . . Only a limited percentage of the refugees die on the way.'

But facing realistically the obstacles which impede the rebuilding of human values, we have to admit that many decent individuals who would normally be the first to help an unlucky

236

neighbour have been rendered impervious by five years' propaganda to the agonies even of the innocent. One example forced itself upon my attention the other day, when the occupants of a London restaurant were reading graphic accounts in the daily papers of grim scenes in the crowded railway stations of Berlin. An acquaintance of ours, the charming young mother of two small daughters whose husband is serving overseas, looked up from her newspaper and exclaimed with savage satisfaction: 'I'm so glad! It's only right they should suffer after what they've done to the Dutch and the Poles!'

So obviously did she expect my enthusiastic agreement, that I hardly hoped to make much impression by replying: 'But the trouble is, the people in the Berlin stations are not the ones who caused suffering in the occupied countries.' 'Yes . . . of course . . . that's true,' she said uncomfortably. Like so many other naturally gentle men and women, she had evidently never questioned the justice of that comprehensive 'they', or contemplated the possibility of discrimination between the most sadistic of the Nazi leaders, and the bewildered peasant children from Silesia and East Prussia.

It is this widespread, press-and-radio-created habit of thinking in 'stereotypes' that threatens, perhaps more than any other factor, the possible constructive evolution of the Dumbarton Oaks proposals and other power-inspired projects for peace. The young London mother was typical of thousands in her belief, fostered by Vansittart propaganda, that the main threat to a future world-order lies in the recurrence of German and Japanese aggression. Such a view springs from the failure of the Anglo-American peoples to grasp imaginatively the degree of devastation, chaos and exhaustion that we shall inevitably find in Central Europe after German resistance has ended. The longer that resistance continues, the greater will be the measure of anarchy and social barbarism when collapse does come. Even the bitter post-Armistice years will not compare with the appalling conditions that will then reveal themselves. They are more likely to resemble and even surpass, the consequences of the Thirty Years' War, which left Germany too stricken to contribute for 150 years to the culture of Europe, and too politically divided to achieve unity for more than two centuries.

If the tentative proposals made at Dumbarton Oaks for a general international organisation 'for the maintenance of peace and security' actually materialise in the form suggested, the threat of failure will arise from the unconstructive character of the proposals themselves. In the first place, the settlement as projected will be based upon the continued division of the nations into conquering and conquered – an arrangement which might not this time lead to the recrudescence of an exhausted Germany, but which would effectually prevent the growth of a democratic Germany and Japan to share in the building of the 'One World' of Wendell Willkie's creative vision. Secondly, the success of the proposals, even within the limits set, depends upon the continuing unity of three great powers whose capacity to develop, maintain and serve a common social purpose in which construction will gradually be substituted for coercion, has yet to be demonstrated.

We are again in the presence of mighty changes which, sooner or later, must lead to the turning of a decisive page of history. The period may be closer than we suppose in which the decisions taken will lead either to an enduring peace, or, within a measurable period, to a third world war. We need not wholly despair. The inevitable swing of the pendulum of opinion now lies in the not-too-distant future, and the cynical realism of mankind's present mood may prove, in the long run, a better specific for peace than the fervent post-Armistice idealism which so optimistically overlooked the baser tendencies of human nature and so signally failed to prevent them from leading direct to World War 2.

But it is useless to hope unless we also inform ourselves, and think – think with that clarity which alone enables politically and socially conscious minorities to assume the leadership of indifferent or lethargic majorities.

'The renunciation of national power and national sovereignty to the degree necessary to establish an effective system of international government remains a first condition of a valid peace', runs the leaflet quoted at the head of this letter. The future of mankind may well depend upon the speed with which those who care for true peace can ensure the acceptance of this idea by the peoples of the English-speaking democracies, and thus send their leaders to the future peace conference committed to the interpretation of a principle more organic than the barren maintenance of coercive power.

At the Crimea conference held at Yalta in February, the decisions taken at Teheran (see p.182) about the post-war spheres of influence in Eastern Europe were confirmed. Russia pledged support in the war against Japan although she did not actually declare war until six days before the Japanese surrender.

The San Francisco conference took place on 25 April when the constitution for the United Nations Organisation was drawn up.

The faith of Abraham ... who against hope believed in hope,
that he might become the father of many nations
– Romans IV, 16, 18

At the Crimea Conference the Big Three and their staffs met in
an oasis hastily reconstructed amid the ruin and desolation of
the South Russian battlefields. Here, according to a detailed
account of the conference arrangements in the *Sunday Express*
for Feb. 18th, their Russian hosts supplied them with rich food,
champagne cocktails and other luxuries, though millions of
people whose fate they were deciding lack the elementary
necessities of life.

We have now had time to read communiqués, hear statements, and reflect upon the work of this triumverate, whose
relationship comes more and more closely to resemble the Holy
Alliance of 1815. But at least their pronouncements are shorn of
the sanctimonious trappings which swathed the declarations
made by the rulers of post-Napoleonic Russia, Austria and
Prussia. The press has used the phrase 'sensible compromises' of
the Yalta decisions – though the retention of 'unconditional
surrender' hardly suggests a compromising spirit. It is at least
possible that early publication of the terms to be imposed would
save thousands of British, American and Russian lives. We know
too, that Germany, under the direction of a special Commission
which is to sit in Moscow, will be expected to make compensation 'in kind' for the damage that she has done – though
whether the massive air assaults of the Allies will leave her
anything to make it with seems doubtful.

Ever since 1914, most thinking people have been aware that
we of this generation are living at the end of that historical epoch
which began with the Renaissance and Reformation; and that
revolutionary changes beyond the comprehension of the
majority have brought tumbling about our heads the apparently
secure world into which those over 35 were born. Within three
decades two great wars have come, largely from the optimistic
belief that a simple method of restoring the lost comfort and

241

security could be found, and that the old happy conditions would re-emerge from the destruction of 'German militarism'.

The British people entered this war, like the last, inspired with those genuinely idealistic motives which persuaded the youth of two generations to take up arms contrary to their own interests and desires. In 1914, the fight was undertaken 'to make the world safe for democracy'. In 1939 it was joined, more simply, for 'freedom' – that freedom from 'fascist tyranny' which in itself was assumed to make possible the organisation of a peaceful human society. In both wars our realistic politicians had, of course, another motive, which was to prevent the political and economic domination of the Continent by a power stronger than Britain. An article recently published in USA by the American commentator, Bill Cunningham, quotes a reply given by Winston Churchill to a question asked him at a Chicago forum in 1938: 'Britain's policy has always been to support the second strongest power on the Continent.' The commentator explains that this policy was put into writing and practised by Canning, but was first enunciated by Cardinal Wolsey, who said in 1513: 'In Europe never throw your power to the side of the strong, but create disunity, create a balance of power by siding with the weak.'

What so far are the actual results of this war, fought by British soldiers for freedom, and by British politicians to maintain the balance of power? Already, I think, we can see four main consequences: (1) The establishment of USA as economically the strongest power in the world – an outcome fortunate perhaps for America, though we must remember that, in economics as in politics, 'absolute power corrupts absolutely', and also arouses the envy of potential rivals; (2) The reduction of the British Empire to a second-rate and of Britain herself to a third-rate power; (3) The transformation of a continent which possessed the finest treasures left by centuries of culture to a condition of ruin, hunger and misery, from which modern civilisation – largely based on a transport system now almost totally destroyed – may have disappeared for a generation or even longer; (4) The domination of that continent, for better for worse, by Soviet

Russia. Britain's fight for 'freedom' has only succeeded in replacing one totalitarian power by another, which may have notable lessons to teach the western world, but is hardly the 'democracy' for which British and American soldiers have died in their thousands. Nothing can prevent that domination, for there is now no 'second strongest power' for Britain to support except France, who has already made her own arrangements with the Soviet Union.

I do not think that any of these results were foreseen by Mr Churchill when he made himself the head of our resistance movement in 1940. They might have been foreseen, for they lay in the logic of history – the more conspicuously after Russia began to repel the Nazi invasion. But Mr Churchill failed to foresee them because, except as an author, he is a man without prophetic vision. He has fought this war without any plan or policy but that of destroying Germany. For this blindness England, and Europe, will pay a heavy price.

As we look towards the San Francisco Conference, can we find in such a picture any grounds for hope? I believe that there are several possible grounds, and I want to conclude this letter by mentioning them briefly for your further consideration. First, despite its lack of far-sightedness and the disappointments which its 'sensible compromises' provide for the more idealistic, the Yalta Conference does seem to have been marked by a genuine desire to reach agreement, and by the realisation that disunity between the three powers which have taken the fate of mankind in their hands will mean the eclipse of civilisation. Divisions doubtless existed behind the optimistic façade, and sometimes, as *The Observer* remarked on Feb. 18th, 'the agreement is in the words rather than in the matter'; but there appears to have been less disunity than some of us had feared.

Secondly, President Roosevelt has committed his country to post-war co-operation with her allies to the limit of which he is capable; and judging by an article entitled 'US Swept by Elation' from F.G.A. Cook in the *Evening Standard* for Feb. 17th this commitment is welcomed by the majority of the American people.. Thirdly, a growing determination in USA to pursue a wise and constructive policy towards the Soviet Union may save Britain from becoming the France of a third world war, and mankind from the threat of such a war altogether. The two greatest world powers are both young countries with immense resources awaiting fuller development, and being divided from each other by two great oceans and a continent, there is no obvious reason why their interests should clash.

Fourthly, I see ultimate good for Europe from the end of the balance of power policy which has divided her for centuries. Domination by Russia may mean a period of persecution for several unhappy countries and peoples; but tyranny shows itself most virulent against opposition. Without an effective opponent, tyrannical regimes are apt to undergo a gradual process of self-modification, and Russia has too much to do in rebuilding and developing her resources to be interested for long years in making war upon any neighbour who does not actually threaten her.

Finally, as civilisation is slowly re-created in Central Europe, the forcible disarmament of Germany – likely this time to be maintained – may prove to be a great constructive experiment which others will want to copy. Once reparations are paid, a re-educated Germany free to spend her national income on education, music, painting, social reform and scientific discovery, might serve as a valuable object-lesson to great powers with no ostensible reason to maintain armaments against one another. An agreement to renounce the use of the bombing aeroplane and of mechanical bombs might come relatively soon after a full realisation of the horrors to which these have led. The fact that the Poison Gas Convention of 1925 has been kept despite the obvious advantages that chemical warfare would have given to some belligerents, suggests that we need not be unduly sceptical over the observation of a convention about bombing.

These are dreams, but they are not mere wishful-thinking, for they are all capable of realisation even in the tragic world that exists. The one thing needed is the will to realise them, the determination to make the coming peace vital and organic rather than vengeful and repressive. It is to the creation of this will that every peace-lover in every land should dedicate himself in the few weeks that precede the San Francisco Conference.

— 19 April 1945 —

Let the fearful be allowed to hope (Liceat sperare timenti)
— Lucan, *De Bello Civili*, Bk. II, c. 14

I write you at the end of a fortnight in which no bombs of any kind have fallen on London. You too, if you are a Londoner have perhaps experienced with me a strange sense of mingled exhaustion and exultation, comparable to convalescence after a dangerous illness, yet still combined with the automatic habit of listening, and of concern for relatives in other parts of 'Southern England', which in varying degrees five years of bombardment must have created in us all. But doubtless you also share the consciousness that our relief – if not yet complete freedom – from fear is a small thing compared with the knowledge that the tragic Dutch are nearer to release from starvation; and that London's approaching final exodus from the firing line should tempt us to no feeling of inhuman triumph over our opponents whose bombs killed 60,000 of our fellow citizens and intermittently made hideous our own days and nights. Our liberation should cause us the more penitently to remember the far more terrible sufferings that our leaders have inflicted in our name, with so little opposition from the bulk of our population.

Today we know that devastation and the complete breakdown of law and order has reduced to chaos the huge industrial centres of the Ruhr, the historic cities of Münster and Frankfurt in which Goethe's house has been destroyed, and the great capital city of Hanover, where war-maddened German civilians wildly looted one another's property. Of Essen the *Daily Herald* war reporter, Charles Bray, wrote on April 12th from the once magnificent office of Professor Eric Mueller inside the wreckage of Krupp's: 'Industrial life has stopped. All other life may end, too, if we are not very careful with disease sweeping the ruins.'

245

The previous Sunday the leader-writer of *The Observer* commented significantly: 'There is something vaguely threatening in the very completeness of the catastrophe which is overwhelming our main enemies. Over vast areas of Europe we see every element both of material civilisation and of political order and cohesion disappear before our eyes. Nothing like it has happened in the many wars of European history. Clearly the consequences of such a cataclysmic event are somewhat beyond calculation. One certain thing is that great care will be needed to prevent them from provoking, merely by their shattering impact and the upsetting of every balance of power, a new world crisis.'

A further horror now overwhelming Europe recalls to my mind a novel that I read some dozen years ago, *Lest Ye Die*, by Cicely Hamilton, who prophetically described the barbaric phenomenon known as 'displacement of population' due to total war. In the *Daily Herald* of April 10th, an article by its war correspondent, Iris Carpenter, read like a chapter from Cicely Hamilton's story. Under the title 'Slaves Wreak Their Vengeance On Their Way Home', she described the spectacle of eight 'angry, dirty, rough men' ransacking a clean and comely little house in a village between Kirchain and Marburg, while 'in the street outside a couple of German hausfraus stood crying and wringing their hands as first chairs, then china dishes, curtains, cushions were flung from windows into the road beside them.'

'Who', she inquires 'were these bandits – for that is exactly what they are?' and goes on to explain that these 'displaced persons' are part of an army of twelve to thirteen million Poles, Russians, Czechs, French, Dutch, Belgians, Norwegians and Danes, who have spent years in concentration camps and prisons, and in farms and factories as 'slaves' of the German people. In spite of military orders to 'stand fast', these men and women make for the already crowded roads as soon as they are free, and live by terrorising the civilian population into giving them food. A similar article by the *News-Chronicle* war correspondent, William Forrest, on April 11th, gave one explanation for this anarchic avalanche; the leaflets issued by the Ninth Army ordering these displaced persons to remain where they are

246

until their repatriation can be organised were printed in English, French, Polish and German, but not in Russian. 'We have not been able to find any Russian printing type,' the Military Government Officer at Army Headquarters explained to William Forrest. If we had not his word for it, this monstrous example of inefficiency would seem like the far-fetched invention of some incredible fantasy. Because no one thought of flying some Russian type to the Western front, or even of sending it to Britain in one of the supply ships returning empty from Russia, the agony of dying Europe is increased by the bewildered wanderings of millions of starving and penniless Russian workers. Yet I myself – presumably because I once signed a letter to the press supporting the lifting of the ban on the *Daily Worker* – regularly receive from Moscow innumerable news-papers and illustrated magazines printed in English!

According to the regulations, these unhappy nomads are cared for first by the burgomasters of the German towns and villages through which they pass, and then by displacement camps in the rear of the armies. At Bonn camp alone, 18,000 DPs a day are being 'processed'. But, admits Iris Carpenter, 'the truth is that, with our advance moving at its present pace, we just have not enough Military Government officials or police in the amount of territory we hold adequately to take care of the problem arising. . . . Why don't we keep them where they are until we can handle their trek back? We try to, but by the time forward troops have moved on to the next objective and other troops can move up to take over policing duties, DPs are well on their way. It is a way which is exacting a price from the German people which the Allied victorious armies as such would never expect them to pay. These nomadic tribes of liberated peoples straggling their way back to civilisation are reducing the civilisa-tion of Germany in their passing to something like that of the middle ages.'

In the similar account given by William Forrest, he reminds us that after the last war Russia was overrun by bands of homeless children whom it took years to round up and recivilise. 'We do not want that sort of thing as an aftermath of this war,' he observes. We do not want it, but we – and especially the Americans – are getting it. William Forrest describes how one American officer who spoke only English was called upon to deal with 9,000 Russians in one liberated camp. 'Six doctors are all that is available to visit the assembly camps where almost every man and woman needs medical attention. This will never do and the army knows it.'

The war correspondents in general seem to take the view that 'the Germans are only getting the retribution they deserve' and do not emphasise the obvious fact that the helpless women whose homes are ransacked are not the Nazi leaders whose ruthless orders enslaved the foreign workers. To say (as Patrick Kirwan said in the *Evening Standard* of April 11th) that all Germans are responsible for Hitler's atrocities is to descend to a morality as primitive as the conditions to which war has reduced the once splendid civilisation of Europe. Patrick Kirwan made the now common accusation that no Germans protested against Hitler's actions – an indictment to which the final section, 'Christianity Speaks', of our anthology, *Above All Nations*, gives the lie in terms of irrefutable evidence. Here, for example, are the protests of such leading German prelates as the bishops of Münster and Berlin, the archbishop of Cologne and Cardinal Faulhaber of Munich, as well as similar courageous acts by lesser men and women pastors. As for the common man, how do we know on what scale he protested? We only know that for twelve years the voices of such brave protestants have been silenced in concentration camps – or in the grave.

The *News-Chronicle* editorial 'Wanderers' (April 11th) faces more responsibly 'the shipwreck of humanity on a scale only comparable to those wanderings of dispossessed nations which followed the fall of Rome. It continues, 'The parallel is a close one. Europe is threatened with a return to the conditions of the Dark Ages. . . . This Army of the dispossessed is an Allied responsibility. We have come to Europe as liberators. Liberation can have no meaning if one of its effects is an intensification of human misery.'

You and I probably agree that the persons most responsible

are the war leaders of the nations; not Hitler only, but all those who, to enlarge and maintain their temporal – and hence temporary – power, have relentlessly sacrificed the lives of millions and destroyed the cultural heritage of centuries. If we are honest, we shall surely now admit that not one of the possible alternatives to war which our leaders rejected in and before 1939, could have brought so terrible a fate to so large a proportion of mankind and to its habitations. Compared with their responsibility, the conscripted youth to which they gave *carte blanche* to wreak havoc to the limits of its technical skill, is innocent indeed. Yet because the infliction of suffering cannot leave the performer immune, these instruments of their policy will have to pay a price the physical and psychological extent of which we cannot yet calculate.

A German exile living in England sends me a report (from the *News-Chronicle*) of an atrocity devised by our own troops in Japan: 'Medieval warfare methods are being used to drive the Japs out of tunnels beneath the pagodas on Mandalay Hill. This morning our men rolled down barrels filled with petrol with the bungs out and then threw grenades into them. The first of these handmade explosive firebombs burned 11 Japs to death.' She concludes her letter with an appropriate and soul-searching question: 'How are these men – sons, brothers, lovers – who have to do these things, coming back to you? How are the airmen, who release showers of death from the skies, going to fit into all our beautiful plans for a better future? Will planned houses, garden cities and public libraries *mean* anything to them? . . . No reconstructed houses and planned cities will be of any use if we have no plans for reconstructing the minds of those, whose one aim for years on end has had to be to kill and destroy. Have we any plans for this? Have we any plans for "switching over" from the propaganda of hate to a propaganda of love? Have the churches? Have even we, who call ourselves pacifists?'

249

The mightier man, the mightier is the thing
That makes him honour'd, or begets him hate.
                    — Shakespeare, *The Rape of Lucrece*

When the death of President Roosevelt was announced to the world on Friday, April 13th – an ill-omened date which for once justified the apprehensions of the superstitious – you must have felt, as I did, that the Allied cause had suffered a blow equivalent to defeat in a major campaign. Even Tokio radio acknowledged the measure of the disaster which had befallen Japan's enemies by introducing a short programme of music 'to honour the passing of this great man'.

Roosevelt was unquestionably, and deservedly, a titanic figure, worthy to stand beside Washington and Lincoln in the Valhalla of history. His ends were noble; the differences between him and his pacifist or near-pacifist critics were mainly those of means. Believing as he did in the expedients and subterfuges of power-politics, it was inevitable that he should deliberately lead his country stage by stage from neutrality through 'non-belligerency' to war. Probably even before his famous speech in the autumn of 1937 urging 'quarantine' for aggressors he had seen hostilities against the Axis as the ultimate course which America would take.

For many individuals, such as myself, sincere grief for Roosevelt's loss must be heightened by this fundamental difference regarding methods of deciding international problems, and also by a measure of personal acquaintance. In December, 1937, I had the privilege – rarer for Britons than for American citizens – of talking to Franklin Roosevelt for fifteen minutes alone in his study at the White House. This conversation, which turned on the contemporary international scene, revealed to me how well-founded was his reputation for charm, benevolence, and that unerring graciousness which sets the humblest acquaintances at their ease. My interview followed a White House luncheon to which I had been invited by his equally remarkable wife. Among those who really knew her, it was an open secret that Eleanor Roosevelt's views were more revolutionary than her husband's. At least part of her considerable lecture earnings were reliably reported to have been given away to the American Friends Relief Service. Many people in USA must be speculating whether she will express her opinions now that she is free to do so, and become a major political figure in her own right.

For a man of Franklin Roosevelt's courage and vitality – so great that it enabled him to master a crippling disease and in spite of it do more than twice the work of most public men – the power to project himself into the situation created by his own death must have been well-nigh unattainable. Some of his critics have asserted that this failure of responsible imagination led him to sacrifice as Vice-President the brilliant, idealistic Henry Wallace, who would have been a comparable successor, to Harry S. Truman the unknown farmer from the state of Missouri in the Deep South whose fulfilment of the cherished 'log-cabin to White House' tradition could hardly be more typical.

But since Roosevelt's death there has been a tendency in some sections of the press – such as the *Observer*, *New Statesman* and *News-Chronicle* – to suggest that this tragedy, which at first seemed so unmitigated, may do more to ensure America's contribution to the organisation of world peace, than the great President's continued survival. Already there is evidence – such as Stalin's consent to send Molotov to San Francisco – that exponents of viewpoints not wholly compatible with those of USA may do more out of piety towards Roosevelt dead than they would have done for Roosevelt living.

President Truman – a mild-mannered, honest, popular man – has none of the enemies whom the dominant, aristocratic Roosevelt inevitably accumulated in twelve years of office. His conscientiousness has led him faithfully to assume the unsought burdens thrust upon him; his modesty will induce him to accept advice; and the qualities which he shares with the common man may make him a leading representative rather than a representative leader. Not only the Senate, which owing to his recent membership and his popularity may grant him concessions which Roosevelt would not have received, but Congress and the American people have obviously rallied to Mr Truman in his predicament, and are determined to do what they can to help him. Whatever the instalment of world organisation created at San Francisco, it may well be seen and accepted as a national popular achievement, rather than as the one-man accomplishment that it would have appeared under Roosevelt.

If this occurs, there will never have been so dramatic a demonstration that not even the most eminent of men is indispensable. It may even be that Churchill and Stalin will accept a salutary reminder that the plans of the great to dominate their neighbours are subject to their own mortality.

There remains the question of what will indeed be achieved at San Francisco, that city which – with the possible exception of Seattle, less familiar to Europeans – is the loveliest of America's many beautiful cities. Picturing my husband at work there amid the galaxy of special correspondents from many nations, I remember seeing the Golden Gate exactly as it should be seen, looking from the train straight across to the Pacific between the twin columns of the famous bridge, with the flaming bars of sunset cloud above them, and the deep blue skyline of the city away to the left. Today that Golden Gate of San Francisco has become a symbol of the New Jerusalem, the Promised Land, in which the war-weary nations would all gladly walk, though their notions of the route thither are as devious as themselves. Writing you now on the actual day that the Conference opens, my knowledge is no better than that of the many newspaper prophets who are so busy with their predictions, and I may be unable to give you any 'inside' story until my husband returns.

One of the best-informed and most interesting pre-views of the Conference appeared in an article by Dr Felix Morley, President of Haverford College, Pennsylvania, in the *Wall Street Journal* for March 8th. In this article Dr Morley inquires whether the San Francisco Conference will take its cue from the 'League of Equals' approved in the Act of Chapultepec on March 3rd by the delegates of twenty American republics at the Inter-American Conference held in Mexico City, or the 'Alliance of Overlords' foreshadowed at Yalta. Far too little is known in Britain about this important American Conference and its resultant document, which correctly described itself as a positive 'act' to improve international amity and minimise aggression in the western hemisphere. For those interested in knowing more about a Declaration morally far superior to that of Yalta, by which 'the juridical equality of all sovereign states was specifically affirmed and a definite programme laid down under which treatment like that accorded Poland would be impossible', the Union of Democratic Control has recently issued a detailed Report of the Mexico City proceedings, obtainable from 34 Victoria Street, SW1 price 6d.

'The virtual coincidence of the Yalta and Mexico City declarations', says Dr Morley, 'emphasises a truly extraordinary situation. The United States is at one and the same time taking leadership in an effort to form a world-dominating Triple Alliance and a co-operative though limited American League of Nations. We seek to control by sheer force in Europe and the Orient while agreeing to, indeed urging, a wholly democratic and legalistic order in the Americas.

'This is a revelation of political schizophrenia and it is to be doubted that even President Roosevelt can indefinitely ride with a foot on the back of two so divergent steeds. Indeed, there are already signs that at San Francisco we shall have to define clearly whether our objective in post-war organisation is a league of equals in which we co-operate as such, or an alliance of overlords in which we intend to dominate by virtue of our material power.'

Despite such basic inconsistencies and the fact that a cynical and disillusioned world does not hope from San Francisco what mankind hoped from Geneva, there is general agreement that the complete failure of the conference would be a disaster outweighing all others. To quote Dr Morley again – this time from the newsletter *Human Events* for March 14th – 'we are engaged in a race to attain some degree of world order before the release of new factors of disorder which must be anticipated when German, and later Japanese, control is finally broken.'

If this race is not won by the protagonists of order, it has become increasingly clear that chaos will prevail in the political vacuum which was Europe. The greater the chaos, the better the chance of power again falling to those elements of sadistic gangsterism responsible for mass murder and concentration camps. Amid the outbreak of horror which the conditions found in these camps have produced, it is necessary to remember that not only German civilians but, between 1933 and 1939, many responsible British politicians ignored their cruelties, despite warnings by such reliable refugees as the well-known Quaker, Dr Richard Ullmann – who was himself in Buchenwald, and on April 23rd reminded the *Evening Standard* readers in a well-balanced letter of his attempts to reveal the terrible truth.

I believe that the discoveries made in these camps are now being given so much space in the press partly, at least, in order to divert public attention from the havoc produced in German cities by Allied obliteration bombing. First described with dismay by war correspondents, the extent of the death and devastation wrought by our bombers was beginning to penetrate the mind of the ordinary citizen. I was recently in a cinema at Southampton – one of the worst wrecked of Britain's smaller cities – when a picture showing the nightmare ruins of Hanover appeared on the screen. An immediate gasp of horror arose from that damage-accustomed audience.

In the neighbourhood of the camps, ignorantly complacent German citizens have rightly been compelled by Allied commanders to tend the victims of their accepted regime. Similar visual instruction in the consequences of war might well be extended to the representatives of safe areas in Britain whose residents demanded the reprisal bombing of Germany. In Hamburg, for instance, though time has doubtless erased much evidence of the agonising deaths of those citizens, roasted alive in shelters, whose estimated numbers vary from 50,000 to 250,000, the aftermath of inferno will still be there on a scale even greater than in Hanover. The guilt of national leaders may not be equal, but not one can wholly disclaim a share. Without repentant humility and the repudiation of hypocrisy and self-righteousness, the foundations of a better international society will not be laid at San Francisco or anywhere else.

—— 17 May 1945 ——

Longumque illud tempus, quum non ero, magis me movet quam hoc exiguum
(I care more for that long age in which I shall not be, than for my small share of time)
— Cicero, *Ad Atticum*, Book 12, Letter 18

Nearly twenty-five years ago, in a book of essays entitled *The Evolution of World Peace*, I first read, quoted by F.S. Marvin, the words which stand at the head of this letter. From the end of the first European war until this moment of writing at the conclusion of the second, they have given meaning and purpose to everything that I have tried to write and to say. I quote them again now because you and I are clearly being given a second chance to create a new society in which our children can walk unafraid. We are privileged in belonging to a nation that, through a series of unlikely historic phenomena rather than by the skill of its leaders, has been spared the worst devastations of war. Left by that war too weak for international domination, Britain is still strong enough to give a moral lead to the world if she chooses. And her choice is yours and mine; we are part of the public opinion which decides what future road she will tread.

Since I last wrote to you, we have all been swept forward by the overwhelming current of events. The final disintegration of the German armies throughout Europe seemed hardly to be interrupted by the summary execution of Mussolini and the reported death of Hitler. Innumerable attempts to forecast the final hours of these world-dominating personalities have been made during the past decade, but not one of the prophets ventured to predict that, within three critical weeks, Roosevelt, Hitler and Mussolini would vanish from the stage. Yet even the sensational coincidence of their exodus – so grandly dignified in the one case, so brutally ignominious in the others – was soon submerged in the cumulative story of German chaos, defeat and surrender. As I listened, in Parliament Square at 3 pm on May 8th, to Mr Churchill's voice proclaiming the end of hostilities in Europe, it was inevitable that I should compare the 'unconditional surrender' of 1945 with the Armistice celebrations that I witnessed, also at Westminster, on November 11th, 1918.

I was glad, on this day of thanksgiving as on the last, to be standing with the crowd on the pavement; that humble position seemed to symbolise the common experience of the Briton and the Londoner which, despite all divergencies of political opinion, I have sought throughout the war to accept. But there, I felt, the resemblance ended. This time the nightmare was not wholly past; even before the Prime Minister reminded the listening throng of the unfinished struggle with Japan, other mothers besides myself must have wondered whether the sons whom they had watched grow from little boys of 11 and 12 to the verge of manhood could count on a future. And, apart from that main difference, there were others. In spite of the flags, bells and ribbons, the bombers circling low over Westminster Abbey, the warm May sunshine struggling through thunder-clouds, and the sense of danger departed which at the Armistice London hardly knew, the occasion lacked the spontaneity of that unstaged outburst of relief which transfigured the drizzly gloom of November, 1918, into an exuberant festival.

Perhaps something of anti-climax entered into those carefully-arranged official celebrations, delayed for 24 hours after we all knew that the war had ended. Perhaps the individuals who composed the orderly, good-tempered London crowds were still a little dazed by years of anxiety and noisy peril, and by the sheer pressure of consecutive events. During the past few weeks I, for one, have had the sense of being continually banged on the head with a very large bludgeon. Listening, on Sunday, April 29th, to the gruesome details of Mussolini's end being given in suave tones by the BBC announcer of the midnight news, I found myself disturbed by the fact that I reacted so little. Having spent nearly six years in the attempt to keep the sensibilities of others alive, had I ended by losing my own capacity for horror and pity?

Surely now, even more than during the recent nightmare, it is vital that you and I should retain the power to feel. Certainly it is less important than the power to think, but both faculties are essential parts of that awareness of which the lack, among the common peoples of the world, contributed so largely to this war and the last. In *The Meaning of History*, Nicolas Berdyaev remarks that it is only experience of historical failure that has proved fruitful, in the sense that the consciousness of humanity has thereby been increased. If this is indeed a fact, it represents the chief and perhaps the only compensation for those periods of historical failure known as modern war, which arise from political unconsciousness, and from the blind absorption of men and women in their own affairs until, too late for the individual to arrest the process, public and private worlds become disastrously one. That is why I see the main task of peace-makers in the years before us as the increase of human consciousness, and a gradual reduction in the numbers of those self-regarding citizens who accelerate catastrophe by their non-perception.

Let us not forget that Dante, the creator of a spiritual cosmos, put the sinners guilty of *accidia* – that quality of indifference which performs neither good nor evil – in one of the lowest circles of his *Inferno*. How many of us, rejoicing on V-E Day in our relief rather than our victory remembered its reverse side and spared a thought for the agony of the German people, twice condemned to defeat and humiliation, mourning for a second time the vainly-spilt blood of their sons? How many who blame these unhappy civilians for their failure to prevent the appalling horrors of Belsen, Buchenwald and Dachau, cared for the sufferings of the Germans who occupied those camps before 1939? How many struggled against official obstacles in our own and other countries to save some Jewish citizen from the fate of the victims whose dead or emaciated bodies we have seen on the news-reels? How many have reason to repent of indifference towards the inhabitants of British slums and prisons?

Yet the very men and women whose political unconsciousness

257

made war possible proved capable, when it came, of rising to superb heights of fortitude and faith. Amid the disillusionment with which, in contrast to the ardent idealism born of the 1918 Armistice, the peoples of the world regard the San Francisco discussions and the possibility of organising world peace, there is a real danger that we may underrate the capacity of the common man to build a new heaven and a new earth. Surely no aspect of 'awareness' is now more important than the realisation that fortitude and faith will be demanded even more urgently for the future life of Europe than by the war just past. The one lesson above all others which these dark years have taught us is that man needs a new conception of human relationships, and a new vision of national and international society; that he can build a finer and more lasting civilisation only by practising a new code of behaviour in which he learns not to take but to give, not to blame but to pity, not to punish but to redeem, not to hate but to love.

And if you remind me, as you well may, that this code of behaviour is not new but two thousand years old, I can only reply that human society is still waiting for its application, and that nothing but its application will transform the subconscious deathward drift of this age into a conscious affirmation of spiritual and moral purpose. For me the first Great War, imping-ing upon the unformed values of immaturity, left behind it the doubt of a divine architect in human affairs. The second, with all its tragedy, its cruelty and its insanity, has at least removed that doubt. Like the girl martyr in the play *Glorious Morning*, 'I know that God lives'; I believe without reservation in His exist-ence, which so many men have denied, and in His laws, which we have all disobeyed. That disobedience, often deliberate, brought us by ever swifter stages to the tragedy of violence and destruction which has just concluded. We of this generation could not have been vouchsafed a clearer lesson that only a different way of living – the way laid down in the Gospels – will bring a different result.

Those of us who claim no share in the military victory of our forces can at least dedicate ourselves, today and for the rest of our lives, to working for the spiritual victory of human society, even though it lie far ahead beyond the distant centuries of that 'long age' in which we shall not be. There, and there only, rests the true goal of undaunted courage; the Jerusalem built by that extension of consciousness known to Blake as 'mental fight'; the Kingdom of God to be entered by those who believe with St Francis of Assisi that

> It is in giving that we receive;
> It is in pardoning that we are pardoned;
> It is in dying that we are born to eternal life.

President Roosevelt asserted in his State of the Nation address to the American people as long ago as 6 January 1941 that there are four essential freedoms: freedom of speech and worship and freedom from want and fear.

Fear of danger is ten thousand times more terrifying than danger itself, when apparent to the eyes; and we find the burden of anxiety greater, by much, than the evil which we are anxious about

– Daniel Defoe, *Robinson Crusoe*

When President Roosevelt, in defining the Four Freedoms, produced the most famous slogan of this war, he rightly put freedom from fear in the list. Fear is the source of all other evils, and the real enemy to be overcome. It creates the conditions which bring want and intolerance: it is the origin of hatred, cruelty, deceit, and even of that self-righteousness which conceals lack of confidence in our own virtues by loudly proclaiming their merits. Only when fear is banished do love, humility, kindness and patience find a real chance to grow.

In so far as the European war was fought to achieve freedom from fear, it has proved a grotesque failure. All it has done is to shift fear from one quarter to another. Every war is inevitably followed by domestic fear – fear of unemployment, of homelessness, of private relationships impaired by separation – but today, unlike 1919, international fears comparable to those which grew with the growth of Hitlerism persist as well. The colossal shadow cast by Russia's unknown and apparently unfathomable intentions lies even darker across the European chaos than the thunder-clouds of the 'little war' in Syria and Lebanon, which blew up largely owing to the fear-based inferiority-complex of General de Gaulle.

The past two weeks, and indeed the whole period since V-E Day, have not improved the tone of the intercourse between Russia and her major allies. Even in pro-Soviet newspapers and journals, such as the *News-Chronicle*, *Evening Standard* and *New Statesman*, we read reluctant references to Russian unilateral action in Poland and Austria; to the Russian refusal to admit newspaper correspondents to Soviet-occupied territories; to Russian intransigence regarding the powers for vetoing the discussion of disputes by the World Organisation, which almost caused complete breakdown at the San Francisco Conference; and finally to the differences between Russian and Anglo-American policy in the administration of Occupied Germany.

Whatever analysis of Russian motives in Germany we may be tempted to make, it seems clear that here, at least, a marked superiority in commonsense and foresight is characteristic of Soviet methods. *The Times* leading article on June 4th pointed out that while the Americans are warning the population of Western Germany that rations are to be reduced to a bare subsistence level insufficient to maintain health and energy, the Russians (who certainly dominate the most fertile German areas) are holding out hopes to Berlin of better rations than its people received in the last days of Hitlerism. Secondly, the Russians are already attempting to set German industry on its feet, while 'few signs of any set purpose or policy have been reported' from the Anglo-American areas.

Finally, the Russians are making reassuring gestures of friend-ship to the non-Nazi masses of the German people, while the British and American commanders have so far maintained a rule of non-fraternisation. This, says *The Times* (whose leader-writer apparently agrees with the packed audience at the Central Hall, Westminster, on May 30, when a suggestion that the non-fraternisation order ought to be revised was loudly applauded), 'is ultimately the antithesis of any principle of sound admini-stration as well as of any sane policy of "re-education", and will certainly prove untenable for any length of time.' According to an article on June 3rd in the *Sunday Express* (which can hardly be accused of pro-German sympathies) the rule has proved untenable already. 'I have seen it broken almost hourly through-out Germany and Austria,' wrote the author, Edward J. Hart, war reporter with the 12th Army Group at Wiesbaden. 'I am convinced', he added from his commonsense knowledge of ordinary – and decent – human nature, 'that it will go on being broken.' On June 5th the political correspondent of the *News-Chronicle* reported that 'our troops may fraternise a little'. 'It has been found impossible', he said, 'to enforce the rule against the troops having anything to do with German children.' One can only add that if this had not proved impossible, our troops would be the inhuman monsters which happily they are not. Whoever supposed that the kindly British and the friendly Americans could be made to ostracise innocent children, is in dire need of re-education himself.

Before this letter is printed, the co-ordination achieved by the recent meeting between Eisenhower, Montgomery and Zhukov, may have eliminated the burden of a foolish regulation which provoked bad discipline by inviting disobedience. But though a plan for greater co-operation in the administration of Germany has emerged from the meeting of the military commanders, the tension produced by the conflict between Eastern and Western political and economic principles is not so easily disposed of. Only the utmost vigilance by men and women of good-will in Britain and America can prevent Russia from rapidly replacing Germany as that 'guilty nation', whose 'threats' justify the retention and increase of existing armaments.

During the recent German war some pacifist journals were wont to emphasise the similarity of German and Russian ideology and behaviour, and *Peace News* especially was criticised for its 'anti-Russian' outlook. The object of these Nazi-Communist comparisons was not, I imagine, to provoke anti-Soviet sentiments, but to illustrate, in the interests of truth, the narrowness of the moral gulf which divided allies and enemies. War thrives on hypocrisy, and to expose hypocrisy is one method of undermining and weakening those war-making elements which find one of their strongest weapons in the gullibility of the politically-unconscious public.

But once a war is over, the purpose of peace-makers is not so much to expose hypocritical propaganda, as to perceive and if possible arrest the growth of the factors making for a new conflict. Hence it is now vital that the people of this country should at once pursue three none-too-easy objectives. First, having seen that war does not eradicate but merely transfers the exercise of totalitarian power, they should make up their minds that under no circumstances whatsoever will they allow themselves to be persuaded that war is the right way to 'smash'

263

Russian ambitions; and that the modification of nationalistic dictatorship, undeniably desirable as it is, can only be achieved by other and more civilised methods. Secondly and thirdly, they should explore these civilised methods.

The first of these is to understand the reasons for Russian behaviour, and the natural fears and suspicions in which it originates; the second is to build up mutual confidence on the basis of that understanding. I do not pretend that either of these objectives is simple when the country concerned is distant, enormous and unfamiliar, with a population made up of over 200 separate peoples whose habits, languages and standards of education differ from one another as well as being widely different from our own. The present Russian policy of limiting the travels of its own nationals and closing its barriers to all but a tiny percentage of visitors from other nations, adds to the current obstacles. Nevertheless, there are practical means of setting out to achieve understanding and build confidence which, if practised on a large enough scale, would themselves modify Russia's own variety of 'non-fraternisation'.

First, the study of Russian history, literature and political theory will explain much that is puzzling in the Russian character. From past history we learn that the Soviet Union's suspicions and alarms derive from the number of invaders who have sought benefits for themselves from Russia's fertile lands and undeveloped mineral resources. More recent history shows us that the 'violent hands' which Mr Churchill, in the most unfortunate section of his Victory broadcast, praised himself for avoiding in the case of Eire, were actually laid by himself on Russia in 1919, leaving Marshal Stalin with no reason for confidence in his present associates who have found his legions so useful to themselves.

Secondly, it is possible to obtain a good deal of information on Russia, published in English, from Moscow itself. For some time, thanks to past sympathetic gestures, I have regularly received *gratis* material which includes back numbers of the *Moscow News*, a monthly periodical entitled *International Literature* containing translations into English from representative

264

Russian writers, an occasional illustrated Bulletin called *Voks*, and one or two paper-covered books by Russian authors, such as the biography of Field-Marshal Kutozov, by Mikhail Bragin. Many of these publications, especially the *Moscow News*, contain crude propaganda but you are well able to distinguish such tendencious material from useful information, of which there is a good deal. For example, a recent article by an educationist describes the Russian victory over illiteracy; another outlines the kind of work being done by the many Russian women who enjoy complete equality with men.

Finally, I strongly urge all students faced with a choice of languages, and any older people who may have the time, to seize the opportunity of learning the Russian language. It is not an easy one, and immediate chances of practising it will probably be few. But when travel to the Soviet Union again becomes possible, the chance is likely to come first to those who can speak with the Russian people, and who know something of their history and ideals. One existing insurance against war with Russia lies in the pro-Soviet propaganda of the war years, which would immediately divide the people of this country if an early risk of conflict were to arise. But more reliable are the sound practical experiments in real knowledge and understanding which I have here ventured to suggest.

— 28 June 1945 —

We need the faith to go a path untrod,
The power to be alone and vote with God.
— Edwin Markham, *The Need of the Hour*

On July 5th, like millions of other British men and women, you and I will be recording our votes in the General Election. If your memory goes back to 1918, you will probably be comparing the mood of that post-war contest with this. There was more keenness then, but it tended to be a savage, war-frenzied keenness, which boded no good to the principles for which peace-lovers stand. The quieter public mood of today is partly a product of the greater suffering and fatigue which British civilians have endured, and partly the consequence of the still-continuing war with Japan which concerns so many sad and anxious families. It is also due to the widespread disillusionment which nourishes cynical doubts regarding the ability of any government whatsoever to bring nearer those happier conditions which Americans describe as 'a made-over world'.

We find, naturally enough, that those who are too young clearly to recall the last General Election are displaying the greatest interest in the artificially engineered but none the less significant political conflict. The most enthusiastic person I have so far met is my own fifteen-year-old daughter, who in the light summer evenings after school has been attending meetings held by the various parties in her constituency. After answering a question which she put at a Liberal gathering on the speaker's views about the nationalisation of the land, the surprised candidate protested: 'Surely this young woman hasn't a vote!' From the standpoint of one whose immediate future depends upon actual rather than potential voters, the protest was natural. Yet there could hardly be a better-justified or more useful form of political self-education than attendance at the meetings of different parties by boys and girls in the years before they reach voting age. My daughter's self-chosen activities recall to me Winifred Holtby's even more drastically impartial methods as an Oxford undergraduate, when she became a member of all three political parties. To one eager partisan who complained about this unconventional catholicity, she responded serenely: 'How can I know what they stand for unless I belong to them all?'

Like many other would-be peace-makers, you and I may well register our votes for candidates whom we hardly know, and policies in which we only half believe. This unsatisfactory compromise is inevitable in any society in which the desires and beliefs of a few are more revolutionary, in the deepest and fullest sense, than those of the majority. In such a situation, the members of the revolutionary minority sometimes decide, or are advised, deliberately to spoil their voting papers. Such a form of negative protest might well succeed, and hence be justified, if it were widely organised in advance, and then carried out at a given moment on a very large scale. If vague and sporadic, it seems to me to be merely ineffective and irresponsible.

Our object should surely be to support by our votes those policies and individuals most likely to further the developments, both national and international, that we desire to see. At the big Central Hall meeting on May 30th, which demanded 'Real Peace This Time!', Victor Gollancz made a vehement plea for the victory of the Left parties in the election. His impassioned sincerity reflected that of his wartime publications, including his own writings. Undoubtedly this campaign against hatred and vindictiveness has brought him much criticism from his fellow Jews. I recently saw a letter in the *Jewish Chronicle* attacking him for publishing, and, in his Introduction commending, *Above All Nations* ('Here in a subtle way an attempt is made to soften the righteous indignation felt by every decent-minded person at the beastly atrocities committed by the Germans. . . . What excuse has Victor Gollancz?').

Similar criticism followed his speech at the Central Hall. This spectacularly successful meeting was virtually boycotted by the ordinary press – with what justification now that the European war is over, and 'Real Peace' is the vital need of every citizen if his children are to survive, it is hard to understand – but the *Christian World* had a leading article on the subject in which the following passage occurred: 'It is encouraging to read that over five thousand people tried to get into the Central Hall, Westminster, at a meeting held by the National Peace Council to demand "radical and constructive peace policies". It is not quite so encouraging to learn that the biggest cheers of the evening came for Miss Vera Brittain's plea for the abrogation of the non-fraternisation order in Germany and for Mr Victor Gollancz's plea for the victory of the Left parties in the general election. . . . We should be very pessimistic about the chances of a "radical and constructive peace" if we believed that such a peace really depended upon a detail like non-fraternisation or on the victory of a particular British party. Peace must have broader foundations than these.'

It seems astonishing that a Christian newspaper should regard the non-fraternisation order as a 'detail' when our behaviour towards a defeated enemy is a basic test of our Christianity, and the standard by which the German nation will judge us in the time to come. Only less astonishing is the apparent belief that a change of standards and a new moral leadership at Westminster could never be part of the 'broad foundations' of peace. Yet this view seems to be widely held. After the meeting, one army officer of high rank took me gently to task for my statement on India, in a letter which was a model of courtesy and tact. It also contained the following comment: 'My other criticism, which applied not so much to your own approach as to that of Victor Gollancz, was on the manner in which the political issue was brought into the discussion on peace. ... My own statement of the case would be very different. It would emphasise how wrong it is to debase great principles by dragging politics into them, a very different aspect. I felt somehow that from the moment party politics were mentioned the tone of the meeting descended to a lower level.'

How does anyone imagine that peace is to be furthered irrespective of 'politics', and what do most people understand by that word? Is not a genuine change of political attitudes at least as relevant to peace as changes in religious education or civic teaching? An idea apparently still persists that 'party politics' are just a kind of extra-rough sport indulged in by political gangsters, whose disreputable game is regulated by a set of primitive rules. I admit that the recent electioneering tactics of Messrs Churchill, Beaverbrook and Bracken do tend to give that impression – as do also the methods of the organised gangs which endeavour to deprive some candidates of free speech by mob obstructionism. But actually 'party politics' is only another name for the process of deciding by what moral, economic and social principles this nation is to live, and by what set of values its behaviour towards other nations, and hence towards the world organisation of peace, is to be conducted.

268

If a speaker on a peace platform thinks that the victory of the Left parties in Britain is the surest road to peace, I cannot see why he should not say so. Indeed, I do not see how he can honestly say anything else. He may be wrong. Some members of Victor Gollancz's audience at the Central Hall may have reflected that the first instalment of woman suffrage – whose leaders only thirty years ago were considered as 'unrepresentative' as the pacifists of today – was granted in 1918 by a coalition government which, like all national governments so far in Britain, had tended to move steadily to the Right; and the second instalment in 1928 by a Conservative government under that least revolutionary of Prime Ministers, Mr Stanley Baldwin. But it is the job of those peace-lovers who listen to Victor Gollancz and other advocates of Left policies, to discover for themselves whether it is the Left or the Right which stands, or is most likely to stand, for the promotion of friendship with other countries, and especially Russia, France and whatever national entity ultimately emerges from Germany; for the progressive delegation of national sovereignty to an international authority through the World Organisation; for the planned distribution to all peoples in fair proportions of the world's available assets in food and raw materials; for the provision, as basic rights, of work, houses and education, which alone can give that feeling of hope and security which is the best guarantee against war; for the organisation of international trade for the benefit of the many, and not for the profits of the few; for the pursuit of justice and freedom for colonial peoples, including the peoples of India; and for the establishment of a Ministry of Peace to counterbalance the three Service ministries.

At the General Election held on 5 July 1945 (the first for ten years) a Labour government was returned with a majority of 247. The Conservatives lost over half their seats and Liberals were reduced from twenty seats to twelve.

I never could believe that Providence had sent a few men into the world, ready booted and spurred to ride, and millions ready saddled and bridled to be ridden.

(Richard Rumbold, When on the Scaffold, 1685)
– Macaulay, *History of England*

Now that the first surging excitement which accompanied the great Labour victory is over it becomes possible to estimate its causes and significance. Judging by such extracts as I have seen from the American press, Britain's move to the Left has apparently been widely misunderstood in the United States. It has been regarded both as gross ingratitude to Mr Churchill as war leader, and as a disquieting indication of prospective revolutionary violence. Actually, it is neither. I hope, therefore, that those American friends who read this letter will do their best to broadcast the contents of the current issue.

In the first place, the huge Labour vote, greatly increased even in those Tory constituencies where socialist candidates were defeated, is the expression of pent-up sentiments which have been steadily growing during six years of hardship and danger, but except in one or two freak by-elections, have been unable to voice themselves for several reasons. One such reason was the party truce, which in most of the by-elections imposed government candidates on totally diverse constituencies. Another and perhaps more widespread explanation was the fear, generated by the arbitrary powers with which the government armed itself during the invasion scare of 1940, of publicising a possibly unpopular opinion. Such minor regulations as those which threatened official punishment to the disseminators of 'alarm and despondency' created a general though normally un-British nervousness of giving vent to honest reactions if they ran contrary to views regarded as 'sound' by wartime Whitehall.

Secondly, the vote was a vehement declaration against the *Fuehrer* principle. With the possible exception of the self-respecting, individualistic American, who has just demonstrated his satisfactory ability to get on without a leader as spectacular

271

as Franklin Roosevelt, there is probably no member of any race who more deeply resents dictation from above than the ordinary British man or woman. In his and her veins flows the blood of a people which, stage by stage and with few periods of violent revolution, has been steadily resisting dictators since the time of Magna Carta. Whether this tradition is consciously realised or all but instinctive, it is responsible for an outlook which sees no incompatibility in gratitude to Mr Churchill for his leadership in a war which no ordinary citizen wanted, and a determination to have no more of it as soon as the terror and tension had ended. From the standpoint of the much-enduring Britisher hoping to take some small share in the future building of 'Jerusalem', the Tories' chief slogan 'Help Him Finish The Job' was as stupid and uninspired a piece of backward-looking propaganda as the cry of 'Safety First!' which lost them the election of 1929.

Thirdly, the size of the Labour majority typified the intensity of the common citizen's desire for a change. Even the youngest voters – so largely made politically conscious by the educational methods of Victor Gollancz, to whom Labour owes a debt of gratitude for the series of publications described by one Conservative candidate as 'those poisonous little yellow books' – fully realised which party was responsible for the two decades of hesitant, humiliating and unillumined international policy pursued by British statesmen between the wars. They knew that the Labour governments of 1923 and 1929–31 were minority office-holders which could take no forward steps in foreign policy, nor prepare one item of revolutionary social legislation, without exposing themselves to defeat by a combined Tory–Liberal majority. And many voters both young and older remembered the bitter words of T.E. Lawrence in *The Seven Pillars of Wisdom*: 'When we achieved and the new world dawned the old men came out again and took from us our victory, and re-made it in the likeness of the former world they knew. Youth could win, but had not learned to keep, and was pitiably weak against age. We stammered that we had worked for a new heaven and a new earth, and they thanked us kindly and made their peace.' Youth's recent vote embodied a determination that this time the 'old men' should not be permitted to come back, and that the party which had never had a real chance, and could hardly do worse than the governments of 1919–1939, should be given its opportunity to do very much better. It was not a vote for Communism; at South Hackney William Rust, editor of the *Daily Worker*, was returned at the bottom of the poll, while Harry Pollitt, the Communist leader, failed to achieve election. The single Communist gain at Mile End, in the heart of much-bombed East London, was probably due to intolerable local conditions, such as primitive housing and widespread homelessness caused by bomb-damage.

A fourth factor in the socialist success was undoubtedly disgust with the Tories' method of conducting their campaign. The attempt to use 'bogies' and 'stunts' in sorry imitation of the Zinovieff Letter scare of 1924 was insulting to the intelligence and irrelevant to the hopes of an electorate which looked for a positive programme of reconstruction, and could not be stampeded into distrust of the honest men and women who had shared the responsibilities of five perilous years. Although it is true that the vote for Labour was a vote against Toryism rather than against Churchill, it would be incorrect to say that the late Premier's election speeches and broadcasts aroused no personal animus. This hostility, however, displayed itself against Churchill's family clique rather than against himself. Among the newly-elected London MPs who made two-minute speeches at the Central Hall, Westminster, on July 26th, no one received warmer applause than Sir Frank Mason Macfarlane, former Governor of Gibraltar, for his victory over Brendan Bracken, and Mr R. Chamberlain, the housing expert who unseated Duncan Sandys at Norwood.

Lastly – but this time far from least – the Labour vote was a vote for peace. Its urgent demand to be saved by new politicians and a new outlook from a third world war did not even exclude the revolutionary values and methods of pacifism. Such pacifist and near-pacifist MPs as Rhys Davies and R.R. Stokes substantially increased their majorities, while similar newly victorious candidates won seats which had been Conservative for a quarter

273

of a century. Chief among these was Mrs Lucy Middleton, once secretary of the No More War Movement, who has been elected for Lady Astor's old seat, the Sutton Division of Plymouth, and will be one of the most valuable of the new women Members.

To the election of such candidates obviously went the votes of many humble people who surreptitiously murmured 'It's not right!' when they read of German civilians slaughtered in their hundreds of thousands by massacre bombing and wrote letters to the Ministry of Economic Warfare begging for food relief to be sent through the blockade to the famished peoples of occupied Europe. Having received little satisfaction either from this Ministry or from the Secretary of State for Air, they have now responded by turning out Mr Dingle Foot and Sir Archibald Sinclair.

There have been many stories, amusing and pathetic, of the people's reaction to the realisation that their hopes and ideals were shared with others throughout the country, but none, I think, was more revealing than the immediate response of my Chelsea hairdresser. A small middle-aged Englishman, and an ardent socialist who secretly hated the war he palpably found my visits a relief amongst those of many local residents who did not share his sentiments. The day after the Labour victory, I found him almost in tears with joy. Three days afterwards, fulfilling my appointment, I noticed in the window a few packets of bronze 'invisible' hairpins, and tentatively asked if he could spare me one. Seizing the precious bundles with both hands, he held them out to me. 'Take two!' he exclaimed. 'Take three! Take four!' And in spite of my protests against having more than my share, the four packets of hairpins were exuberantly thrust into my bag. I shall keep one as a souvenir which oddly symbolises the universal hopes and aspirations of struggling mankind.

On 6 August 1945 the world's first atomic bomb was dropped on Hiroshima and on 9 August another on Nagasaki. The total number killed – almost all civilians – was over a quarter of a million. Neither the public – nor, probably, the scientists – were fully aware of the lingering, lethal effects of radioactive fall-out.

There are certain deeds which science should not do. There are certain actions for which scientists should not be made conscripts by any nation. And surely the extermination of any civilian population by any nation is one of these
– The Bishop of Chichester in a letter to *The Times*, Aug. 14, 1945

I had intended to write to you this week about the decisions of the Potsdam Conference, but the total change of perspective which involved humanity when the first atomic bombs descended on Japan and concluded the war, relegates every other topic to insignificance. It is difficult for the lay mind to grasp the full apocalyptic meaning of the mysterious power hitherto pent within the infinitesimal units from which the material structure of the universe is made, but now twice released. What is quite clear is the possibility of unlimited destruction which this release unfolds.

During the past two weeks, many of us have been sickened by the usual plethora of excuses and justification put forward by those who seek to quieten their latent misgivings. We are told that the instantaneous extermination of huge populations is 'more merciful' than the prolonged and cumulative raids which were indeed evil things unworthy of civilised mankind, but which, being less 'total', at least left the individual with some possibility of self-defence and some hope of escape. From all cities which endured long-sustained aerial attack, the most vulnerable sections of the population – young children, pregnant women, invalids, the aged – were in fact largely removed.

Again, it is said that Japan started the whole war by invading China in 1931, and therefore this awful visitation was, in the words of a *News-Chronicle* headline, her 'Day of Judgment'. As usual this argument overlooks the fact that when man, in his satanic pride clumsily usurps God's prerogative of exacting the divine 'vengeance' which ensures that causes produce their effects, it is invariably the innocent rather than the guilty upon whom his punishment falls. The Japanese children 'vaporised' at

Hiroshima and Nagasaki were unborn when the China incident began. The only crime committed by them and their mothers was that of living in an industrial city.

Finally, the apologists for mass extermination seek, as always, to justify themselves by arguing that the use of the atomic bomb (like the high-explosives, incendiaries, phosphorus cans, etc, in the 'saturation raids' before it) has 'shortened the war' and 'saved lives'. These lives are, of course, Allied lives. The lives of the Japanese do not count. They are regarded with no more compunction than the farmer shows towards the wasps in the nest which he burns to save his fruit.

Obviously, since a point of terror had been reached which no flesh and blood could survive, the Japanese war was shortened by its compulsory ending – something for which we can at least be thankful, whatever we may think of the manner of its conclusion. But do those who maintain that the speedy ending of a war justifies extreme abomination ever stop to consider the real significance of their argument? It means that for the first time in the history of Christendom, human life is no longer to be regarded as sacred in terms of its *humanity*; and that the national leaders who have used, or permitted the use of, the atomic bomb (which logically follows the 'obliteration' raids that preceded it) are deliberately repudiating the tremendous spiritual and moral revolution which occurred in human thinking when Christ said: 'The very hairs of your head are all numbered.'

On this and kindred sayings has been founded for centuries the Christian doctrine – accepted as true by many civilised non-Christians – that human life is sacred in the eyes of God who made man in His own image. This principle lies at the heart of the greatest political institutions of modern society – democracy, for instance, and international law. Its repudiation – as a letter in the *News-Chronicle* of August 14 from an Indian woman, Mrs Haidri Bhuttaoharji, makes clear – debases the currency of Christian civilisation in the eyes of all non-Christian Asiatic peoples.

By whose authority has the great principle on which Western

277

civilisation has rested for twenty centuries been denied? Some writers of letters to the newspapers have blamed the scientists for allowing this discovery to be made, though some of these were never told for precisely what purpose their work was to be used, and others apparently evaded that uncomfortable knowledge. It is, of course, open to scientists who realise that an evil use is to be made of their discoveries to become conscientious objectors in exactly the same way as conscripted soldiers, and refuse to contribute their trained intelligence to destructive ends. Their critics are doubtless justified in wishing that the scientists of today had an outlook as moral and realistic as that of Leonardo da Vinci, who refrained from making his researches on submarines available to the society which he knew would misuse them. But the scientist, as his name implies, is merely the servant of knowledge, and his normal task is to follow wherever it leads. The real enemies of man are not scientists, but those representatives of national sovereign states who prostitute and degrade scientific invention.

The morality of sovereign states, more primitive even than that of individuals, sanctions the use of ever more terrible weapons in pursuit of ends which, for all their selfishness, are held to justify the employment of any means. It is this false doctrine which is the antithesis of Christian values and has now become an immediate threat to human survival.

The Americans who, for national ends, dropped the first atomic bomb, obviously felt uneasy about its use, for *The Times* correspondent in a dispatch from Washington dated Aug. 7, stated that 'the decision to use the new weapon was apparently taken quite recently and amounted to a reversal of previous policy.' It seems vital to establish the reason for this change, which led two states claiming a high degree of civilisation to sanction and carry out two appalling massacres far exceeding in size and terror any previous massacres of history. It is indeed time to implement and develop the San Francisco decisions, unless, as I suspect, these decisions are incapable of development and already obsolete. In that case, let the world leaders call a new conference in the light of the new knowledge. If this knowledge involves the abandonment or reversal of 'settlements' made at Potsdam or the Pacific, so much the better. With the power of universal death now culpably unleashed, the provocation of hatred and vengeance is more than ever likely to prove fatal in its effects. Men dare no longer be cruel or unjust to their neighbours, lest semi-informed attempts at retaliation destroy our planet itself.

Amid the fear and depression which the atomic bomb has engendered, let us not overlook certain sources of hope. What would have happened to our civilisation if this unleashing of atomic energy had occurred in say, 1942, and been made available to Hitler, Mussolini and Stalin? – or even to Roosevelt, who had forgotten by 1944 the appeal that he made to the combatants of 1939 to refrain from bombing civilians; or to Churchill, who stated on September 21st, 1943: 'There are no lengths to which we will not go to destroy Nazi tyranny' – and doubtless knew even then what further 'lengths' would soon become possible. At least the first atom bombs have been made when all the peoples are war-weary, and Britain has a Labour government which, though involved, perhaps to its own embarrassment, in the atomic bomb project immediately after attaining power, is composed of honest men and women who want to do better than their predecessors, and must respond to the will of the people who put them where they are.

A revulsion against war and its inhumanity was already beginning amongst those people – whose vote for Labour was one way of expressing it – when the atomic bomb came to increase it, and to place clearly before democracy the choice between life and death. The same revulsion against war already exists in most of Europe, including Germany and Italy. It has always existed in China. It will certainly come in America. It may even come in Russia – and in Japan, though here the inevitable desire for revenge, and a bitter contempt for Western professions, will first have to be overcome. Certainly it is now clear that armies, navies and large-scale air forces are automatically rendered obsolete by the atomic bomb. Hence military conscription and the controversies which rage round it will soon be seen as obsolete also.

This will remain true whether war is abolished or not. The leaders of mankind have to deal with atomic energy, and with that alone. All subsidiary weapons, and the manpower needed to use them belong to the past.

The constructive possibilities of atomic energy are, of course, immense. In pointing this out, *The Week* for Aug. 10, condemned those critics who regarded the discovery with horror instead of rejoicing over the new opportunities made available to mankind. Here, however, it is not *The Week* but the horrified critics who are realistic. The memories of the past six years are still too close for us to forget man's perverse habit of using his intelligence and financial resources to destroy rather than build. On the shoulders of this demoralised generation rests the responsibility for deciding whether the human race is to continue or not.

Finally, the crimes of Hiroshima and Nagasaki reduce to hypocrisy the self-constituted 'right' of the Allied leaders to put 'war criminals' on trial. The populations of their countries are quite intelligent enough to ask what moral difference there is between Nazi 'extermination camps', and the mass extermination by atomic bombs of helpless civilians. It may well be that some, at least of the 'war guilt' trials will be abandoned or their procedure altered, as a result of the growing public feeling that, instead of sitting in judgment on others, the victorious Allies should rather be entreating God's forgiveness for their misuse of the cosmic forces which He alone can be trusted to control.

___ 6 September 1945 ___

In his will is our peace
– Dante, *Paradiso*, Book III, 1. 85

With Japan's formal surrender, rather than with the celebrations of VJ Day, the Second World War came to its end. This series of Letters, begun on October 4th, 1939, in the hope of creating a war-time link between peace-lovers, also ends with the present issue.

At last, after nearly a decade and a half the exhausted world finds itself in a condition which is technically, though incongruously, described as 'peace'. Thanks partly to the method by which peace was enforced, and partly to the festering national slums left by years of fighting and its political aftermath in Europe and Asia, the weary peoples enter the post-war period with none of that sense of release from nightmare which, illusory though it was, lightened the dark landscape of 1919.

On August 15th, the *Evening Standard* and other newspapers published a grave warning, from Generalissimo Chiang Kai-Shek, which might have served as a model for all the Allied leaders. After enjoining the peoples of the world, and the soldiers and civilians of China, against revenge or the heaping of abuse on 'the innocent people of Japan', he continued: 'We have always said that the violent militarism of Japan is our enemy, not the people. We have won victory. I urge all our friends in the Allied nations, and all my own countrymen, to face the fact that the peace we have gained by arms is not necessarily the beginning of permanent peace.'

This warning recalls to my mind an article published during 1939 by Mr Harold Nicolson, in which with less prophetic foresight than he displayed in the descriptions of the atomic bomb in his novel, *Public Faces* (1932), he gave his reasons for believing that this country must go to war. It was impossible, he said, to make any plans with the certainty that they would be fulfilled. We could feel no security about the future. Only by the removal of the aggressors who threatened us could that security be restored.

Can we honestly say today that our future looks more secure than it looked in 1939? The major consequences of this war are fourfold, and, failing that determined moral revolution which still may save us but alone can do so, not one of these consequences holds less reason for apprehension than the anxieties of the summer before war began. First, through the search for destructive power to which scientific knowledge and skill have been prostituted, a force has been released which is capable not only of annihilating an enemy but of ending man. Secondly, the totalitarianism which the democracies of 1939 set out to fight has merely shifted, unconquered, from two dominant nations to a third more powerful than both combined. Thirdly, we are faced with a fearful winter in which millions of human beings – exiled, deported, 'displaced', or struggling to exist like rats beneath the rubble of once great cities – face slow death from starvation, disease and cold on a scale greater than the total casualties of the war. Finally, the moral fervour and spiritual strength which alone can nerve mankind to fight their real enemies, the four Horsemen of the Apocalypse whom war has resurrected, have themselves been undermined to a degree never experienced in history.

In 1939, as the earliest letters in this series show, I did foresee that a long war was bound to produce, as it produced between 1914 and 1919, a steady demoralisation which would again make peace and reconstruction difficult to achieve. I began these letters with the idea of compelling myself at frequent intervals to confront the world situation and try to see it in a perspective which might help my readers. I wanted to keep alive in myself the values which I believed that we, as individuals and as a nation, would progressively lose. And I hoped that by struggling to hold on to them personally, I might contribute towards their survival in at least a few others.

But I could not have foreseen, six years ago, the full measure of moral degradation which would darken the human mind and spirit throughout the world. Any writer would have been condemned as a false Jeremiah who had prophesied the widespread abandonment of Christianity even by so-called Christian nations, the growing worship of 'toughness' and cruelty, and the base identification with 'weakness' and 'sentimentality' of those humanitarian standards on which Western civilisation has been built. The extent to which fascist ideology – which some of us have resisted for twelve years in our own way – has taken hold of the minds and spirits of men and women who believed themselves to be fighting it, is one of the most alarming consequences of the war.

Another result, and one which such classics as Lord Ponsonby's *Falsehood in Wartime* made it possible to foresee up to a point, has been the corruption of truth. In the 1914 war, this process was carried to its limits through such media as were then available, but in the late war broadcasting added a new and enormous region of misrepresentation to the 'wishful thinking' and confusion already existing. In Volume II, No. 31, of the American News-Letter *Human Events*, Dr Felix Morley ascribes to 'our abandonment of the great American tradition of objective reporting' the shock caused by the British election results to many citizens who thought themselves well-informed. 'As a result of four years of war psychology, both press and radio have now almost wholly succumbed to the practice of "slanting" or editorialising news . . . Of course most people realise that truth is the first casualty in war. Less well understood is the subtle way in which subordination of truth to propaganda destroys the power of political analysis. Today this loss of the scientific attitude is at least as pronounced in our universities and colleges as in the editorial offices of our newspapers. And this attrition of the essential critical faculty, withering that hard and honest and courageous thinking which is rare at best, has become a matter of national urgency.'

Finally, I did not foresee when I began these letters that upon the survival of the standards which I sought to preserve would depend not only the moral and spiritual but the actual physical continuation of man. I am not suggesting that I regard physical as worse than moral extinction. The words: 'Fear not them which kill the body, but are not able to kill the soul: but rather fear him which is able to destroy both body and soul in hell', have been newly revealed to us in their terrible truth during the past six years. I believe, and throughout the war have maintained, that from the Christian standpoint the most pitiful victims of bombing and starvation were not even the mothers and children murdered by these weapons, but the men who used them, and, still more, those who contrived and ordered their use. I merely record that as recently as V-E Day I saw humanity, as a species, continuing to exist through the centuries of that 'long age' in

283

which I should not be, and waging a constant spiritual struggle in which it might win or lose. I had not then faced the possibility that, unless the values triumph for which a few have striven throughout the war, the human race will not be there to struggle at all.

Henceforth, whatever their religious or political denomination, most thinking people will recognise that only these values, and the revolutionary conduct that they involve, can save us either from physical or from spiritual death. The history especially of the past century has shown us that there is no safeguard in 'remaining strong', nor in the invention of weapons so fearful that men will refrain from their use. Occasionally, as in the general self-denial of poison gas, the nations have avoided certain lethal expedients, though not from motives on which their potential victims could rely. But the bulk of human experience points in the opposite, fatal, direction. For the last month, in newspaper after newspaper, bishops, dons, scientists and politicians have been saying what few but pacifists dared to say during the war: that only a complete revolution in personal and national behaviour can rescue us from doom.

'I am convinced', wrote Professor A.V. Hill, FRS, in *The Spectator* for August 17th, 'that if these terrible fears for the future are not to be realised some drastic decisions are necessary very soon. Political isolationism, aggressive nationalism and secrecy in preparing scientific methods for mutual destruction, must stop. Scientific men throughout the world must be allowed to work together in mutual confidence and sincerity. Ethical standards in their world must be restored, so that the misuse of scientific knowledge and discovery (the common property of mankind), either for selfish exploitation or for general destruction, will be regarded – like cowardice in a soldier or dishonesty in a banker – as the unforgiveable sin.'

Or, as John Betjeman put it two days earlier in the *Daily Herald*: 'For the first time thousands of people who can think seriously and who have hitherto believed that, thanks to scientific discovery, the world was getting better and better, are doubtful of the truth of that nineteenth-century heresy. They have seen that the soul matters more than the body, that all those religious preachings against envy, anger, pride, sloth, lust, greed, and all those calls of religion to faith, hope and charity, may have been right after all. For kind fairy godmother Science has given the child a toy with which it can kill itself and its family. Only those old religious teachings are going to prevent it from being so anti-social as to make an end of the human family on earth.'

These thousands of people are not powerless, any more than you and I are powerless, though the restrictions of wartime often made us feel as though we were. The millions of individual votes which brought about the silent revolution of the General Election showed that what we want, we can obtain. If only we can stimulate in ourselves and others that moral determination on which the redemption of mankind depends, we shall have fulfilled at last our aspiration to be not only lovers but makers of peace.